D0425103

The Feminist Legacy of Karen Horney

The Feminist Legacy
of Karen Horney

Marcia Westkott

Yale University Press
New Haven and London

WITHDRAWN
LVC BISHOP LIBRARY

Excerpts from *The Adolescent Diaries of Karen Horney* by Karen Horney, © 1980 by Basic Books, Inc., Publisher, are reprinted by permission of the publisher.

Excerpts from the following are reprinted by permission of W. W. Norton and Co., Inc.: *Feminine Psychology*, ed. Harold Kelman; © 1957 by W. W. Norton and Co., Inc. *The Neurotic Personality of Our Time*, by Karen Horney; © 1937 by W. W. Norton and Co., Inc.; © renewed 1965 by Marianne von Eckardt, Renate Mintz, and Brigitte Swarzenski. *New Ways in Psychoanalysis*, by Karen Horney; © 1939 by W. W. Norton and Co., Inc.; © renewed 1966 by Marianne von Eckardt, Renate Mintz, and Brigitte Swarzenski. *Self Analysis*, by Karen Horney; © 1942 by W. W. Norton and Co., Inc.; © renewed 1969 by Marianne von Eckardt, Renate Mintz, and Brigitte Swarzenski. *Our Inner Conflicts* by Karen Horney; © 1945 by W. W. Norton and Co., Inc.; © renewed 1972 by Marianne von Eckardt, Renate Mintz, and Brigitte Swarzenski. *Neurosis and Human Growth*, by Karen Horney; © 1950 by W. W. Norton and Co., Inc.; © renewed 1978 by Marianne von Eckardt, Renate Mintz, and Brigitte Swarzenski.

Copyright © 1986 by Yale University.
All rights reserved.
This book may not be reproduced, in whole
or in part, in any form (beyond that
copying permitted by Sections 107 and 108
of the U.S. Copyright Law and except by
reviewers for the public press), without
written permission from the publishers.

Designed by Sally Harris
and set in Melior type by
The Publishing Nexus Incorporated, Guilford, Conn.
Printed in the United States of America by
Murray Printing Co., Westford, Mass.

Library of Congress Cataloging-in-Publication Data

Westkott, Marcia, 1943–
    The feminist legacy of Karen Horney.

    Bibliography: p. 215
    Includes index.
    1. Women—Psychology. 2. Femininity. 3. Identity
(Psychology) 4. Horney, Karen, 1885–1952. I. Title.
HQ1206.W47 1986   305.4'2   86–9201
ISBN 0–300–03706–6 (alk. paper)

The paper in this book meets the guidelines for
permanence and durability of the Committee on
Production Guidelines for Book Longevity
of the Council on Library Resources

10   9   8   7   6   5   4   3   2   1

Contents

Acknowledgments

I wish to express my gratitude to the many individuals who assisted and supported this work. At the University of Colorado at Colorado Springs my colleagues in the Department of Sociology created an environment of intellectual freedom and adventure that encouraged my endeavors. The members of the University Seminar in Feminist Theory critically nurtured my emerging ideas. Lee Chambers-Schiller in particular has been a mainstay of intellectual and personal support, reading several drafts with discerning intelligence and sharing her knowledge with characteristic generosity.

Gila Hayim shared the excitement of my early formulations and gently prodded their development with wisdom and friendship. Jean Baker Miller gave generously of encouragement, knowledge, and insight. Janice Hays read several drafts, often on short notice, with a writing instructor's rigor and a poet's sensibility. Diane Hill offered invaluable suggestions from a subtle and sensitive clinical perspective. Jim Westkott read the manuscript with characteristic care and encouraged me to clarify my own ideas. I am indebted to Robin Post for alerting me to Karen Horney's significance and to Hans Speier for sharing his memories of Horney as well as his humane intelligence.

Editor Gladys Topkis's careful and perceptive attention to both substantive and editorial issues helped significantly in clarifying the presentation of my thoughts. Gay Francis assisted in the details of manuscript preparation with unwavering commitment, determined exactitude, and good-humored intelligence. Lynn

Scott and Elaine Schantz were not only proficient in typing the manuscript but steadfast and calm in the face of revisions and deadlines. I am grateful to Judy Conroy for helping to unravel some German knots, to the librarians at the University of Colorado at Colorado Springs for assisting with friendly and unflagging expertise, and to the Women's Counseling Center Study Group of Colorado Springs for analyzing and celebrating with spirit.

Not least, I have been fortunate to share the pleasures and responsibilities of daily living with Jim, Pete, and Matt Westkott, who in supporting this endeavor and in being themselves have helped to make life grand.

The Feminist Legacy of Karen Horney

Introduction

Our whole civilization is a masculine civilization. The State, the laws, morality, religion, and the sciences are the creation of men. . . . If we are clear about the extent to which all our being, thinking, and doing conform to these masculine standards, we can see how difficult it is for the individual man and also for the individual woman really to shake off this mode of thought.
—Karen Horney

This book develops a social psychological theory that explains women's personality development as a consequence of growing up in a social setting in which they are devalued. The protagonist is the conflicted female psyche who sweetly complies with her devaluation and rages to triumph over it. My focus is this female conflict, its historically embedded development, its manifold psychological expressions, and its possibilities for creative transcendence.

Three interrelated strands of inquiry led me to write this book. First, I wanted to understand an array of personality traits that writers have recently identified with women. These traits emphasize women's disposition to relate to and care for others. They include, for example, a need for affiliation (J. Miller, 1976), a nurturing dispostion (Chodorow, 1978), and sense of responsibility for other people (Gilligan, 1982). Converging in the idea that female identity is relational, the writings on these traits have exerted a compelling influence on contemporary feminist thought, especially because they place positive value on women's qualities.

I wanted to understand the psychological development of these qualities and their relationship to a whole personality or character. I also wanted to know how these traits—regarded so postively—emerge from a historical setting in which women are less highly valued than men. This paradox suggested an underside to the nurturance and affiliation that invited further exploration. Finally, I was concerned that, in the absence of contextual understanding, the traits would be mystified and unreflectively idealized as an inherent female essence, thereby undermining a tradition of feminist scholarship that takes gender patterns to be historically created, contingent, and thus subject to change.

Second, I wanted to understand the linkage between culture, the psychodynamics of family relations, and the development of female character. I was dissatisfied with existing approaches to explaining these links. On the one hand, socialization studies trace gender patterns to the ways girls and boys are treated in families, schools, and other social institutions (for a review see Weitzman, 1979), but they leave unexplained exactly how these differences are internalized as feminine or masculine personality types. Psychological theories, on the other hand, explain personality development, but often by abstracting it from the social contexts in which development actually takes place. Both the social and the psychological approaches leave important gaps in understanding. I sought an alternative that would bridge them, that would integrate the causal influence of social relations with an idea of the developing person.

The most influential theory of female development, Nancy Chodorow's *The Reproduction of Mothering* (1978), has contributed much to the awareness of development as both a social and a psychological process as well as to the idea that female identity is relational. But I struggled on both theoretical and empirical grounds with Chodorow's assumption that mothers overidentify with daughters and not with sons. First, her argument that mothers keep their daughters in an extended, "pre-Oedipal" depen-

dency conflicted with others' observations that girls are expected
to detach themselves from being mothered and take care of themselves at an earlier age than boys. (see Caplan, 1981). Second,
Chodorow's explanatory emphasis on the mother-child relationship minimizes the influence of both the father and wider
cultural values on family relations. These differences with
Chodorow led me to look for an alternative theory of female
development, one that would proceed from different (and for me
less problematic) assumptions and would emphasize the historical specificity of women's psychological development.

Finally, I was interested in exploring more fully a notion of
female alienation that I had identified elsewhere (Westkott, 1977,
1979). I had begun to describe women's alienation as a consequence of growing up in a context where females are devalued.
My own experience, both scholarly and personal, led me to
believe that women incorporate their devaluation as well as
oppose it; we internalize the values that presume female
inferiority, but we also struggle against them. I wanted to understand the historical patterns of the devaluation as well as the psychological dynamic of incorporating and opposing it. This
dynamic is, I believe, the source of the most exciting—and sometimes the most difficult—self-understanding as well as the basis
for envisioning and creating social change.

These lines of questioning eventually led me to the work of
Karen Horney, an early twentieth-century psychoanalyst.
Horney's early work, which is critical of Freud's ideas on women,
is well known to contemporary feminist scholars. But it was her
later work that captured my attention. For in these mature writings, Horney created a theory of character development that
emphasized the causal influence of cultural values and social relations. She perceptively analyzed character conflict—its complex-
ities and nuances—so as to illuminate the depth of its influence.
And she described childhood experiences that seemed to form a
characteristically female pattern. Clearly, in Horney I found the

elements to create the theoretical approach that I had sought.

Drawing from Horney's theory, I describe a female character that both internalizes and opposes cultural expectations of femininity, one that needs others for identity and yet strives to realize an autonomous sense of self. The inner conflict explains women's emphasis on relationships as it forms a tension with opposing responses. For example, the ethos of female care for others that Carol Gilligan (1982) identifies is from my perspective not simply an alternative to the predominant male values of strategic intelligence and abstract moralizing; rather, it emerges from a context that assumes female inferiority and powerlessness. Similarly, the cultural devaluation of women and the female moral dispositions, and the ideology of female inferiority and women's relational traits are dialectically related. This theory links the psychological to the social through an explanation of development as a process in which devaluation is both internalized and struggled against. It is a social-psychological theory of conflict: nurturing is related to subordination, sexualized identity to fear, caring to anger, affiliation to powerlessness, and sweet compliance to the rage to triumph.

Although I found in Horney the framework for this explanation, I took an interpretive leap beyond her to develop it. Horney intended her theory of development and character conflict to apply to men and women alike. Yet the sexualizing and devaluing experiences that she associated with conflicted development struck me as characteristically female. Moreover, the personality type that is central to her theory is the one she associated with women. For these reasons, I interpret Horney's gender-neutral theory as one that specifically explains women's psychology.

My book, therefore, is not a conventional study of an author: I have not written an exegesis of all of Horney's writings. Nor have I focused on her work within the context of the history of psychoanalysis in general or of the cultural neo-Freudians in particular.[1] I have not written a profile that highlights Horney's contribution to psychoanalysis as a woman (see O'Connell, 1980). And I include very little biographical information on Horney herself. (There is one biography in print [Rubins, 1978], and another forthcoming [Quinn, 1987].) My approach is rather to articulate the feminist voice implied in Horney's theory and to use it to create a new social psychology of women.

Before proceeding to these ideas, I want to clarify two methodological issues. First, to speak of female character or women's conflicts as if they were universal would be misleading. All psychological theories, including those that claim universal aplicability, are grounded in the experiences of particular people, the theorist notwithstanding. Karen Horney was born in Germany at the turn of the century and emigrated to the United States in the 1930s. Her theory, written in the 1930s and 1940s, explains the relational traits that subsequent psychologists have more recently identified. But Horney based her ideas on her own experience and that of her acquaintances and patients, women like herself, who were white, middle class, and predominately heterosexual. Although there may be a basis for extending this interpretation of Horney's theory to women in other social categories— particularly its notion that in our culture women are sexualized and otherwise devalued—I think that it would be unwise to do so without further research and testing of its validity in explaining their experiences.

1. For analyses that address these intellectual exchanges, see, for example, Witenberg, "American Neo-Freudian School: The Interpersonal and Cultural Approaches" (1974); Fine, *A History of Psychoanalysis* (1979, pp. 109–13, 138–40); Kelman, *Helping People: Karen Horney's Psychoanalytic Approach* (1971, pp. 1–50); Moulton, "Early Papers on Women: Horney to Thompson" (1975); Fliegel, "Feminine Psychosexual Development in Freudian Theory" (1973); Walter James, "Karen Horney and Erich Fromm in Relation to Alfred Adler" (1947); Freeman, "Concepts of Adler and Horney" (1950); Cameron, "Karen Horney: A Pioneer in the Science of Human Relations" (1954).

Finally, in drawing together works from various disciplines, especially history, psychoanalysis, and the psychology of women, I delve into areas that lie outside my expertise. With an awareness of the limits to such an approach, I have nevertheless attempted to understand the specialized knowledge, preserve its intellectual integrity, and create a synthesis that is appropriate both to specialized concepts and to my purposes. Inevitably, specialists in each of these disciplines will identify topics that they would develop more fully, additional points that they would address, and ideas that they would interpret differently. This response is normal and vital to interdisciplinary work such as women's studies. I hope that my interpretation will not be contradicted by specialized knowledge but will be used to initiate a dialogue within these disciplines to enhance our understanding of women.

*   *   *

When Karen Horney wrote about "masculine civilization," she was referring to Western civilization and its powerfully determining presumption of male superiority and female inferiority. Following the analysis of sociologist Georg Simmel,[2] Horney argued that this presumption informed the state and its laws, economic and political orders, and social institutions, as well as systems of morality and thought. These male-created forms constitute the social landscape in which women are routinely devalued: "No matter how much the individual woman may be treasured as a mother or as a lover, it is always the male who will be considered

2. Horney's criticism of masculine civilization was drawn from her reading of Simmel's analysis of male-dominated culture (Simmel, 1911, 1984). For a discussion of Simmel's writings on this subject, see Coser, 1977. Simmel used the word culture (*Kultur*) to refer to the entire spectrum of historically created social, political, religious, moral, intellectual, and artistic forms of social life. This definition of culture, which Horney followed, is the one that I assume throughout this book. In this respect, the term *masculine civilization* is more correctly *masculine culture*, referring to the idea that the cultural forms are creations of men and reflect their values (See Horney, 1926, pp. 55–57).

more valuable on human and spiritual grounds" (Horney, 1926–27, p. 82). The devaluation of women, Horney claimed, pervades the atmosphere in which female character develops. "In actual fact a girl is exposed from birth onward to the suggestion—inevitable, whether conveyed brutally or delicately—of her inferiority" (Horney, 1926, p. 69). The effect is to impress upon girls a belief in their own inferiority. They become women who act on this belief, adapting "themselves to the wishes of men and ... [feeling] as if their adaptation were their true nature" (p. 57).

As concerned as she was about this wound to female development, Horney was also interested in how women rebel against their devaluation. The rebellion can take subtle psychological forms, appearing, for example, as a rejection of traditional female roles (Horney, 1926), frigidity (Horney, 1926–27), or resentment and envy of men (Horney, 1934). All these symptoms represent women's opposition to the submission required by their inferior status. Thus women may incorporate masculine civilization's devaluation of them, but they also struggle against that identity.

The conflict that informs her work is one that Karen Horney also lived. She was born Karen Clementine Danielsen on September 16, 1885. Her mother, Clothilde ("Sonni") Van Ronzelen, was descended from a well-known Dutch-German family. Horney's father, Berndt Waekels Danielsen, a middle-class sea captain of Norwegian origin, was a widower with four teenage children when he married Sonni, seventeeen years his junior. They had two children, first a son, Berndt, born in 1881, and four years later Karen (Rubins, 1978).

The Danielsens' marriage was conflicted. Horney's father was stern, religious, authoritarian; he believed in the necessity of female subservience. Her mother was beautiful, sophisticated, better educated than her husband, and more liberal in her views (Rubins, 1978, p. 11). She was also, according to her daughter's adolescent diaries, depressed, irritable, and domineering toward

Karen. The diaries record a guilt-ridden sympathy for her mother and impatience toward, yet fear of, her father (Horney, 1980). She found refuge from her parents' strife in school, where teachers encouraged her intense curiosity (Moulton, 1975, p. 207). As an adolescent Karen began to question the inherited authority of the patriarch, both that of her father and that of her Christian upbringing. When she was fifteen, she recorded in her diary: "Today I read in a book that one should honor one's father not for his personal characteristics but to honor the authority God has vested in him. But it is awfully difficult" (Horney, 1980, p. 22).

The "awfully difficult" struggle to be obedient to a patriarchal authority that she felt she should respect but did not accept continued well into Karen's intellectual and professional career. Ironically, the expansion of educational and career opportunities for women enabled Karen to study and practice within male intellectual and professional domains and, thus, to question further their assumptions. Soon after these institutions opened their doors to women, Karen entered the gymnasium in Hamburg in 1901 and medical school, first at Freiburg in 1906 and then at Berlin in 1908 (Eckardt, 1980, p. ix). She was one of the first psychoanalytic patients, entering therapy with Karl Abraham, a colleague of Freud and president of the Berlin Psychoanalytic Society. While she finished her medical education and began her apprenticeship, Karen married Oscar Horney, a business lawyer (in 1909) and gave birth to three daughters (from 1911 to 1915). Karen Horney practiced psychoanalysis in Berlin and became one of a handful of women throughout the world who were members of this expanding profession (Rubins, 1978).

But Horney's privileged education and training presented ideas that conflicted with her own understanding of reality, especially about herself. After two years she terminated analysis with Abraham with a sense that the process was not leading toward an authentic sense of herself (Horney, 1980, pp. 270–71). Her first publication on therapeutic technique revealed an early deviation from Freud in its more holistic approach to therapy (Horney, 1968/1917; Moulton, 1975). And her first public presentation before the international psychoanalytic community, in 1922, took exception to Abraham's influential paper which stated that penis envy is a fixed and universal characteristic of women (Horney, 1924; Abraham, 1927/1920; Moulton, 1975). Like her other papers on female psychology written in the 1920s and early 1930s,[3] Horney's response was a courageous attempt to reform the accepted psychoanalytic ideas on women. Over time her essays became more daring in their challenge to a system that derived female psychology from a male standard. They demonstrate Horney's creative independence of mind and her willingness to challenge authority. Clearly, she had moved beyond her youthful effort to be obedient to patriarchal thought and authority.

The essays also reveal another characteristic of Horney's work: her intellectual explorations of issues that she was personally experiencing. For example, her study of female development and her awareness of young girls' interest in their own bodies were influenced by her having raised three daughters (Moulton, 1975, p. 211). After her marriage to Oscar Horney ended in separation in 1926, Karen Horney wrote six essays on the problems of marriage (Horney, 1927b, c, d; 1928; 1931a; 1932b). And later, in a book aptly entitled *Self Analysis* (1942), she described a patient called Clare whose childhood experiences and adult conflicts closely resemble those of her own life (Kelman, 1971, p. 23). Thus, although her professional writing is evenhanded and remarkably objective, the origins of the problems she addressed are deeply personal.

Horney's early essays on female psychology are not simply critiques of Freudian orthodoxy; they are also attempts to reform psychoanalysis so as to enable her to find an authentic place for herself within the profession. But her arguments were more radi-

---

3. Some of these were published posthumously in *Feminine Psychology* in 1967.

cal than the Freudian paradigm with its ontology of instinct could allow. Thus, from a theoretical perspective, her early efforts to reform Freud's ideas on women while conforming to his framework were ultimately unsuccessful.

Only after she emigrated to the United States did Horney move ahead with the theoretical implications of her earlier challenge to Freud. With political conditions deteriorating rapidly in Germany she accepted a position at the University of Chicago Medical School in 1932. Two years later she moved to New York City and became a part of the growing community of refugee scholars (Coser, 1984). Although she continued to be involved in the intellectual debates and institutional schisms among psychoanalysts in New York, Horney clarified and deepened her ideas there. In the company of other dissidents she developed her alternative to Freud's theory.

Her ideas are consistent with those of the cultural psychoanalysts with whom she associated, including Clara Thompson, Harry Stack Sullivan, and Erich Fromm. These thinkers emphasized cultural rather than instinctual determinants of psychological development. In this intellectual setting, Horney created a theory of the development of adult characterological conflict—neurosis—explaining it as a consequence of contradictory and devaluing childhood experiences. She expanded upon her theory of neurosis in five books and numerous articles published from 1937 until her death at the age of sixty-seven in 1952.[4]

Horney's later work on neurosis is frequently interpreted as intellectually distinct from her earlier essays on the psychology of women (see O'Connell, 1980). There is good reason to take this position. First, while the early essays raised the issue of cultural determinants of character—that is, the debilitating consequences

4. Horney wrote five books on her theory on neurosis: *The Neurotic Personality of Our Time* (1937), *New Ways in Psychoanalysis* (1939b), *Self-Analysis* (1942), *Our Inner Conflicts* (1945), and *Neurosis and Human Growth* (1950a). She edited and contributed to another, *Are You Considering Psychoanalysis?* (1946a).

of masculine civilization—they did not take culture to be the primary influence on development as did Horney's later work. In the early essays she tried to maintain the primacy of Freud's instinct theory, and posited—unsuccessfully in the judgment of some recent feminist theorists (for example, Mitchell, 1974, pp. 125–28; Chodorow, 1978, p. 148)—separate female instincts. Her later work, by contrast, is a rejection of instinct theory; instead, it elaborates cultural determinants of character. Second, Horney's early essays focus almost exclusively on women's psychological problems, while the later work is intended to explain the neurotic conflicts of both men and women. Her early essays are more critical and polemical and are regarded by some to be more feminist (for example, Garrison, 1981), while the later work is more self-assured, systematic, and appears to be gender neutral. Thus, in her early, explicitly feminist writing, Horney does not provide a theoretical alternative to Freud, and in the later work, where she does provide a theoretical alternative, her concerns do not appear to be feminist. Those who attend to her early writings are primarily feminist theorists who find it wanting, and those who are interested in her later work are often clinicians who are not asking the questions that inform feminist theory (for an exception, see Symonds, 1971, 1973, 1974, 1978, 1979). Her early and late periods therefore appear to be divided both by Horney's separate concerns and by the responses those concerns have generated.

My interpretation, however, is to view Horney's early and late periods as dialectically related. I see in the early essays the roots of her later theoretical solutions, and in her later work a continuation of the earlier feminist questioning. The writings from these different periods form a continuity that displays a relationship to the intellectual journey of a lifetime. It is that continuity that I want to emphasize.

Accordingly, I juxtapose Horney's early and late writings to interpret her later theoretical work as a social psychology of women. This is an interpretation that Horney herself envisioned.

In an essay entitled "The Flight from Womanhood" (1926), she argued that women's questioning of traditional female roles was a rejection of the inferior status that masculine civilization had imposed upon those roles. To understand female psychology, she proposed, one must account for this male-created social subordination of women. Thus, a psychology of women should be a social psychology, an explication of the interaction of psychic and social factors. These analyses would reveal problems "so grave and so important that they require a separate investigation" (p. 170). Horney herself never undertook that investigation, but she created the theoretical framework for such a project.

The framework, which emerges in her later work, explains neurotic conflict in terms of the cultural contexts and psychodynamics of child development. Unlike Freud, Horney did not hold that psychological conflict was the inevitable consequence of an ontological opposition between human nature and civilization (Freud, 1930). Rather, for her, inner conflict is the avoidable consequence of the contradictions and dehumanizing elements of civilization as transmitted by parents to their children. The neurotic shares the same cultural context as the non-neurotic but experiences its effects more intensely. In this respect neurotic conflict is simply an extreme version of the psychological conflicts that are typical in a given culture, and the neurotic individual is that culture's prototype. Neurotic suffering reflects critically on the cultural context to which it is a response. Thus, Horney's theory of neurosis is not only an explanation of character development and conflict but also a critique of the social relations and cultural values that give rise to psychological suffering.

Horney's concept of neurosis may appear unusual or confusing to contemporary readers. First, although she was in agreement with Freud that neurosis is psychological conflict, her culturally grounded etiology differs substantially from Freud (Horney, 1939b). Foreshadowing the antipsychiatry of R. D. Laing (1967), Horney argued that the neurotic is a victim whose suffering is not an individual failure but the rational human response to a culture that is sick. Unlike Laing, however, Horney did not romanticize madness as liberating (Laing, 1967, p. 127). Her approach is closer to the cultural anthropology of Ruth Benedict (Benedict, 1959/ 1934; Horney, 1937). To Horney the neurotic is not mad but supranormal: the paragon of what a neurotogenic culture produces. In her view therapy was deconstruction of the neurotic (culture) type as a condition of social change (Horney, 1947b). Thus, Horney's concept follows neither the traditional Freudian explanation nor the approach of modern antipsychiatry.

From the perspective of clinical diagnosis Horney's usage of neurosis is dated. Contemporary clinicians no longer refer to a conflicted character structure as neurosis but as personality disorder (DSM-III, 1980, p. 10). The various personality disorders—for example, dependent, narcissistic, passive-aggressive —are diagnostic categories that do not correspond to Horney's etiology and concept of neurosis, but they do refer to many of the symptoms that she associated with neurotic conflict (DSM-III, 1980, 305–30). An additional confusion for the contemporary reader is the problem of popular usage. The word *neurotic* is often popularly employed today as a term of derision or criticism (for example, Wood, 1986). In sorting through these definitions and the confusions surrounding the concept of neurosis, one must remember that Horney was attempting to understand and explain a particular social-psychological configuration. For her neurosis is human suffering caused by historically created cultural values and social relations.

Horney intended her theory of neurosis as an explanation of the characterological conflicts of both women and men. Her explicit criticism in this body of work is leveled against dehumanizing social contexts in general rather than against masculine civilization's devaluation of women in particular, as in her earlier work. Yet, I shall argue, the gender neutrality of the theory does not run deep. Although Horney, like Freud, sought to create a theory of psychological development that was applicable to men and women alike, like Freud she created a theory that reflects her own gendered experience. Because of its foundation in female experience, Horney's social-psychological theory can most appropriately be read as one of female development and characterological conflict in response to the social and cultural contexts that devalue women. From this critical perspective, implied in Horney's theory, female character conflict is the intelligible consequence, the subjective experience, and the objective criticism of masculine civilization.

A key to my interpretation of Horney's later work as a psychology of women is her concept of the "common present-day feminine type" first portrayed in an essay entitled "The Overvaluation of Love" (Horney, 1934). In this remarkable profile, Horney described the psychological conflicts that she witnessed both in her patients and among other middle-class women (pp. 184, 212). She linked the psychological struggles to conflicting definitions of femininity: a patriarchal ideal of womanhood versus a more independent female identity. The former defines "woman as one whose only longing is to love a man and be loved by him, to admire him and serve him" (p. 182); the latter refers to new opportunities for women to become economically independent of men by developing their own abilities and skills and pursuing careers (p. 183). The modern independent indentity conflicts with the traditional patriarchal one, and modern women are caught between wanting to make themselves desirable to men and pursuing their own goals. The competing purposes elicit conflicting behaviors: seductive versus aggressive, deferential versus ambitious. Modern women are torn between love and work and are consequently dissatisfied in both.

The patriarchal ideal of women to which Horney referred received a new emphasis in both Germany and America in the early decades of the twentieth century, especially during the 1920s. Romantic love, marriage, the relaxing of sexual mores, and the media exploitation of the sexualized female body all contributed to a female ideal and identity that emphasized a woman's relationship to and dependency on a man. Historians have termed this emphasis the "heterosexual imperative" (Ryan, 1983, pp. 238–44) or the "heterosexual revolution" (Rapp and Ross, 1983, p. 93). During this same period, the male standard of success, defined in terms of middle-class career ambition, was extended to women (Bledstein, 1976; Kessler-Harris, 1982; Showalter, 1978, pp. 14–16). Consequently, in the early decades of the twentieth century middle-class women had new, if limited, opportunities to engage in the public world of work and to dream of career success.

The feminine type's conflict reflects these historical changes. She pursues heterosexual attachments compulsively; indeed, according to Horney, she overvalues being loved by a man. She also desires middle-class career success, which she associates with being like a man. Yet, the feminine type deprecates her own skills and abilities even while she craves fame and fortune. Horney called this combination of overvaluing male love and achievement and disparaging one's own real abilities an "objective falsification of values" (p. 187). Her analysis implies that it is not love per se that is overvalued, but men. Being loved by a man and succeeding on male terms are the ideals that contrast with the lowly image that the feminine type has of herself. Out of a sense of her own worthlessness this male-identified woman turns to men as a source of false self-esteem.

If Horney had only described these conflicts, she would have provided an excellent portrait of the psychological consequences of the heterosexual imperative. But she went beyond description to posit a startling explanation of the feminine type's compulsive and indiscriminate desire for male love and approval. The reason, she argued, is not a primary heterosexual desire; the craving for a man is instead a secondary expression of an underlying rivalry with other women (Horney, 1934, p. 201). The feminine type compares and judges herself—especially her appearance—against other women. She is envious of all women who are attractive to men or are successful in male domains. She wants to humiliate other women by surpassing them in the accumulation of male admirers or by triumphing through public acclaim. But even if she is successful, she does not gain enduring satisfaction, for she fears retaliation from other women and loss of interest from men (Horney, 1934, pp. 186–92).

This uncertainty fosters anxiety and self-doubt. The women from whom Horney drew her definition of the feminine type suffered from a deep sense of inadequacy and shame through comparison with other women. They felt irremediably ugly; they perceived their bodies, especially specific aspects—weight, hair, complexion, and so on—as not right, even inordinately repulsive. In attempting to hide their perceived ugliness (according to Horney, most were actually attractive), they placed a great emphasis on dress. But their perfectionistic obsession with clothing only heightened their sense of anxiety about their bodies; nothing was ever quite good enough to hide their flaws. And, because their clothes were not perfect, their feelings of shame and inadequacy were heightened (Horney, 1934, pp. 196–97).

Horney probed deeper into explaining the rivalry between women. She argued that it emerges from a childhood in which a girl grows up in competition with her mother and sisters to be the favorite of the more powerful males in the household. This desire for male favor is socially rather than instinctually based. It emerges from a family setting of male prerogative and power and female subordination and sexualized identity. A girl learns early to devalue her abilities and regard herself as a sexual object. She competes with all other females to become the favorite of a sexualizing and powerful male. If she is humiliated by defeat when discarded for another (which is likely given the chaotic nature of the sexualizing treatment) she later wreaks her revenge on other women, whom she perceives as enemies.

The feminine type wants to triumph over other women by securing the love of men, but she feels fundamentally unlovable.

She therefore deprecates her successes and discounts any man who is attracted to her. Yet she panics at any suggestion of loss of interest on his part. Similarly, she is often dependent on women, with whom she also feels in competition. The stronger the woman on whom she is dependent, the more she fears her dependence and envies the other's strength. Her relationships with other women are fraught with conflict as she simultaneously clings to their strength and attempts to erode it. The feminine type, then, needs to destroy other women and to secure the love of men in order to convince herself that she is not the worthless creature that she believes herself to be (Horney, 1934, pp. 188–93).

"The Overvaluation of Love" is Horney's first fully developed attempt to understand in social contextual terms the kind of woman she found prototypical to her times. Her feminine type is an exaggeration in two respects. First, as an *ideal type* she personifies in the extreme the conflicts that Horney believed were common among other women. Second, the feminine type reflects the extremes of her time. The conflicting identities for women that have remained well into the twentieth century were first brought into competition with each other when the feminine type was a young woman. Today, the idea that women juggle personal and career goals is commonplace, but fifty or sixty years ago it was considered a contradiction, despite the fact that many did it. To the extent that elements of that contradiction remain in the lives of contemporary women, the feminine type's struggle can illuminate them.

Yet, the tension between love and work is only part of a larger picture of female conflict personified by the feminine type. The male identification, the rivalry among women, the childhood experiences of being treated as an inferior female and as a sex object, the shame and self-doubt, the desire for vindication are all part of a pattern that Horney first identified in 1934. In her analysis of this pattern I see the foundation for the major elements of her subsequent theory of neurosis.

Thus, I interpret Horney's theory of neurosis through the lens of her feminine type. In this way I cast her theory as a critical social psychology of women, explaining the feminine type's development and the dynamics of her conflicts. The critical basis of this interpretation is Horney's concept of neurosis as inner conflict, especially between self-hatred and an idealized self-image informed by cultural stereotypes and values. The cause of neurosis is not the failure of the individual but the dehumanizing conditions that she encounters in the social world. Devalued by masculine civilization and expected to comply cheerfully with this condition, she adopts dependent characteristics as a strategy of safety. Her dependency may be an individual solution, but it reflects the misogynistic values that engendered it; her inner conflict may create psychological pain, but the fact that it eminates from cultural patterns gives it social meaning.

In appropriating neurosis as a critical concept, I follow Horney's usage and underscore its importance for a social psychology of women. From this perspective the neurotic is not abnormal but supranormal, not socially deficient but the cultural ideal. She is the feminine type, the female paragon who exaggerates the qualities that masculine civilization promotes in women. Her success, however, is achieved at the cost of suffering experienced as inner conflict. This psychological conflict represents a flight from social criticism: the feminine type acquiesces to masculine civilization and internalizes its devaluation of her.

My goal is to explore the psychological basis for socializing the conflict—transforming self-criticism to social criticism. But this requires something other than projecting the inner struggle upon the world. It necessitates understanding the conflict itself—its development and dynamics—for purposes of working it through and creating a new critical basis for engaging in the world.

In an effort to create this understanding, I analyze the psychological conflict of the feminine type. Chapter 1 describes the historical setting in which she lived. Chapter 2 examines the development of Horney's thought leading to her theory. That the-

ory, which I interpret as a social psychology of women in chapter 3, explains the feminine type's behavior. The following five
chapters elaborate this interpretation by examining the girlhood
experiences of sexualization (chapter 4) and devaluation (chapter 5), and their consequences in dependency (chapter 6), anger
(chapter 7), and detachment (chapter 8). Finally, chapter 9
explores an idea of overcoming and socializing women's psychological conflict.

1 | Historical Contexts and Psychological Conflicts

Horney's description of the feminine type was published in 1934, two years after she emigrated to the United States. Most of the middle-class women who reflected the type were born around the end of the nineteenth century, In order to illuminate the feminine type and Horney's subsequent elaboration of her in the later theory, it is necessary first to understand the life and identity of middle-class women in turn-of-the-century America.[1]

The Domestic Ideal

The feminine type was born into a nineteenth-century middle class that had created an ideal of female domesticity. According to Barbara Welter (1973), this ideal was defined in terms of religious piety, sexual purity, wifely submission, and motherly domesticity. Central to the code of behavior was the presumption that women would cultivate their elevated qualities in the home, the "private" sphere of domestic care-taking.

Nancy Cott (1977) claims that the development of the "separate sphere" of domesticated womanhood occurred between 1780 and the 1830s among the white native-born middle to upper middle classes of the northeastern United States. These people created a cult of domesticity that emanated into other classes and regions in the nineteenth century and eventually became a powerfully influ-

1. It is likely that in her elaboration Horney was describing white women only, since she based the feminine type on characteristics of her patients, who at this time were likely to be white and middle class (cf. Garfield, 1978, pp. 199–201).

ential definition of female identity (pp. 9–10). The domestic cult was created in response to rapid economic growth and social change, especially the shift from a mercantile to a capitalist economy, which removed the production of household goods from the home to the factory. Middle-class women who formerly produced items their families needed—such as candles, soap, or cloth—could now purchase them relatively cheaply. As a result, married women's work, which had always been carried out in connection with the home, was transformed; it now focused primarily on household upkeep and child care and shifted from producing commodities to consuming them (pp. 44–58). At the same time the work of middle-class men now took them away from the household to shops, offices, and factories. Thus, the working worlds of middle-class women and men became separated as home and wage labor became differentiated (pp. 58–62).

The different spheres of men and women were considered complementary. A husband's wages were necessary to purchase necessities. Although a wife's domestic duties focused on housekeeping and child care, they also involved creating a home as a place of refuge from the uncertainties, intense pace, and ethical compromises associated with the public world of industrial labor and business. The rapid social and economic changes of the early 1800s bred a quest for stability and a desire to reaffirm the traditional religious and ethical values that seemed to be eroding (Griswold, 1982, p. 14). The domesticated world of women became the locus of preservation, the private substitute for community solidarity, and the individual defense against chaos and moral decay.

Women's very separation from the competitive treachery and pecuniary contagion of the marketplace elevated their moral station in a society perceived to be dominated by self-interest and greed (Cott, 1977, pp. 67–69). In contrast to the ethical compromises exacted by the marketplace, women were expected to be unconditionally loving and unflinchingly committed to traditional religious principles. In opposition to the self-serving individualism that the business world required, women were held to be naturally selfless, desiring only to live for others (pp. 70–71). A middle-class man thus sought in a wife both the morality that was vanishing from the outside world and the maternal qualities that would assuage the insecurity created by his engagement in that world. In effect, he looked to his wife as a spiritually elevated and unconditionally loving mother, "tolerant, constant, and forgiving" (Barker-Benfield, 1976, p. 13).

The idea of the motherly wife creating what Christopher Lasch (1979) calls a "haven in a heartless world" was entwined with a middle-class ideology of repressed female sexuality. At first associated with the early nineteenth-century belief that women were spiritually above sex, the idea of inhibited female sexuality came during the second half of the century to be linked with the notion that women lacked sexual drive (Cott, 1978). Historians note that during this period middle-class men and women alike were subject to the strictures that equated respectability with control over sexual impulses (Haller and Haller, 1974; C. Rosenberg, 1973). However, for the middle-class Victorian woman, self-control was presumed to be physically inherent (Cott, 1978, pp. 235–36). This presumption undergirded the ideal of spiritual motherhood: mothers were above the "baser" instincts. The idea of women's inborn prudery also formed the psychological basis for the imperative of maternal selflessness. Without desires, a wife was considered to live only for others—especially husband and children. As Victorian Eliza Duffy saw it, women had "more of the motherly nature than the conjugal about them.... Their husbands are to them only children of larger growth, to be loved and cared for very much in the same way as their real children. It is the motherly element which is the hope, and is to be the salvation of the world. The higher a woman rises in moral and intellectual culture, the more is the sexual refined away from her nature, and the more pure and perfect and predominating becomes her motherhoood.

The real woman regards all men, be they older or younger than herself, not as possible lovers, but as a sort of step-sons, towards whom her heart goes out in motherly tenderness" (quoted in Haller and Haller, 1974, pp. 100–01).

The good woman, the hope and salvation of the world, was the asexual mother, whose very refinement was guarded by the domestic sphere she created as a stable moral refuge from the chaos of industrial expansion in nineteenth-century America. To trespass outside that sphere of asexual domesticity was to risk losing the identity of virtuous womanhood. Advice columns in women's magazines exhorted mothers to protect the reputation of their daughters by cultivating in them the virtues of "true womanhood." Welter (1973) cites examples from popular literature in the mid-century of moralistic tales describing the unfortunate fates of young girls of good standing who were either intemperate or not vigilant enough in protecting themselves against the profligate intentions of sophisticated young men. Mrs. A. J. Graves recorded the sad tale of Amelia, a middle-class girl who "died in the almshouse, 'the wretched victim of depravity and intemperance,' and all because her mother had let her be 'high-spirited—not prudent.' These girlish high-spirits had been misinterpreted by a young man, with disastrous results. Amelia's 'thoughtless levity' was 'followed by a total loss of virtuous principle' and Mrs. Graves editorializes that 'the coldest reserve is more admirable in a woman a man wishes to make his wife, than the least approach to undue familiarity'" (p. 99).

The protection of nineteenth-century women from the dangerous world of men meant their separation from the compromising business of wage-earning. This image, of course, contradicted the lives of scores of working women. As Alice Kessler-Harris (1982) documents, the proliferation of manufacturing in the early 1800s required workers; men and women alike were encouraged to join the expanding labor force. Moreover, less production within the home meant extra female help was no longer needed there (pp. 20–27). Thus, while affluent middle-class women developed their separate spheres of domestication, other women—married and single—worked for the wages that their families needed (p. 30). Married women generally performed work at home, such as sewing, while their daughters worked as domestics or as "mill girls" (Lerner, 1969). However, after the economic depression of the late 1830s, fewer women worked outside the home. This trend was reinforced by the growing influence of the ideology of separate spheres (Kessler-Harris, 1982, pp. 45–53). Some women—especially new immigrants and black women—continued to work outside the home, but the cult that elevated female domesticity denigrated those who needed to work for wages. Reflecting the belief that women belonged in the home, employment opportunities for women were reduced; employers paid only "supplemental" wages to females; and some women were forced into prostitution (pp. 53–59). Thus the domestic cult sharpened class differences as it prescribed acceptable femininity in terms of middle-class resources and lifestyle.

The domestic cult contained a contradiction that created conflicted female identity. First, all women were supposed to be motherly; wives were expected to provide for the physical and spiritual well-being of their husbands as if they were needy sons. Steven Mintz's analysis of Robert Louis Stevenson's letters to his fiancée records this expectation: "'You must help me!' he implored, 'and I must live to honour your help.' In return, he would be her 'son,' her 'faithful friend,' her 'priest'" (Mintz, 1983, p. 108). Mintz claims Stevenson's exaltation of his fiancée's virtues is a means of compensating for his own flaws. "Her moral idealism counteracts his vulgar ambition; her capacity for self sacrifice corrects for his vulgar egotism; her moral purity compensates for his weakness. Idealizing her virtues is a way of indicating that his vices and flaws are inconsequential. This attitude, which glorifies women as moral supports and guides of men, recurs again and again in Stevenson's love letters and contributes to an image of men as not wholly responsible for their actions."

The morally superior wife not only compensated for her husband's shortcomings but also excused them with indulgent sympathy and cheerful understanding. In a popular novel of 1850, the author fantasized the motherly wife who smilingly forgives all: "A home! . . . it is the Presence . . . that there at least you are beloved; that there you are understood; that there all your errors will meet ever with gentlest forgiveness; that there your troubles will be smiled away; that there you may unburden your soul, fearless of harsh, unsympathetic ears; and that there you may be entirely and joyfully—yourself!" (quoted in Barker-Benfield, 1976, p. 13). The motherly wife was a husband's spiritually elevated counterpart who redeemed his flaws through her own spotless behavior. She was the unconditionally loving and gently forgiving mother who, in contrast to employer or competitor, accepted her husband as he was. She nurtured him emotionally and indulged him physically.

But women were to be more than responsible mothers; they were also defined as weak and incapable dependents. This contradictory definition derived from women's financial dependency upon men. If men were needy sons who required the motherly wife's responsible caretaking, women were incapable and delicate children who had to rely on their husbands' superior intellect and strength. "Ladies" lacked the mental and physical capacity to work outside the home. To some, this female delicacy was thought to be anatomically based.

Woman, according to one nineteenth-century physician, "has a head almost too small for intellect but just big enough for love" (Welter, 1973, p. 103). Women's inborn delicacy and their financial dependence on men were the basis for their submission to male authority. Although often couched in terms of the religious image of the husband as God's delegate, a nineteenth-century wife's deference to her husband was required by the order established by the separation of spheres, which made him the breadwinner and her the dependent (Mintz, 1983, pp. 54–61).

The imperative to nurture men and the condition of being financially dependent upon them called out opposing attitudes and behavior. Women were supposed to be both strong and weak, self-reliant and dependent, maternal and ladylike, responsible for men and deferential to them. According to Carroll Smith-Rosenberg (1972), these opposing expectations led to a crisis among middle-class daughters during the last three decades of the nineteenth century. Daughters reacted to the "child woman" contradiction by developing symptoms of hysteria (p. 656), which became a legitimate means for expressing dissatisfaction with the conflicting expectations. By taking to her bed with headaches, nausea, pains, or paralysis—taking her passivity to its extreme—a young woman could reject the responsibility thrust on her. This passive aggression released her rage against social expectations and preserved her dutiful inhibition against expressing it directly (pp. 662–78).

Thus, not all women cheerfully embraced the domestic cult and its contradictions. Others found means more direct than hysteria to express their dissatisfaction and their independent wills. According to Lee Chambers-Schiller (1984), a significant segment of antebellum women rejected marriage and motherhood and made their livings as teachers or missionaries, arguing that liberty was "a better husband." Others who did take husbands tried to democratize their marriages at the same time that they struggled to create equal rights for women as citizens (Hersh, 1978). These were the early feminists who identified their exclusion from voting as the public sanction of male privilege and thus made female suffrage the goal of the struggle for women's political equality (Baker, 1984). Still others, instead of opposing male privilege, enhanced their influence through emphasizing the female maternal role. For example, some early nineteenth-century women coopted the ideology of female sexual "passionlessness" and enhanced their opportunities as human beings by minimizing their sexual reproductive functions (Cott, 1978). This created, according to Daniel Scott Smith (1973), a "domestic feminism" whereby women were able to reduce the size of their families.

The same type of approach that emphasized traditional female qualities led other women to capitalize upon their maternal influence and extend it beyond the traditional domestic sphere. Catharine Beecher sought to transform the home through a domestic economy that would elevate housekeeping to a professional calling (Sklar, 1973). In the 1830s women in New York and New England inaugurated moral reform societies to attack prostitution and thereby to control men's sexual behavior (Smith-Rosenberg, 1971). In the 1820s and 1830s educators like Emma Willard founded new schools for women, which ostensibly provided instruction in household skills but also included a curriculum in the liberal arts and sciences (Cott, 1977, pp. 122–25). And after the Civil War women throughout the United States founded literary clubs that permitted them to leave the confines of the home to meet together for intellectual exchange. They justified this activity by claiming that it enhanced maternal capability (Blair, 1980).

Thus, the feminine type was born into a late nineteenth-century middle class whose reverence for a domesticated ideal created a powerful definition of female identity: woman's place was most definitely in the home as a motherly dependent. Yet, this identity was neither unanimously interpreted nor universally available to women in all economic classes. Moreover, the imperative to nurture men contradicted the expectation of female weakness and subservience. The world in which the feminine type grew up inherited this domestic ideal and its conflicts; it also underwent major social and economic changes that transformed them.

The New Woman

The contradiction between women's submission to male authority and their duty to nurture men and children—the paradox of "powerless responsibility," to use Adrienne Rich's phrase (Rich, 1976, p. 52)—did not disappear in the twentieth century. Rather, it was transformed as the separation between home and work and the definition of women's roles interacted in new and more complex ways.

In the 1870s the middle classes began the migration to the suburbs that, according to Gwendolyn Wright (1980, 1981), established the pattern of contemporary urban landscapes. This shift in middle-class residency was a response to the tremendous industrial growth and sweeping social changes occurring at the turn of the century: the increase in transportation and industrial production, the proliferation of new technologies and consumer products and services, the rapid expansion of the population (especially urban) through immigration, the doubling in per-capita income (Wright, 1980, pp. 82–87), and the continuing decline in the size of the average family (from eight to ten children in 1755 to three in 1900) (Kennedy, 1970, p. 42). As middle-class families became more numerous, smaller in size, and more affluent, they sought to escape the perils that they associated with city living—"poor health, social unrest, and vice. The private dwelling in a safe residential neighborhood would protect the wife and children from the dangers of the wicked city" (Wright, 1981, p. 96).

The home as a suburban haven was made possible by the increase in production, the effects of which the suburbanites were fleeing. New technologies allowed mass production of building products such as wooden ornamentation, shingles, and lead pipes, and created a deluge of decorative items, furniture, bric-a-brac, and wallpaper (Wright, 1980, pp. 81–102). The suburban home—the haven of repose and comfort away from city and market—was the showcase for a husband's material success and a wife's consumer expertise and decorating talents; indeed, the home came to represent the commercialized individualism of the family itself (Wright, 1981, pp. 109–13). As home and wage labor—the private and public spheres—became geographically more separated through suburbanization, the lives of middle-class women were physically separated from the areas of industrial production and the crowded cities. Married women focused on individualizing the home by consuming "artistic" household products, and caring for husbands and children.

The contrast between middle-class affluence and display and the poverty of many city dwellers did not go unchallenged. In his trenchant critique *The Theory of the Leisure Class* (1953/1899), Thorsten Veblen called middle-class women a "vicarious" leisure class whose frivolous attention to domestic adornment and tidiness served merely as a conspicuous display of their husbands' pecuniary success (pp. 68–69). But Veblen's critique was preceded by that of many middle-class women themselves, who from the 1880s until World War I extended the limits of domesticity by engaging in the major reform activities associated with Progressivism. By finding new public arenas for maternal influence, middle-class women participated in activities that Mary Ryan has termed "social housekeeping" (Ryan, 1983, p. 198).

Women's clubs began to shift their attention from literary topics to social problems such as slum housing and child labor (Blair, 1980, pp. 98–99). The Women's Christian Temperance Union, under the leadership of Frances Willard, expanded its cause in the 1890s to attack social abuses affecting women and children (DuBois, 1975). Between 1890 and 1900 the number of women graduating from college increased significantly from less than 25 percent to 40 percent of all graduates (Ryan, 1983, p. 201). Many of these young women sought to put their education to use in settlement-house work and labor organizing. Among them was Jane Addams, who in 1887 with Ellen Star founded Hull House in

Chicago "to provide a center for higher civic and social life; to institute and maintain educational and philanthropic enterprises, and to investigate and improve the conditions in the industrial districts of Chicago" (Addams, 1961/1910, p. 89). By 1910 there were over four hundred settlement houses in the United States which allowed thousands of young worker-settlers, predominantly women, to "put their talents as well as their compassion to work" (Ryan, 1983, p. 202). These women engaged in numerous neighborhood and civic activities—established cooperative neighborhood organizations, educated mothers in the middle-class virtues of good nutrition, health care and child welfare, created kindergartens, assisted in dealing with public officials, and participated in political campaigns and legislative reform (S. Rothman, 1978, pp. 112–27).

The various social housekeeping activities involved many middle-class women in what Estelle Freedman (1979) has termed "female institution building." These women created female-directed institutions, based on shared values of maternal caretaking, that were alternatives to male-controlled public institutions and political activities. In the process, individual women became publicly successful. Florence Kelley, an early advocate of child labor reform, became an influential head of the State Board of Labor and Jane Addams became a widely recognized leader in civic and national politics as well as in international peace organizations (Ryan, 1983, pp. 201–03).

Many other individual women reaped the benefits of the professionalization that women's institution building and social reform efforts produced. The reformers created new state and municipal bureaucracies to implement social welfare policies. As government grew, so did professional careers in social service (Bledstein, 1976). According to Kessler-Harris (1982), many of these new jobs went to women who had been volunteers in areas where men had no traditional influence or experience. "Jobs as factory inspectors, child labor investigators, visiting nurses, and truant officers; jobs in bureaus of labor statistics and in the personnel offices of large industries now opened to women as part of their social role" (p. 115). As careers in social service expanded, women sought the education that would prepare them to be professionals. Through the jobs that came to be defined as women's professions—teaching, nursing, social work, and librarianship—middle-class women entered the labor force (Bledstein, 1976, pp. 38–39; Kessler-Harris, 1982, p. 116). Although these careers were less well-paid than comparable careers for men, they nevertheless formed a new legitimate opportunity for middle-class daughters to choose a vocation that was as respected as homemaking. While many women pursued their careers only briefly until marriage, others chose to devote themselves to a profession and never married at all (Matthaei, 1982, pp. 181–83).

Women professionals were a small percentage of working women (Matthaei, 1982, p. 226), but they were taking advantage of a new alternative for middle-class female autonomy and purpose. The alternative emerged along with and sometimes as the result of other changes in the early decades of the twentieth century: the social housekeeping of the club women, settlement workers, and volunteers; the sharp increase in the number of women graduating from college, the rise in women's overall participation in the labor force from 14.7 percent in 1890 to 24 percent in 1920 (Wilson, 1979, p. 6); and the increased support for women's suffrage (Baker, 1984, p. 624). All of these changes loosened the traditional bonds on women and led to the emergence of a "new woman" who was free to take on responsibility and pursue self-improvement. She fought against the submission required of the "true woman" by extending her maternal responsibility into the public world of social reform and engaging in independent actions that sometimes challenged male political authority. By extending maternal responsibility, social housekeepers helped create the new professions that in turn contributed to women's individual advancement in careers. The expansion of social services and the shortage of men during World War I further extended women's opportunities in the professions and civil service (Kessler-Harris, 1982, p. 116). The new woman appeared to be creating a world in which male and female roles were no longer defined in terms of the separation of spheres.

The changes, however, seemed more dramatic than they actually were. First, the majority of wage-earning women were single, and most of them eventually left their jobs to marry and rear families (Matthaei, 1982, p. 143; Degler, 1980, pp. 385–92). Moreover, the idea of women's domestic role hung on strongly into the twentieth century, receiving new emphasis in the backlash against the freedom and self-assertion associated with the new woman. When combined with nativism and racism, this reaction frequently expressed fear that native white middle-class women were abandoning their maternal responsibilities while immigrant and black women were producing large families (Filene, 1974, p. 37). In fact there was a substantial increase in the number of daughters of native-born parents in the labor force between 1890 and 1920. They formed, according to Kessler-Harris, an advance guard of new women professionals and office workers (Kessler-Harris, 1982, p. 119). Moreover, college-educated women were having fewer children than the national average and fewer of them were marrying (R. Rosenberg, 1982, p. 23).

The fear of "race suicide" thus prompted some to exhort middle-class white women to return to their traditional roles. Writing in the *Atlantic Monthly*, Margaret Deland (1910) implored, "Oh, let us learn to wait . . . there seems to me a certain unhumorous arrogance in this bustling, feminine haste to make over the world—it is as if we thought ourselves so important that nothing could go right without us" (p. 301). Deland feared that feminist demands would upset the pattern of ethnic and racial dominance. She claimed that she was not opposed to female suffrage but only to *universal* female suffrage: "Shall the suffrage therefore be given to your cook?" (p. 298). Teddy Roosevelt made the connection between racial dominance and female domestic compliance most succinctly: "A race is worthless and contemptible if its men cease to be willing and able to work hard and, at need, to fight hard, and if the women cease to breed freely" (quoted in Filene, 1974, p. 39).

The reaction against the new woman was also combined with men's fears that the opportunities for masculine expression and vocation were being limited by economic and social changes. According to Peter Filene (1974), the expansion of business and the rationalization of labor undermined traditional masculine definitions of independent hard work (pp. 73–75). Some men in the clerical fields that women were rapidly entering felt especially threatened (Hantover, 1978). Moreover, women's reform activities in organizations like the Women's Christian Temperance Union appeared to be assaulting masculinity itself. In response, men reasserted the traditional roles of male dominance and female submission, symbolized best by Teddy Roosevelt's glorification of the strenuous life for men and motherhood for women (Filene, 1974, pp. 71–94). Even the less threatening club woman seemed dangerous. In 1905, Grover Cleveland, fearing that the female domesticity that undergirded male stability was eroding, complained, "There are women's clubs whose objects and intents are not only harmful, but harmful in a way that directly menaces the integrity of our homes" (quoted in Blair, 1980, p. 105).

Middle-class male fears of unbridled female autonomy were economically unfounded. Men still dominated the professional world, and the vast majority of middle-class women continued to marry and have children. Muckraker Ida Tarbell, herself an example of new womanhood, argued that the changes in women's roles were less dramatic and disruptive than they appeared to be. The contemporary woman, Tarbell contended, "Is no larger factor in industrial life than she has always been, but the form of industry has changed. It draws her into great groups, and those groups collect in cities and manufacturing towns. We see her more often than we did when she canned and wove and sewed in small isolated groups. She is more obvious" (Tarbell, 1916, p. 15).

Tarbell was correct in linking the new woman's paid labor out-

side the home to the production that women had formerly performed in the home, but she glossed over the significance of
women's increased visibility. Working-class women especially
became increasingly "obvious" not just at work in department
stores, restaurants, and factories but in their leisure activities as
well. According to Kathy Peiss (1983), many of these "working
girls," "dressed in the latest finery, negotiated city life with ease,
and sought intrigue and adventure with male companions"
(p. 76), especially at dance halls, vaudeville shows, and amuse-
ment parks. Their behavior reflected that of the performers: they
were openly flirtatious and drew attention to themselves by wearing elaborate dresses, hair styles, and makeup (pp. 77–78). These
women, who worked several years before they married, dated men
who treated them to drinks, theatre tickets, or gifts. "Treating was
not a one-way proposition, however, but entailed an exchange
relationship. Financially unable to reciprocate in kind, women
offered sexual favors of varying degrees, ranging from flirtatious
companionship to sexual intercourse, in exchange for men's
treats" (p. 78). Those who did reciprocate with sex were termed
"charity girls" and distinguished from prostitutes because they
did not accept money (p. 81).

Although most working women were not charity girls, the relax-
ation in sexual standards and the openly suggestive behavior of
many working women blurred the Victorian distinction between
the lady and the prostitute. Observing the phenomenon,
sociologist W. I. Thomas (1956/1923) noted, "Thus fifty years ago
we recognized, roughly speaking, two types of women, the one
completely good and the other completely bad—what we now
call the old-fashioned girl and the girl who had sinned and been
outlawed. At present we have several intermediate types—the
occasional prostitute, the charity girl, the demi-virgin, the equiv-
ocal flapper, and in addition girls with new ... social behavior
norms who have adapted themselves to all kinds of work"
(pp. 230–31).

The blurring of the distinction between good women and bad women was part of a social phenomenon in which all women were sexually defined. As a result of this identity, wage-earning women were frequently subject to sexual harassment (Peiss, 1983, pp. 78–79) and their sexual attractiveness became an increasingly important job qualification. Sociologist Frances Donovan (1920) noted that the emphasis on working women's appearance created competition among women as well as discrimination in hiring practices (p. 209). "Restaurants want women who are young and good looking; the advertisements announce it and most managers insist on it. 'There ain't no chance for an old hen, they all want chickens and they want 'em slender,' is a remark which defines the situation" (p. 211). In her history of women office workers, Margery Davies (1982) cites a businessman's specification for his new secretary: "An exceptionally attractive, intelligent young woman, not over twenty-five; must be educated and well-bred, with charming personality; a natural blonde, five feet eight inches tall, and slender; a smart wardrobe necessary" (p. 153).

The expectation that women be sexually attractive was not confined to wage-earners. In her history of women's beauty in America, Lois Banner (1983) argues that the sexual freedom of the dancehall performers imitated by working-class young women set a new standard for middle- and upper-class women as well. The sexualized new woman portrayed an image of "new self-assertion and vigor and new sensual behavior, a desire for pleasure that flew in the face of Victorian canons of duty and submissiveness. Throughout American society, women began to respond to new sexual themes expressed on the stage and in popular music and newspapers" (p. 187). The new female sexual identity was taken up by the advertising, fashion, and cosmetic industries in an explosion of mass media portrayal of what Mary Ryan calls the "sexy saleslady" (1983, p. 223). Scantily clad models urged men and women alike to buy new products from automobiles to soap. Women were expected to emulate the idealized advertising models. "Sex and sales were so tightly conjoined with the female gender that women themselves began to resemble marketable commodities. Female bodies paraded through the popular culture and advertising copy like standardized, interchangeable parts coming off an assembly line" (p. 225).

Mass media, fashion, beauty contests, and other forms of popular culture created not simply a new and more sexual standard of female beauty. More important, they reflected a new emphasis on sexual attractiveness as the most important aspect of woman's identity (Banner, 1983, pp. 249–70). Lydia Commander ruefully observed the consequence of this in *The American Idea* (1907). "In the old days a married woman was supposed to be a frump and a bore and a physical wreck. Now you are supposed to keep up intellectually, to look young and well and be fresh and bright and entertaining" (p. 182).

The universal emphasis upon sexual attractiveness trivialized women: What they did mattered less than how they looked. No image captured this trivialized femininity better than that of the flapper of the late 1910s and 1920s. The flapper was apolitical, fun-loving, and energetically disdainful of Victorian prudery. She rejected the social housekeeping, women's clubs, and reform activities of the Progressives (Ryan, 1983, p. 220) and instead sought the company of indulgent men and the individualistic pleasures of acquisitiveness. According to Smith-Rosenberg (1985) the image of the sexually liberated flapper, promoted by male writers and sex experts, redefined female autonomy by separating it from political and economic structures. "The daughter's quest for heterosexual pleasures, not the mother's demand for political power, now personified female freedom" (p. 283). But female sexual liberation was channeled into superficial images of sexualized attractiveness and used to undermine women's claims to be taken seriously. "Glamorous, economically independent, sexually free, and of course single, the flapper represented what a business community would like its young women workers to be.

In return for limited economic and sexual freedom, women were encouraged to adopt a flighty, apolitical, and irresponsible stance. That image was meant to guarantee only peripheral involvement in the task of earning a living" (Kessler-Harris, 1982, p. 226). Those women who persisted in pursuing economic and political power were castigated as "unnatural" and "mannish lesbians who violated natural order" (Smith-Rosenberg, 1985, pp. 265–83).

The image of the frivolous young woman who worked only until marriage was promoted by a segregated labor force that distinguished between men's and women's jobs. Women's jobs were viewed as temporary; they were underpaid and offered little opportunity for advancement. The division of labor created by management in the early twentieth century established hierarchies in which women's jobs, such as clerical work, were at the bottom of the ladder. When opportunities for advancement arose within an office, they automatically went to men (Davies, 1982, pp. 38–50).

Thus, job segregation and sexualization combined to trivialize working women. "Hired because employers needed a transient yet educated labor force, female typists, receptionists, clerks, and stenographers found their rewards not in high pay and promotion but in glamour, paternalistic amenities, and the opportunity to serve" (Kessler-Harris, 1982, p. 233). Further devalued by the expectation that women workers should serve their bosses, many women—especially clerical workers—became the equivalent of professional wives. Margery Davies (1982) documents the ways private secretaries served as "office wives": they were expected to be attractive, utterly loyal, maternally sensitive to their bosses' needs, and efficient and competent in running the office (pp. 154–57).

Similarly, women's careers were defined as sub-professions that assisted the real work of men (Matthaei, 1982, p. 181). Even within female occupations, women lost control over administration and the setting of standards. Women were librarians, but men were library directors; women were dental hygienists, but men were dentists; women were the majority of teachers, but the principals were men. "Women were entering the professions, but the professions remained largely gender divided" (Kessler-Harris, 1982, p. 117; cf. Bledstein, 1976, p. 120).

Trivializing women workers by emphasizing their sexual attractiveness and by pushing them into subordinate jobs palliated the impact of women's public participation in the paid labor force. The "working girl," no matter what her age, was continually reminded that she was not taken seriously as an autonomous actor in the public world of men because her fate was ultimately domestic. Those who resisted this definition were derogated as "mannish lesbians" and lesbianism itself was attacked because it threatened the socio-economic order (Smith-Rosenberg, 1985, p. 267). In this way, wage-earning women became privatized. Subordinated to men and responsible for implementing male wishes, they encountered in the working world the same "powerless responsibility" that had characterized the nineteenth-century domestic cult.

If wage-earning women were privatized by being subordinated in a segregated labor force and assigned nurturing responsibilities, married women encountered the opposite effect: they became partially professionalized as homemakers and mothers. This "public" transformation of women's traditional family roles resulted from the development of new expertise in the areas of housekeeping and childrearing, specialized knowledge that was part of what Burton Bledstein (1976) termed the "culture of professionalism." Gradually developing during the latter half of the nineteenth century, the culture of professionalism exploded at the turn of the century with the strengthening of scientific technique. Professionalism as a means of social mobility was rooted in the authority of science. "Professionals controlled the magic circle of scientific knowledge which only the few, specialized by training and indoctrination, were privileged to enter, but which all in the name of nature's universality were obligated to appreciate" (p. 90). Professional knowledge was wedded to the ideology of method that disseminated twentieth-century scientific-technical mentality into all areas of life. According to Jacques Ellul (1964), this process represented the belief that there exists a most efficient means for every area of human endeavor (p. 21). In a period of capitalist development and competition, employers felt it was in their interest to develop the techniques of scientific management, which promised to increase profit by guaranteeing the most efficient use of employees' time (Braverman, 1974, pp. 37–38). Those who designed and employed such techniques were considered experts whose knowledge elevated the status of their occupation to that of a profession (Bledstein, 1976, p. 34).

In this setting the new profession of home economics was formed to apply the principles of scientific management to housework. The president of the American Home Economics Association, Ellen Richards, in 1911 claimed the purpose of home economics was to discard past traditions and employ scientific techniques to improve home life (Wright, 1980, p. 154). As college home economics courses burgeoned—from 4 in 1890 to 195 in 1916 (p. 153)—middle-class young women learned the expert knowledge that would give them a new sense of importance as homemakers (Kessler-Harris, 1982, p. 118). Women were encouraged to think of themselves as "home administrators" and of their kitchens as "laboratories" or "domestic factories" (Wright, 1980, pp. 272–73). Unlike Catharine Beecher, who advocated women's control over their domestic environment (Sklar, 1973), the domestic scientists of the early twentieth century ignored the housewife's needs and experiences in favor of abstract models of efficiency. According to Gwendolyn Wright (1980), "the domestic scientists wanted to produce trained workers who would operate smooth-running machines according to the precise instructions of the managers. Their expectations necessarily meant that housework would consume more of the woman's time and effort, as she struggled to keep up to the ever rising standards. The semblance of modern functional planning became an end in itself. Few people stopped to inquire whose needs were actually being met in this arrangement" (p. 273).

Other experts instructed women in the science of human development and the techniques of childrearing. At first, psychologists like G. Stanley Hall (1907) emphasized women's maternal instinct, giving scientific justification to the nineteenth-century ideal of woman as natural mother. This underscored the imperative that women must be mothers (Shields, 1984, p. 266). Later, the behaviorists, influenced by John Watson (1919, 1924), complicated the maternal task by arguing that women are not natural mothers but only necessary managers of child development. Thus, according to Watson, they must be instructed in how to provide the proper environment to mold the child's behavior into a socially acceptable product. Mothers became instruments of the behaviorist professionals who defined precise feeding and toilet training routines for them to implement. Watson's writings expressed an underlying suspicion of women whose traditional or commonsense approach to their children threatened to interfere with scientifically determined regimens (Contratto, 1984, pp. 236–37). Women must implement the childrearing regimens but must not overindulge their children; on the other hand, they must be at home and in control but not overbearing or intrusive. These conflicting expectations produced a kind of tightrope mothering. In the words of Sheila Rothman (1978), "The mother was, in effect, in a terrible trap. Her devotion to the child would warp his growth; her ignoring the child would foster neglect. Thus, the new child-rearing experts made the mother into a shadowy figure— hovering in the background, distrustful of her impulses, wary of her emotions" (p. 217).

The home economics experts sought to elevate women by professionalizing housework, but instead they created routines that became ends in themselves and produced more work and anxiety for women. The child experts attempted to raise healthier children by making child care a science, but instead they established regimens that overrode the needs of both mother and child. By making housewives and mothers the instruments of technique, the experts undermined the basis for independent judgment. The culture of professionalism was a powerful ideological force in women's lives. By attempting to make the home into a professional laboratory, the experts gave new meaning to housework and child care and increased their importance as vocations for middle-class women. But by providing externally defined procedures for this work, professional intrusion actually devalued women by undermining their choices and encouraging self-doubt.

Thus the period between 1880 and 1920 did create a "new woman," but she was more multifaceted than the image—often identified with the flapper—suggests. At first concerned with bringing their domestic values into the public world, middle-class women made significant changes through social reform. But these very changes contributed to the professionalism that undermined women's separate institutions and instead emphasized their individual success in a male world. In working for wages women both transcended the nineteenth-century domestic cult and encountered it in the workplace, where they occupied jobs that were controlled by male authority and were support roles to men's work. While wage-earning women were being domesticated in the workplace, homemakers and mothers were professionalized at home. For all these women, the ideal of middle-class career success represented an increasingly powerful image of personal identity, despite the fact that women were expected ultimately to prefer their domestic roles as wives and mothers. Finally, all women were encouraged to evaluate themselves in terms of an externally imposed and narrow definition of sexual attractiveness. The traditional distinction between the sexual, bad woman and the asexual, motherly, good woman was blurred and eventually became inconsequential. Now all women—both in the home and at work—were expected to be sexually attractive, deferential to male authority, and maternally capable. How did these conflicting expectations relate to women's recently released taste for independence as wage-earners and their desire to achieve middle-class career success? During the 1920s the conflicts were tentatively resolved through the ideal of romanticized marriage.

Romanticized Marriage

Although many male sex reformers rejoiced that women were shedding their inhibitions against heterosexual pleasure, some sounded a note of concern about the implications of female sexual freedom (Freedman, 1974–75, p. 379). Samuel Schmalhausen (1929), for example, voiced a common ambivalence. On the one hand he applauded "the strange sexual awakening of woman . . . sweetly learning to enjoy erotic comradeship as a most precious experience, promising a rediscovery of her true self" (p. 380). Yet he feared that women might be going too far and forsaking maternal steadfastness. "Can human nature continue to undergo a civilizing . . . development if the casual sweetheart replaces the more permanent wife and mother . . . in the experience of the younger generations? What shall be the new relations between the mother ethic in human behavior and the emerging sexual ethic if the minds of men are to remain whole, psychoanalytically in equilibrium? What are the finer potentialities of civilized promiscuity?" (p. 407).

Despite Schmalhausen's fears, despite the visibility of titillating "working girls" and the "sexy salesladies" of advertising copy and the sexual freedom associated with the flapper, women's sexual activity was still expected to occur only within marriage (Fass, 1977, p. 81). Indeed, women's concern with sexual attractiveness—the attention to clothes, the frequenting of beauty parlors, the experimentation with makeup—were all supposed to have a single purpose: getting and keeping a husband. High schools and colleges provided new opportunities for heterosexual socializing, especially, as the Lynds (1956/1929) noted in the Middletown study, with the increased availability of cars. Cars enabled adolescents to escape the watchful eyes of parents and to congregate at dances and parties (p. 134). They also allowed them to go to movies to watch the latest romantic films (pp. 138–39).

The attention to appearance, dating, partying, and romantic images in the media emphasized young women's heterosexual identity. The separate institution building among women during the Progressive era now seemed old-fashioned and boring (S. Rothman, 1978, p. 181). Membership in female organizations was no longer viewed as desirable in itself but merely as a means to become popular with men. According to one college dean of women, "These girls come to college to get a fraternity pin as well as a sorority pin! The college age is the mating age and many fine friendships ripen into love and marriage follows" (p. 182). The Lynds found that the most popular clubs for girls were not female organizations, like the YWCA, that took them away from coed social life but the pep clubs and booster clubs that promised the greatest heterosocial contact. "What makes a girl eligible for a leading high school club?" the Lynds asked. "The chief thing is if the boys like you and you can get them for dances" (Lynd and Lynd, 1956/1929, p. 216).

The emphasis in the 1920s upon women's relationships with men—the emphasis Mary Ryan has termed the "heterosexual imperative" (1983, p. 238)—defined a young woman's chief concern as making herself into an attractive prospect for marriage. "For while men looked toward marriage as a vital part of their lives, women looked toward it as their primary and almost exclusive goal; all other aspirations became secondary" (Fass, 1977, p. 80). In the 1920s the romantic image of marriage in popular culture and textbooks alike reinforced it as the most attractive life goal for women (p. 71). This image drew on a century-long tradition of marriage as a result of romantic choice by the marriage partners rather than economic arrangement by their parents (Lindsey and Evans, 1972/1927; Degler, 1980, pp. 29–47; Griswold, 1982, pp. 10–13). But the romanticized marriage of the 1920s added to the earlier companionate ideal an emphasis upon sexual pleasure, and particularly the fulfillment of female sexual desire (M. Gordon, 1971). The increased availability of birth control was an important factor contributing to loosening of women's sexual inhibition (Kennedy, 1970, p. 140).

According to Fass (1977), emphasis upon sexual gratification in a companionate marriage reaffirmed the traditional restriction of sex to marriage. "In large part, the sexual revolution of the twenties was not a revolt against marriage but a revolution within marriage, and as such it recharged the momentum toward marriage as the consummation of love" (p. 75). The revolution created by the romanticized marriage absorbed the early twentieth-century revolt against the prudishness and patriarchal control associated with Victorian family life. The threat of that earlier revolt—symbolized in the sexually free flapper and the economically independent lesbian—was to release sexuality from marriage for women (Simmons, 1979). Hence, in advocating the fulfillment of sexual pleasure in marriage, popular writers, social scientists, and health professionals were, in effect, limiting sexuality—especially women's sexuality—to heterosexual marriage. This same conservative use of liberalizing sex appears in the reaction to birth control in America (Kennedy, 1970). The distribution of birth control, which was opposed so vehemently by religious groups in the early decades of the twentieth century because it gave women sexual freedom, was eventually endorsed by those same groups. They accepted the practice of birth control because they saw it as fostering romantic heterosexual love, marriage, and the conservation of the family (pp. 160–61, 272).

Romanticized marriage may have restricted women's sexual pleasure to marriage, but it also presented a new expectation for women. The expectation for mutual sexual fulfillment did not replace other ideals of married life; instead, it was added onto them in ways that produced conflict. In her study of divorce in New Jersey and California in 1920 , Elaine May (1980) describes a major component of that conflict in a summary of the 1919 film *Why Change Your Wife*. It tells the story of a husband who is bored at work and looks forward to enjoying sensual pleasures with his wife, who, alas, disappoints him by being too prudish and serious. He divorces her and marries a model, who is sensuous and fun-loving. But she wants to play around too much, so he divorces her. Meanwhile, his first wife wises up, "buys a new wardrobe of seductive clothes and takes on a flirtatious personality. . . . Soon after, the husband meets [her] at a fashionable resort, clad in a revealing swimsuit and surrounded by admiring men. He is attracted to her before he realizes who she is. They reunite, and the exciting style is then brought back into the moral home" (p. 61). As May interprets the message of the film, men want both sexual excitement and domestic responsibility in their wives. "A satisfying union has to maintain a delicate balance between old-fashioned duties and modern excitement. Only then, presumably, can the home fulfill new demands for happiness" (p. 61).

The combining of old-fashioned duties and modern excitement was more easily achieved in Hollywood fantasy than in everyday life. Analyzing the divorce records of 1920, May finds conflicting expectations. One man complained that after seven years of marriage, his wife's looks "annoyed" him: she was too fat (May, 1980, p. 77). Another complained that his wife was getting too old. Yet, "although he was enamored with youth, and enjoyed young girls, he also wanted a mate who was a good wife and homemaker" (p. 78). May found that by 1920 there was an increasing stress on romance and youth, but that wives were still expected to accept the responsibility for nurturing husbands and children.

These competing expectations upon women actually emerged from a historical conflict between sexual freedom and domesticated motherhood, debased desire and middle-class respectability, sex as the individual's secret and family life as the fulfillment of personal bonding. The expectation that all women lose their heterosexual inhibitions as well as nurture men preserved the conflict in a contradictory female identity. A woman was expected to be desirable sex object and responsible caretaker, sexualized female and asexual mother.[2] Although in the 1920s these opposing identities tentatively merged in the concept of romanticized marriage, they nevertheless remained conflicted as the rising divorce rate indicated (May, 1980, p. 2). The tenacity of this conflicted female identity extended well into the twentieth century, exemplified in the image of the attractive, maternally capable, sexy, young, selflessly giving wife caricatured in *The Stepford Wives* (Levin, 1972) and promoted in *The Total Woman* (Morgan, 1975).

If the nineteenth century domestic cult was extended into the 1920s in the idea of the nurturing (albeit sexily nurturing) wife, it was also conserved in the belief that the husband is the primary breadwinner. May (1980) found that many marriages collapsed because the couple was unable to integrate the wife's job into the marital relationship (p. 118). Many of these husbands "believed that if a wife went to work, she was exposed to bad influences which could lead to sexual immorality. Moreover, she would neglect her household chores, and the home would fall apart. And on top of it all, her husband would suffer the stigma and humiliation of having a working wife—an affront to his dignity" (p. 134).

But these traditional expectations were complicated by twentieth-century changes. The period after World War I was a time of increasing ambition and acquisitiveness. "Women, like men,

2. Two of Adrienne Rich's works can be read in terms of these compulsory demands for being heterosexual object and responsible, nurturing subject. See Rich's "Compulsory Heterosexuality and Lesbian Existence" (1980) and *Of Woman Born* (1976). For a discussion of the contradictions of the concept of asexual motherhood, see Susan (Contratto) Weisskopf's "Maternal Sexuality and Asexual Motherhood" (1980).

demanded their share of the world's rewards. Ambition crept into their vocabulary. To aspire, to achieve, not merely to do a job, became at least a possibility for daughters as well as for sons" (Kessler-Harris, 1982, p. 226). Ambition as well as the desire for new consumer items encouraged women's participation in the labor force. Popular magazines and lectures advised them how to get ahead, and women formed professional organizations to foster individual advancement (p. 227). A rapidly expanding consumer economy and advertising industry encouraged families to purchase new appliances, cars, and household furnishings (Matthaei, 1982, pp. 235–45). Married women supplemented their husbands' income with paid labor so they could buy more, and wage-earning women decided not to give up their jobs when they married (Kessler-Harris, 1982, pp. 228–29). It appeared as if women could have both marriage and career, and, indeed, the number of married women in the labor force increased from two million in 1920 to three million in 1930 (p. 229).

Although the expanding economy needed women's labor, many feared their ambition. As Kessler-Harris (1982) and Davies (1982) have documented, the business community resolved this problem by employing women in low-paying, dead-end jobs that encouraged high turnover and discouraged working after marriage. The idea that young women should marry and retire to domestic bliss supported this practice and also created a backlash against hiring married women. Librarians and teachers were fired if they married because they were considered poor examples for their unmarried colleagues (Kessler-Harris, 1982, pp. 234–36). Thus, despite all the talk about women's ambition and career opportunities and the hopes of combining home and career, the segregation of the labor force and job discrimination meant that women actually lost ground in the 1920s. Women "were paid less, had fewer important jobs, and faced discrimination in appointments and promotion" (Lemons, 1973, p. 229). Their numbers in male-dominated professions declined: "the 1930 census revealed what woman physicians, surgeons, and dentists had feared: their number declined since 1920, the number of dentists falling nearly 30 percent" (p. 230).

Thus, despite the fact that more married women held jobs in the 1920s, they were encouraged to think of themselves first and foremost as wives and mothers. Suffrage, won in 1920, did not lead to an expansion of women's opportunities but signaled a new era of romanticized domesticity and exploitation in the labor force. The idealization of marriage created greater expectations, isolation of families, and suspicion of bonds between women, especially in the form of feminist organizing (Becker, 1981, p. 5). By the late 1920s and early 1930s the professional woman—Horney's "feminine type"—was experiencing these conflicting expectations, exacerbated by the financial insecurity and destruction of opportunities brought on by the Great Depression.

The feminine type did not spring in full bloom from American soil. Karen Horney had her in mind before she emigrated from Germany in 1932; indeed, she had begun to identify some of the typical characteristics in her psychology of women as early as 1926.[3] Clearly Horney's experience of growing up in turn-of-the-century Germany influenced her definition of the prototypical woman.

German Women

Despite differences—especially in political economy, postwar recovery, and the history of feminist organizing[4]—America and Germany in the first three decades of the twentieth century posed

3. See "Inhibited Femininity" (1926–27); "Problems of Marriage" (1932b); and "Maternal Conflicts" (1933b). But Horney did not pull these characteristics together into her complex character type until she wrote the 1934 essay.

4. For analyses of the turn-of-the-century women's movement in Germany see Evans (1976); Hackett (1972, 1976); Bridenthal (1984); Kaplan (1984); and Honeycutt (1979). For women's participation in politics see Koonz (1976).

similar conflicts for women. Like her American counterpart, the German "new woman" of the 1920s was defined in terms of sexual liberation and participation in the labor force. During World War I, German women entered the industrial world and assumed men's jobs. After the war they filled positions in the bureaucracies mushrooming in government and business and served as saleswomen in department stores and shops. A few women were able to pursue professional careers in law and medicine, but for the most part segregation kept women in low-paying, low-status jobs (Bridenthal and Koonz, 1984, pp. 47–53). Nevertheless, the postwar new working woman was more visible in office and factory. She used makeup, smoked in public, and flaunted her freedom. The 1918 Weimar government gave her the right to vote; she had access to contraception, obtained illegal abortions, and earned her own wages (Bridenthal, Grossmann, and Kaplan, 1984, p. 11; Grossmann, 1983b, 1984).

The new woman in Germany, like her American sister, was not as autonomous economically as her behavior might suggest; nevertheless her image threatened the traditional cultural emphasis on motherhood and family stability. Conservative German politicians as well as middle-class feminists had always emphasized women's unique role as mothers (Bridenthal and Koonz, 1984; Hackett, 1976; Honeycutt, 1979). By flaunting her sexual freedom and economic independence the new woman challenged this popularly supported maternal ideal. The decline in the birth rate in early twentieth-century Germany appeared to confirm the worst fears of many that new women were shirking their maternal responsibility (Allen, 1985, pp. 419–20). This fear was not of the loss of population per se but of the reluctance of the superior— that is, Nordic, hard-working, middle-class—women to propagate the race. Fearing "race suicide" and overpopulation by "inferior" types—the mentally deficient and financially poor—many diverse groups after World War I advocated sterilization of undesirables and promoted an increase in reproduction of the "fit" (Bock, 1983, pp. 400–07).

In the 1920s German women were encouraged to renounce the autonomy associated with wage earning and to reaffirm the values of Kinder, Küche, and Kirche that undergirded traditional family life (Bridenthal and Koonz, 1984, p. 34). Conservatives began promoting Mother's Day as an expression of old-fashioned female morality and German nationalism (Hausen, 1984). Experts warned of the dangers of mannish women who brutally struggle for power and threaten national stability (Koonz, 1984). Drawing upon the deep cultural belief in the maternal ideal, experts in the sex reform movement sought to tame the new woman by limiting her sexual freedom to marriage and family life. She was to be both emancipated and domesticated: "the movement posited a sexually satisfied mother, lover, comrade, and wage earner, outfitted with time-saving household aids, birth control methods, and a sensitive husband in command of the latest sexual techniques. . . . The Mother of the Race was integrated with the new Emancipated Woman" (Grossmann, 1983b, pp. 158–59; 1983a). For German women, as for American women, the integration created a double bind between liberated sexuality and self-sacrificing maternalism, a contradiction that formed in both countries the heart of the new ideal of romanticized marriage (p. 159).

Psychological Conflict

Thus the feminine type that Horney found in America faced conflicting social expectations that German women had also experienced. The expanded educational and career opportunities for the middle classes were undermined by the realities of a sex-segregated labor force. Women were permitted to pursue education but expected to become mothers. They were encouraged to be sexually emancipated but supposed to limit sexual desire to monogamous marriage combined with asexual motherhood. They were told that they could have careers but were expected to defer to men at work and at home. They were enticed by ambition but taught to find salvation in love. It was in the web of conflicting expectations that the feminine type, derived both from Horney's German experiences and from her new American setting, struggled to make her life.

The feminine type's psychological conflicts, described in the introductory chapter, unfolded in this historical setting of the heterosexual imperative and the middle-class ideal of professional success. She was caught between affection and ambition, marriage and career, trying to make herself attractive to men and desiring to emulate them. Her overvaluation of love to the detriment of career is understandable, given the cultural backlash against female ambition and the focus on romanticized marriage. If giving up ambition caused deep resentment and rage, that too is intelligible in the context of the universalized ideal of career success.

The feminine type's focus on men as both sexual partners and ego ideals complemented her devaluation of and competition with women. Her identification with men reflected widespread suspicion of the bonds between women. If heterosexuality had become compulsory in the twentieth century (Rich, 1980), in the 1920s it had also become identified with normality. The loving friendships and intimacy among women that were accepted as normal in the nineteenth century had been redefined as deviant, unnatural, and "inverted" by the new generation of sex experts (Smith-Rosenberg, 1975; 1985, pp. 245–96). Lesbians were taught to suspect their own natural desires (Faderman, 1981) and heterosexual women were expected to "prove" theirs. Attractiveness, male attention and admiration, sexual intercourse, and ultimately marriage were regarded by the feminine type—and by the culture—as necessary conditions of normality for women.

Horney's feminine type is the compulsive heterosexual, yet her struggle reflects the expectations of all women in the early twentieth century. The twentieth-century heterosexual imperative includes not only the equation of heterosexuality with normality but also a new definition of femininity, masculinity, and their relationship. Women were not only expected to be heterosexual but also to express their heterosexuality (that is, their normality) in self-effacing, seductive, alluringly compliant behaviors. In the pursuit of normality each woman had to be extraordinary; she had to outshine every other woman in conforming to a narrowly defined and unattainable standard of beauty. This complex of behaviors created suspicion and envy of other women and obsessive attention to the judgments and needs of men.

The feminine type reflected the cultural setting in which she lived, but she also internalized her culture in more complex ways. Horney's theory of neurosis provides an explanation of this internalizing process. The following chapter traces the evolution of her break with Freud, which preceded that theory.

2 | Karen Horney's Critique of Freud

Horney is probably best known for her writings of the 1920s and early 1930s opposing Freud's ideas on female psychology. Her stand brought her immediate notoriety among Freud's colleagues and supporters (Fliegel, 1973); more recently, it has come under attack from theorists seeking to reconcile psychoanalysis with feminism (Mitchell, 1974; Chodorow, 1978). This more recent criticism both highlights the polemical nature of Horney's early debate with Freud and illustrates the limitations of taking only her early work into consideration.

Briefly, Horney opposed Freud's notion of the female version of the castration complex: the girl's disappointing discovery of the "fact" of female castration and its inevitable consequence, penis envy (see Abraham, 1927/1920). The yearning to compensate for the lack of a penis, according to Freud, explains female heterosexual desire, rivalry among women, and the gratification of motherhood. It also explains female homosexuality, masochism, and jealous imitation of male behavior. In sum, the Freudian concept of penis envy explains all one needs to understand of female behavior, from passivity and self-denial to active striving and desire (Freud, 1925b, 1931, 1933a).

In a series of essays written between 1922 and 1933, Horney struck against this basic tenet with daring, force, and wit, arguing that Freud's concept of female psychology was simply a reflection of the boy's narcissistic self-absorption when he first sees the naked female body. When he realizes that a girl does not have a penis, he assumes that she has been castrated, which he believes makes her inferior to him. He fears, however, that her fate may await him too. He especially fears her desire for revenge against him for the "fact" of her inferiority and deficiency. His attitude toward females is thus one of dread of their envy of him (Horney, 1926, pp. 57–58). Horney later expanded on this notion by emphasizing the boy's fear of genital inadequacy in relation to his mother (Horney, 1932a). If in the 1926 essay the boy fears castrating revenge, in the later one he fears humiliation through rejection. If the former fear produces a castration complex in males, the latter produces a kind of compulsive masculinity, "an overwhelming inner compulsion to prove their manhood again and again to themselves and others" (p. 145). In effect, the fear of rejection is an extension of the fear of castration; the castrating woman is the dissatisfied, humiliating woman. Laughing at the puny penis is equivalent to removing it. By implication, even sexual intercourse returns the male to flaccid insignificance. Horney argued that lurking beneath the narcissistic glorification of the penis is trembling dread of the vagina.

Horney countered the male bias of penis worship with the primacy of parturition. She asserted that the desire for children is not a secondary manifestation of penis envy, as Freud contended; the child is not the woman's substitute penis. The desire for children is instead "primary and instinctually anchored deeply in the biological sphere" (Horney, 1931b, p. 106). Moreover, males envy the uniquely female capacity to bear children because the primary wish for motherhood is characteristic of both boys and girls (Horney, 1926, 1933a). Hence, the male attribution of penis envy to women is not only the consequence of their fear of women; it is also a projection of their underlying envy, the inversion of their wish for motherhood. Later, when this envy is superseded by castration anxiety, the boy represses his early wish to be a mother and denies even the existence of the vagina. Horney argued that the boy's denial of the vagina corresponds to Freud's phallic stage, which is characterized by heightened phallic narcissism (Horney,

1932a, pp. 144–45). Boys never seem to outgrow this narcissism and the underlying fear of inadequacy. It even, as Horney's 1926 critique claimed, forms the premise of the psychological theories they create.

Horney thus took direct issue with Freud's mystification of female sexuality and capacity to bear children by asserting both the primacy of motherhood and the existence of "a specifically feminine, primary, vaginal sexuality" (Horney, 1933a, p. 161). Similarly, she opposed the idea that female heterosexual desire is a secondary manifestation of penis envy with the notion of a primary "attraction to the opposite sex" (Horney, 1926, p. 68; 1933b, p. 178). In both instances Horney was attempting to extricate an understanding of female sexuality and psychology from an explanation that assumed a "primary phallic sexuality" (Horney, 1933a, p. 161). In her effort to rescue female psychology from the concept of penis envy, she struggled to assert separate female instincts. To her female heterosexuality and the wish for motherhood were not derivatives of the male symbolic; they were primary.

The limitations of this stance have been underscored by such recent critics as Mitchell (1974, p. 128) and Chodorow (1978, p. 148). The female instincts Horney postulated are in fact the realization of social roles. To claim that the role behaviors of heterosexuality and motherhood are instinctual is to remove the possibility for social criticism of the particularities of these roles. Thus, in delivering female psychology from Freud's phallic authority, Horney created a separate vaginal symbolic, but she lost a critical perspective. Primary instincts replace secondary penis envy, but women continue to be locked into social inferiority.

Like her contemporary critics, Horney herself recognized the problems inherent in this reductionism and ultimately went beyond it. To stay within the terms of the discourse that Freud had established and on the metatheoretical foundation of psychoanalysis, Horney had to accept the validity of instinct theory. Her assumption of primary female instincts led her to others that she pitted against Freud's: a biological envy for a biological envy, a female sexual instinct for a male one, a female superiority for a male superiority, a vaginal symbolic for a phallic one. Horney's is a confrontation by alternative, the posing of assumptions and concepts that in their startling sexual imagery and dramatic opposition serve to expose the speculative and male bias of Freud's theory. Unfortunately, her alternative not only kept her in the realm of polemic speculation (an area in which she appears to be least comfortable) but also continued to ground her thinking in instinct theory, which, despite her reformulation, devalues women.

To Freud, instinct was drive, desire, and the force behind human behavior and civilization. Its basic components are sexual and aggressive. Instinct is inherently irrational and therefore must be curbed for the sake of orderly, civilized social relations. The task of inhibiting instinct as well as mediating drives with moral demands belongs to the ego. But no matter how well tamed it might become, instinct remains in fundamental opposition to the organizing limitations to which it is forced to accede. Neurosis is the consequence of a poorly resolved compromise to this opposition: it is in effect a failure of the rationalizing ego, characterized by frustration, guilt, and irrational instinctual release (symptoms) (Freud, 1915a, b, c; 1923; 1926).

Psychological health, by contrast, derives from the robust ego, which is not only a psychological standard for Freud but a cultural ideal. The triumph of the rational ego over the irrational forces of the instinctual id represents the progress of civilization, the ascendance of organized control, and the realization of a dispassionate, calculating intelligence (Hayim, 1978, p. 321). It is also the triumph of the clean, organized, logical male principle over the demanding, odoriferous, primal female (Freud, 1930, pp. 99–107; Gallop, 1982, pp. 27–29). With the controlling ego, modern man is no longer tormented by raging urges and desires or dominated by traditional patriarchal demands (especially as transmitted by the mother). He censors his urges by managing (sublimating) instinct; similarly, he realizes himself in the methodical, not the moral, act (Hayim, 1978, p. 318). By mastering the claims of both id and superego, modern man (ego) releases himself from the demands of irrational femininity: neither female passion nor patriarchal motherhood, neither desire nor family, shall contain him (see Van Herik, 1982).

Horney's early criticism of Freud can be interpreted as an attempt to rescue instinctual femininity from a theory in which it is devalued. By asserting independent female sexual and mother-ing instincts, she attempted to create a female psychology that was not derived from male psychology. Not compensating for what she is not but revealing what she is: this was to be the basis upon which a woman's actions are rendered intelligible. Horney failed because she had not realized that Freud's notion of instinct and his misogyny were intertwined. By identifying separate female instincts, she only deepened the misogynistic aspects of Freudian theory. From the Freudian perspective Horney's revision would keep women mired in menstrual blood and lust, without even penis envy to lift them to a quasi-rational level for a glimpse of male civilization; they would be stuck in instinct (See Mitchell, 1974, p. 28). Moreover, by creating separate and equal instincts for women, Horney overlooked the fact that to Freud modern men were not to be instinctual. The ego not the id and civilization not the instinct-ridden horde were to triumph. This ascendence shifts the feminist critical task from creating parity in instinct to con-fronting the products of the male ego: culture and social and eco-nomic organization. This is the level on which women's inferiorization—including the idea that they are primarily and negatively instinctual—is created.

The strand of cultural criticism that weaves through Horney's early essays on female psychology is a countertheme to her emphasis on female instinct. It does not emerge as a central the-oretical construct until later when she challenged Freud's instinct theory. This challenge, while reflecting her earlier suspicions and influenced by others' similar criticisms, primarily derived from the failure of Freudian theory to create positive therapeutic results for her patients (Horney, 1939, p. 7).

Critique of Instinct Theory

New Ways in Psychoanalysis (1939b) is Horney's explanation of her break with Freud's instinct theory, which had been occurring gradually over the previous fifteen years and is clearly established in her first book, *The Neurotic Personality of Our Time* (1937). The rejection of instinct theory, as Horney recorded it in *New Ways*, proceeded from an ethical as well as an empirical basis; in both cases it was a response to instinct theory's implicit fatalism. As Horney interpreted it, Freud's instinct theory, while emphasizing the need for the ego to control the id and for the environment to foil the instincts, nevertheless assumed a certain theoretical primacy of instinct. The drive of instinct lies behind its rational transformation, and the frustration of instinct explains neurosis. Furthermore, beneath both rational and neurotic behavior lies the ahistorical unconscious—the locus of repressed wishes and imperatives—which reduces concrete, specific acts to manifestations of universal, ahistorical patterns. Thus, the cunning of the instinct-repressed unconscious foils any pretense to choice. Not only is change merely cosmetic; in a certain sense it is a lie (Horney, 1939b, pp. 7–78; 133–53).

Horney struggled with the contradiction between Freud's therapeutic emphasis on the ego and his theoretical emphasis on instinct. While the former holds up the possibility of change in psychological capability through the strengthening of the ego, the latter fatalistically denies the importance of such changes. The notion of universal libidinal development according to fixed stages simply structures the path of instinct. Both the healthy adult who makes it to the genital stage and the neurotic who is stuck in an infantile stage are explained via the same mechanism. The healthy adult sublimates instinct that had reached genital ascendancy while the neurotic's fixations are repetitions of lower instinctual experience. While the healthy ego creates a phallic culture, the neurotic sputters around in oral-aggressive or anal-compulsive circles. But for both healthy and neurotic persons, the instinct-dominated unconscious is the reason behind apparently rational and conscious choices.

This creates a problem for the psychology of women. First, maturity is clearly seen as the realization of phallic ascendancy. Even Freud's attempt to create a parallel, heterosexual female genital ascendancy—the move from clitoral to vaginal pleasure—does not serve to obscure the primacy of the phallus in libidinal development. Penis envy, not vaginal heterosexual pleasure, is the theoretical basis of female behavior in Freud's analysis. If women are denied the highest stage of libidinal development (and thus adult maturity) because of physiological "incapacity," then the sexual instincts themselves remain mired in a feminine, immature stage characterized by a wish for something nature has denied. The female unconscious is dominated by this repressed wish, and female behavior is explained by its release in penis envy. Penis envy is thus the concept of theoretical irreducibility for Freud's female psychology: that is, all female behavior can ultimately be explained by reference to it. It leads to a fatalism that characterizes his entire instinct theory.

Horney rejected this fatalism and its ethical consequences. If penis envy is inevitable, then women can only resign themselves to that which they cannot change. If it explains all female behavior, it also serves to justify that behavior. A woman's anger at her husband, for example, can be explained away by penis envy. "That such interpretations befog the real issue," argued Horney, "is my most stringent objection to them, particularly from the therapeutic angle" (Horney, 1939b, p. 110). By mystifying what she regarded as the real causes of the woman's anger, the concept of penis envy serves to maintain the conditions that cause anger and to resign the woman to the inevitability of those conditions as well as to repress, and finally to trivialize, her rage. The therapeutic consequence is not only to teach the woman to accept a world and a self that she cannot change but also to deny her responsibility for her own actions. If the former produces an attitude of "why fight the inevitable?" the latter suggests "what can you expect from a mere woman?" Both serve to keep a woman in her place: obedient and infantilized.

Penis envy is the central aspect of the fatalism that Horney identified in Freud's instinct theory. Another aspect is Freud's idea of destructive instincts and their cosmic explanation in the death instinct, the desire to return to an inorganic state free of tension. Like his concept of penis envy, Freud's assumption that "humans have an innate drive toward evil, aggressiveness, destructiveness, cruelty" (Horney, 1939b, p. 125) has harmful ethical and therapeutic implication. It can serve to justify the release of hostile impulses as well as produce resignation to the status quo. "Such an assumption paralyzes any effort to search in the specific cultural conditions for reasons which make for destructiveness. It must also paralyze efforts to change anything in these conditions. If man is inherently destructive and . . . unhappy, why strive for a better future?" (p. 132).[1]

Horney's opposition to the fatalistic elements of Freud's theory cannot be explained simply by her more optimistic viewpoint. The fundamental difference between Freud and Horney rests in their approaches to psychoanalysis. Freud's main interest was in the development of theory, and his clinical practice provided grist for this intellectual mill. Horney, in contrast, was interested primarily in clinical practice, in helping people make changes in

1. Horney used the male pronoun generically. I have retained her usage here, but I want to emphasize her gender-neutral intention. In subsequent chapters where I interpret Horney's work to refer to women specifically, I change her male pronouns to female.

their lives. She challenged existing theories or developed new ideas when she found that people were not being helped by the old ones. These different purposes create different ethical visions. Freud's emphasis on theory allowed him to hold a more fatalistic attitude. While sympathetic to patients, he was nevertheless detached from their pathos (Rieff, 1959, pp. 9–11). His theoretical assumptions concerning the limits or even the inconsequence of change could be maintained at a distance from those who struggled to change their lives. For Horney, understanding psychic struggle was always a means to resolving patients' concrete problems. She found that the concept of inevitable instincts created only roadblocks, not avenues for change. It not only befogged the real conflicts but denied the patient responsibility for solving them. The practical therapeutic goal of helping patients to take responsibility for their lives therefore led Horney to reject the fatalism of an instinctual determinism.

Her rejection of instinct theory had an empirical dimension as well. The real conflicts that she saw in her patients were different from those that instinct theory predicted and explained. The foundation of Freud's concept of neurosis is frustration of sexual instinct (libido). Neurotic symptoms—anxiety, compulsion, regression—are self-defeating releases from the tension created by the repression of instinct. The symptoms are, in effect, conversions of frustrated instinctual drive; hence, beneath the neurotic symptoms lie desire, frustration, and ahistorical conflict. But this is not what Horney heard from her patients. She heard desire, but it was entwined with fear; and instead of imperfect attempts at instinct resolution she heard strivings for safety. Instinct theory and its implications did not square with what Horney's patients were telling her. And what she heard from them formed the basis of her cultural theory of human development.

Horney saw the origins of neurosis in childhood disturbances of human relations as well as in intrapsychic conflict. The core of the neurotic character—anxiety and hostility—develops from a child's experience of fear and hostility at the hands of devaluing or uncaring parents rather than from necessary frustration of instinct. "Man does not collide with his environment as inevitably as Freud assumes; if there is such a collision it is not because of instinct but because the environment inspires fears and hostilities" (Horney, 1939b, p. 191). Consequently, the neurotic conflict is something that can be overcome rather than an unchangeable condition that needs to be managed more efficiently.

This shift in theoretical emphasis from instinct to social relations led to a fundamental rupture with the basis of Freud's theory. To Horney the healthy self is a whole, integrated self, not a self that successfully manages inevitable internal conflict. The Oedipal conflict is a neurotic situation not a natural one, created by sexually exploitative and intimidating parents, not by the incestuous desires of the child. The superego represents a neurotic drive toward perfectionism which Horney identified with the "proud" or "idealized self," not the normal locus of conscience. Narcissism and masochism are neurotic expressions of the striving toward safety rather than primary and secondary expressions of instinctual drives. And the unconscious does not harbor timeless repressed wishes, like the myths of "persons who are transplanted into some mountain cave, where they remain unchanged for hundreds of years while life around them continues its course" (Horney, 1939b, p. 133). It is rather the locus of historically produced conflicts and feelings that are inconvenient for the proud self to acknowledge. Thus the behavior and processes associated with fixation, regression, and transference, which Freud interpreted as repetitions of the past, Horney regarded as neurotic attempts to find safety through a present character structure that is a response to the past but is dominated by emergent, irreducible conflicts.

The ego—the part of Freud's tripartite psychic structure that is presumably most consistent with Horney's concept of the real self (see chapter 3)—comes in for special criticism. "It will be seen that the 'ego' approximating Freud's description is not inherent in human nature but is a specifically neurotic phenomenon" (Horney, 1939b, p. 189). Because it lives off the borrowed energy of the id and allocates moral judgment to the superego, the ego is a superficial, cynical agent. "It means that theoretically there is no liking or disliking of people, no sympathy, no generosity, no feeling of justice, no devotion to a cause which is not in the last analysis essentially determined by libidinal or destructive drives" (p. 187). A patient who begins to think in these tripartite terms learns to suspect his or her own feelings. "A more or less conscious awareness [that] 'it is only because' will easily jeopardize the spontaneity and depth of emotional experiences. Hence the frequent impression that although an analyzed individual is better adapted he has become 'less of a real person,' or, as one might say, less alive" (p. 188).

This condition of being "less alive" is consistent with the ego's adaptive managerial function, which is built on alienation from the self. The tripartite psychic structure is itself a managerial model of the psyche, a differentiated self with the calculating ego at the controls. The ego's adaptive managerial mode also aligns itself unreflectively with the rational, managed existence of external reality (see Hayim, 1978, p. 318). "In such a model," argues Horney, "the individual has lost his center of gravity in himself and shifted it to the outside world" (Horney, 1939b, p. 189). Relying on the judgment of others (*externalized living* in Horney's terminology) and believing that methodical processes govern life are nothing but neurotic. Neurotics "cannot reconcile themselves to the fact that life is not calculable like a mathematical task, that it is to some extent like an adventure or like a gamble, subject to good and ill luck, full of unpredictable difficulties and risks, ... unforeseeable perplexities" (p. 243). If something goes awry in the methodical world that they depend upon, neurotics must blame either others or themselves. And because life is never as predictable as the managerial ego requires it to be, the neurotic is frequently in a state of self-reproach or injured innocence.

Hence the task of therapy is not to strengthen the externalized living of the ego but to overcome the neurotic need to do so. "The analyst ... must deliberately work toward the ultimate goal of having the patient retrieve his spontaneity, and ... faculty of judgment, or in James' term, his spiritual self" (Horney, 1939b, p. 190). Not control but release, not managing feelings better but unblocking and recognizing them, not diminishing the moral demands of the superego but casting off the perfectionist proud self and creating in the whole, real self the basis for feeling and judgment. In this effort the specialized and deficient ego in Freud's rendering must be rejected.

Horney's substitution of cultural factors for Freud's instinct theory was not simply a shift in emphasis; it was the creation of an alternative theoretical basis. If Freudian theory reflects male stereotypes in its emphasis on instinct and the supremacy of the ego, Horney's reflects the female experience. In place of the concept of the newborn as a bundle of irrational and powerful energy seeking only gratification of its own needs, Horney identified a vulnerable being in need of care, love, protection, and respect. Instead of emphasizing frustration and the transformation of narcissistic desire as the hard knocks required for growing up, Horney emphasized the necessity of parental warmth and nurturing for the development of a mature, whole self. Whereas the ego for Freud was the triumph of the adult capacity for calculating and managerial control, for Horney it represented an alienated compulsion for externalized living. Neurosis, according to Freud, was the consequence of a weak ego unable to reconcile pleasure with manmade reality, but for Horney it was the outgrowth of the sickening reality itself. Freud detached himself from the pain of his patients in the name of scientific objectivity and created a theory endorsing a social reconciliation. Horney could neither subordinate helping others to the abstract pursuit of science nor resign herself to accepting the world that men had made. Thus, if Freud's instinct theory reflects the narcissism of the rebellious son and the triumph of the modern, detached, managerial man, Horney's sociological explanation reflects the wounding of the devalued daughter and the hope for a new woman.

3 | A Social Psychology of Women

In her later work Horney built on her critique of Freud to create an alternative explanation of character development and conflict. This was her theory of neurosis, which substituted experience for instinct in explaining psychology. But with this alternative foundation Horney did more than give primacy to cultural context and social relations; she feminized psychoanalysis. More specifically, she universalized female experience as the basis for understanding human development and conflict.

The Theory of Neurosis

For Horney neurosis is the consequence of cultural contradictions and constricting expectations that block the development of a whole self. All members of a culture, healthy and neurotic, experience these detours. In American culture, for example, a strong element of competitiveness, which promotes interpersonal hostilities and undermines self-esteem, creates fertile ground for the development of neurosis (Horney, 1937, p. 287). Moreover, conflicting cultural values and social conditions—competition versus brotherly love, or conspicuous consumption versus the reality of limited economic resources—foster neurotic conflict. Thus the neurotic, "the stepchild of our culture" (p. 290), reflects culturally engendered problems in the extreme. The stepchild is in this sense the one who shows the most obvious resemblance to its cultural parent. The implication of this explanation is, of course, cultural criticism: some cultures are healthier than others.

Some people become neurotic because they experience the neurotic elements of society and culture more intensely than others. Their family settings transmit and replicate rather than mitigate the competition, hostility, and contradictions of the culture. A parent who is anxious about competing with others, who needs blind admiration as a bulwark against a hostile world, who has difficulty giving genuine warmth and nurturing to others passes these traits along to his or her child. The neurotic parent is too egocentric to cope with the normal egoism of a child. The child, in turn, develops neurotic defenses in response to the fear and hostility generated by inadequate parenting. The parent creates for the child the very conditions that the parent fears in the outside world, thus perpetuating the neurotic cycle (Horney, 1937, pp. 79–94).

Horney also believed that our culture creates values which foster neurotic personalities. While she did not coin the concept of inadequate parenting as a mediation between culture and psyche, it is clearly implied in her analysis. Horney would have agreed that neurosis is produced not only by the child's embeddedness in neurotic culture but also—and especially—by the parents' continuing unsuccessful struggle with that culture, which leads to inadequate parenting and hence reinforces the child's neurosis.

The concept of inadequate parenting implied in Horney's analysis has been developed more fully by ego psychologists and theorists of object relations. The latter emphasize the mother-child relationship in the earliest months of life as the foundation for the child's psychological health. They claim that either too little or too much maternal involvement during various stages in infant and early childhood development can create serious personality disorders in the child. If the mother herself lacks ego strength, she will transmit these problems to her children.[1]

From the perspective of Horney's analysis, the problem with these more recent works is that they treat the mother's mental health as a means to the health of the child, and they abstract the mother-child relationship from the contexts of family and culture in which they are embedded. Thus they make an independent variable of a factor that Horney implied was a mediator between culture and psyche. The notion that neurosis is perpetuated by transmission from a disturbed mother to her children, among whom the daughters ultimately become disturbed mothers themselves, ignores the cultural and social contexts of neurosis.

Horney's work asserts the contrary: a disturbance in particular social relations can never be abstracted from the cultural contexts in which they are embedded. "In fact the cultural conditions not only lend weight and color to individual experiences but in the last analysis determine their particular form. It is an individual fate, for example, to have a domineering or a self-sacrificing mother, but it is only under definite cultural conditions that we find domineering or self-sacrificing mothers, and it is also only because of these existing conditions that such experiences will have an influence on later life" (Horney, 1937, p. viii).

The key to Horney's linking of culture and psyche is her assumption that human beings are "ruled not by the pleasure principle alone but by two guiding principles: safety and satisfaction." Safety, because it is the condition for the realization of satisfaction, is the primary requirement. "People can renounce food, money, attention, affection so long as they are only renouncing satisfaction, but they cannot renounce these things if without them they would be or feel in danger of destitution or starvation or of being helplessly exposed to hostility, in other words, if they

1. The literature on object relations theory is extensive. The major works include Fairbairn (1952); Klein (1964); Jacobson (1964); Balint (1965); Kohut (1971, 1977); Kernberg (1976); Mahler (1979); Bowlby (1969, 1973, 1980). For a review of object relations theories see Greenberg and Mitchell (1983).

would lose their feeling of safety" (Horney, 1939b, p. 73; cf. Wolman, 1960).

The concept of safety introduces social and ethical elements to Horney's theory of human development. Whereas satisfaction refers to the need for an object world—a world of people, and food and other things that are the objects of one's needs and desires—safety refers to conditions that others must create. From the perspective of the developing infant, safety implies caretakers and a human community. The theoretical primacy of safety suggests that the human infant is not simply—or even primarily—a bundle of desires but a being at risk, dependent upon the ethical conduct—the care—of others.

> Only the individual can develop his given potentialities. But, like any other living organism, the human individual needs favorable conditions for growth "from acorn into oak tree"; he needs an atmosphere of warmth to give him both a feeling of inner security and the inner freedom enabling him to have his own feelings and thoughts and to express himself. He needs the good will of others, not only to help him in his many needs but to guide and encourage him to become a mature and fulfilled individual. He also needs healthy friction with the wishes and wills of others. If he can thus grow *with* others, in love and in friction, he will grow in accordance with his real self. (Horney, 1950a, p. 18)

Foreshadowing Erikson's assumption that an infant needs first and foremost to experience "basic trust" in relation to his or her caretakers (Erikson, 1968), Horney claimed that a child's fundamental need is for a loving and warm atmosphere that provides inner security (Horney, 1937, p. 80). Inextricably linked to that inner security is inner freedom, the feeling that one is free to become oneself without risking the loss of parental love. Horney was not so naive as to believe that becoming oneself occurs without conflict. Echoing Freud's concept of the reality principle

(Freud, 1920), she suggested that in pursuing one's wishes one will inevitably clash with reality, which includes the wishes of others. But in calling for "healthy friction," she interjected a parental ethic into the conditions of reality. That ethical imperative is the parents' genuine care for the child as a unique human being. This permits friction to occur without fear and with the assurance that despite differences with the parent the child will continue to be loved and cared for, promoting, to use Horney's term, a feeling of "we" (Horney, 1950a, p. 18).

Inner security is the condition necessary for the realization of inner freedom, which allows the development of the real self. The *real self* is Horney's concept of the ideal outcome of human development: a person who has been loved and is able to love and care for others in return, who has been free to develop his or her potentials without feeling compelled to live up to externally defined expectations. In the real self desire and judgment are not the functions of separate components (as in id and superego) but are integrated into a whole thinking, feeling, and judging being. Horney appears to have hedged on whether the real self is discovered or created, an essence to be uncovered or a product of human choice. On the one hand, she stated, "Whatever the conditions under which a child grows up, he will, if not mentally defective, learn to cope with others in one way or another and he will probably acquire some skills. But there are also forces in him which he cannot acquire or even develop by learning. You need not, and in fact cannot, teach an acorn to grow into an oak tree, but when given a chance, its intrinsic potentialities will develop. Similarly, the human individual, given a chance, tends to develop his particular human potentialities" (Horney, 1950a, p. 17). This suggests an essentialist perspective: the core of the oak is determined by the acorn. Yet when describing the release of the real self from neurotic conflicts, Horney emphasized that the basis of the real self is choice. If so, the real self is created; and freedom to create oneself implies ethical responsibility for the choices one makes (Horney, 1947b, p. 86).

Horney's apparent vagueness on whether the real self is an essence to be discovered or a product of creative choice reflects, I think, her assumption that it is both. Individuals are born with unique physical and mental faculties that can be tapped and developed. These potentialities and limitations are not rigidly determined; what one does with them is a matter of choice and chance. "Under favorable conditions man's energies are put into the realization of his own potentialities. Such a development is far from uniform. According to his particular temperament, faculties, propensities, and the conditions of his earlier and later life, he may become softer or harder, more cautious or more trusting, more or less self-reliant, more contemplative or more outgoing; and he may develop his special gifts. But wherever his course takes him, it will be *his* given potentialities which he develops" (Horney, 1950a, p. 18).

The concept of human growth captures both the discovered and the created components of the real self. By engaging with the world, one both discovers one's unique characteristics and creates one's future. From this perspective growth is self-directed life itself, and at its core is the central inner force that is the real self (Horney 1950a).

If safety and satisfaction, inner security and inner freedom form the conditions necessary for the growth of the real self, it was their absence that captured Horney's attention. Her concern with the conditions that foster neurotic conflict reflected both her therapeutic purpose and her criticism of culture.

Being abused, unloved, or treated solely as an object for parental satisfaction or control is both a personal fate and a circumstance that occurs within a wider cultural context. The cultural pattern that Horney critiqued most sharply was the rampant competitiveness that she associated with capitalist industrial societies:

Modern culture is economically based on the principles of individual competition. The isolated individual has to fight with other individuals of the same group, has to surpass them and, frequently, thrust them aside. The advantage of the one is frequently the disadvantage of the other. The psychic result of this situation is a diffuse hostile tension between individuals. Everyone is the real or potential competitor of everyone else. This situation is clearly apparent among members of the same occupational group, regardless of strivings to be fair or of attempts to camouflage by polite considerateness. It must be emphasized, however, that competitiveness, and the potential hostility that accompanies it, pervades all human relationships.... It remains one of Freud's great achievements to have seen the role of rivalry in the family, as expressed in his concept of the Oedipus complex and in other hypotheses. It must be added, however, that this rivalry itself is not biologically conditioned but is a result of given cultural conditions and, furthermore, that the family situation is not the only one to stir up rivalry, but that the competitive stimuli are active from the cradle to the grave. (Horney, 1937, pp. 284–85)

In Western society, pervasive competitiveness forms a normal cultural pattern of social relations. According to Horney, it generates psychic consequences in feelings of hostility and fear, which serve to undermine genuine self-confidence and self-esteem. Competitive culture also creates a paltry substitute for the self-esteem it destroys: the *image* of success, an other-directed emphasis upon valuing people for "what they appear to be [rather] than for what they are" (Horney, 1942, p. 98). Predominant cultural values of competition and success also foster an obsession with presenting the appearance of having socially valued qualities. Superficially cultivating the grandiose image of superiority constitutes the self-inflation that Horney associated with narcissism. "A striving for admiration may be a powerful motor toward achievement, or toward developing qualities which are socially desirable or which make a person lovable, but it involves the danger that everything will be done with both eyes on the effect it has on others. An individual of this type chooses a woman not for her own sake but because her conquest would flatter him or add to his prestige. A piece of work is done not for its own sake but for the impression it might make. Brilliancy becomes more important that substance" (Horney, 1939b, p. 94).

The illusion of success belies its rickety basis in feelings of insecurity (Horney, 1939b, p. 94). Self-aggrandizement is a false substitute for genuine self-acceptance. Horney called it the *idealized self*, which is fundamentally alienated from the real self. An individual consumed with narcissistic self-inflation desires most of all the respect, admiration, and affection of others. "He loses any understanding of the fact that friendliness and love can include an objective or even a critical attitude. What falls short of blind adoration is to him no longer love; he will even suspect it of being hostility" (p. 93). Thus, the narcissist needs constant affirmation from others that the created illusion of desirable qualities—the idealized self—is admired. Consequently, this type "is incapable of loving either himself or anyone else" (p. 100).

Parents who are insecure, vulnerable to the ideals and stresses of a competitive society, and obsessed with an other-directed image of success reproduce these insecurities in their children by creating the same conditions within the family that they fear in the world outside. Their self-absorption interferes with their capacity to care. The danger to the child can take many forms; the most extreme is physical or sexual abuse (Horney, 1937, pp. 80–87). Less obvious but more pervasive, according to Horney, is the absence of genuine love and concern for the child. "People in the environment are too wrapped up in their own neuroses to be able to love the child, or even to conceive of him as the particular individual he is; their attitudes toward him are determined by their own neurotic needs and responses. In simple words, they may be dominating, overprotective, intimidating, irritable, overexacting, overindulgent, erratic, partial to other siblings, hypocritical, indifferent, etc. It is never a matter of just a single factor, but always the whole constellation that exerts the untoward influence on a child's growth" (Horney, 1950a, p. 18).

Particularly destructive is the pattern of treating a child as a narcissistic extension of the parent's idealized self. In their desire to take on the image of success, they may use the child to achieve their own social aspirations. When treated in this way, "a child may be led to feel that his right to existence lies solely in . . . living up to the parents' expectations—measuring up to their standards or ambitions for him, enhancing their prestige, giving them blind devotion; in other words he may be prevented from realizing that he is an individual with his own rights and . . . responsibilities. The effectiveness of such influences is not diminished by the fact that they are often subtle and veiled" (Horney, 1942, p. 44).

Abuse, disregard, or the more subtle self-absorbed use and control of a child form a pattern—particularly, in Horney's examples, among the middle class—of childhood danger in a competitive society. Horney did not equivocate about this source of neurosis: the danger in the home is a basic theme in her analysis of character development. The type and intensity of family danger can vary considerably; some of the children in a family may experience it more than others, and certain families may escape it altogether. For some its impact may be lessened through some mitigating circumstance such as a loving relative or friendly teacher (Horney, 1937, p. 88). But, like the competitive, hostile world that it reflects and reproduces, the dangerous family was for Horney a fact of modern life.

In the face of such jeopardy, the child's response is fear and anger. Horney saw this fear as a realistic reaction to hostile conditions that the child cannot control. Powerless and devalued, he or she feels weak, helpless, and worthless. At the same time, the child feels hostile toward the devaluing or abusive parents. This, too, is a realistic response. Horney implied that the hostility is a healthy way of fighting back, an expression of self against feelings of worthlessness. The problem, she argued, is not in the protest but in its repression, which forces the child to repress his or her legitimate feelings (Horney, 1937, pp. 79–84).

Unfortunately, the conditions that give rise to hostility also foster its repression. Neurotics cannot tolerate criticism or hostility, especially from those who are expected to be under their control. Criticism from people of lower status is the ultimate humiliation. The neurotic parent thus responds to a child's hostility by employing the same abusive or devaluing means against which the child is protesting. Expression of hostility thus intensifies the child's danger, while repression of his or her legitimate anger serves to diffuse it, creating the illusion of being protected, cared for, and loved as a "good" child. Fear, then, overpowers the assertion of hostility and becomes the foundation of repression. The consequence of this repression is the development of basic anxiety (Horney, 1937, pp. 83–89).

As mentioned, Horney considered fear a realistic reaction to parents' devaluing behavior rather than an inevitable response to biological helplessness. "In children growing up under adverse conditions helplessness is usually artificially reinforced by intimidation, by babying or by . . . keeping a child in a stage of emotional dependence" (Horney, 1937, pp. 85–86). Fear can also be aroused by "threats, prohibitions, and punishments, and by outbreaks of temper or violent scenes . . . ; it may be aroused also by indirect intimidation such as impressing the child with the great dangers of life—germs, street cars, strangers, uneducated children, climbing trees" (p. 86). In the face of parental hostility and fear of life's dangers, a child may also fear loss of the illusion of love and protection that the parent offers. "When genuine affection is absent there is often a great emphasis on how much the parent loves the child and how they would sacrifice for him up to the last drop of their blood. A child, particularly if otherwise intimidated, may cling to this substitute for love and fear to be rebellious lest it lose the reward for being docile" (p. 86).

Thus, out of fear of reprisal or loss of love, the child represses hostility; the feared and resented parent becomes admired and the child becomes the object of his or her own hostility. This "shift from true rebellion to untrue admiration" (Horney, 1942, p. 51) is a solution to interpersonal danger. By admiring the powerful parent and accepting his or her devaluing judgment as true, the child eliminates interpersonal conflict and thus diffuses danger. Horney recorded this conversion in the patient Clare, who, as I have indicated, was probably a representation of Horney herself.

> This shift from essentially true and warranted accusations of others to essentially untrue and unwarranted self-accusations had far-reaching effects . . . [it] entailed more than an acceptance of the majority estimate of herself. . . . She repressed all grievances against the mother. If everything was her own fault the grounds for bearing a grudge against the mother were pulled away from under her . . . it was much safer to find shortcomings within herself than in the mother. (Horney, 1942, p. 50)

By reversing hostility, the child loses touch with the real self, the locus of judgment and feeling. "Clare lost the feeble vestiges of self-confidence she had. To use a somewhat vague term, she lost herself. By admiring what in reality she resented, she became alienated from her own feelings. She no longer knew what she herself liked or wished or feared or resented" (Horney, 1942, p. 51).

Repressing legitimate anger also intensifies fear. In rejecting protest, the child accepts his or her helplessness and dependency upon the gratuitous good will of others, in effect conceding his or her susceptibility to danger. "Repressing a hostility means 'pretending' that everything is all right and thus refraining from fighting when we ought to fight, or at least when we wish to fight. Hence the first unavoidable consequence of such a repression is that it generates a feeling of defenselessness" (Horney, 1937, p. 64).

The world is seen as a dangerous place and other people as intimidatingly powerful figures. These perceptions constitute *basic anxiety*, which "may be roughly described as feelings of being small, insignificant, helpless, deserted, endangered, in a world that is out to abuse, cheat, attack, humiliate, betray, envy" (p. 92).

Thus the neurotic character foundation is reproduced in basic anxiety. Realistic fear of a person is internalized as irrational fear of the world in general. Those who deserve hostile protest are, paradoxically, admired, and the repressed hostility is not only turned back on the self but also diffused and projected onto others. The neurotic feels threatened by a menacing environment, which in turn generates additional feelings of defensive hostility. A cycle is created: fear and anxiety lead to hostility, which is projected and experienced as an external threat. This heightens anxiety, provoking hostility in defense. "This effect of reciprocity between hostility and anxiety, one always generating and re-enforcing the other," creates the underlying dynamic of the neurotic personality (Horney, 1937, p. 74).

The Neurotic Types

Horney's best-known theoretical construct is most often identified with her typology of neurosis. The neurotic types are character strategies that individuals create to cope with the anxiety-hostility conflict. If anxiety predominates, the sense of helplessness and fear prevails. Like the child's admiration for what it fears, the solution for neurotic anxiety is self-effacement, compliance, and excessive admiration. This is the *compliant* or *dependent* type. Conversely, when hostility is employed defensively, aggression, power, and domination prevail. These are characteristics of the *hostile* or *domineering* type. Because anxiety and hostility are interlocking components of neurotic character structure, each type incorporates the other. Hence, beneath neurotic compliance and admiration smolders a rage for revenge, and beneath neurotic aggression and domination naked terror hides.

These two neurotic types represent logical solutions to the problem of feeling helpless in a hostile world: relying on others to protect one from hostility, or overpowering the aggression of others through one's own hostility. The third solution is flight from the problem, an attempt to quell anxiety and avoid hostility by withdrawing from social relations. Basic anxiety and hostility remain, but the social contexts that aggravate them are avoided. Like the other two, the *detached* type strives for safety in a dangerous environment.

Horney described four neurotic patterns in *The Neurotic Personality of Our Time* (1937): (1) seeking affection, (2) submissiveness, (3) gaining power over others, and (4) withdrawal. Eventually, however, she came to understand the first two as aspects of a single type and collapsed them into a category of dependency (1942). She used this threefold typology throughout her subsequent work. In *Our Inner Conflicts* (1945) she termed the patterns (1) moving toward people (emphasizing helplessness), (2) moving against people (emphasizing hostility), and (3) moving away from people (emphasizing isolation). In her last book, *Neurosis and Human Growth* (1950a), her terminology emphasized the intrapsychic over the interpersonal: (1) self-effacing, (2) expansive, and (3) resigned. Each book emphasizes different aspects of the neurotic types and her understanding of them became more complex, but the three types remained. For consistency, I shall call them *dependent, domineering,* and *detached,* terms that Horney herself used at various times.

The dependent type attempts to gain reassurance and protection against basic anxiety through the affection of others. Dependent types believe that others will protect them from the hostile world and make them feel safe (Horney, 1945, p. 53). To attain this protection they adopt attitudes of helplessness, docility, and self-effacement (Horney, 1937, pp. 119–20; 1945, pp. 51–53; 1950a,

p. 168). The behavior of the dependent type conveys the message, "if I give in, I shall not be hurt" (Horney, 1937, p. 97). Various techniques—including belittling or denying oneself, living according to others' expectations, and being unassertive, placating, and self-effacing—comprise this defense. Dependent people learn to "like" others because they are essentially afraid of them. They are often naively accepting or enchanted by the goodness of everyone and are genuinely shocked to discover that people can hurt them, a denial of their own unconscious fears.

If dependent types subordinate themselves as protection against a hostile world, domineering types control and overpower others to protect themselves. While both types resort to egocentric use of other people, dependent individuals make themselves appealing so others will express protective affection rather than hostility, and domineering types intimidate others so they will not dare treat them badly. While both types fear their own weakness, dependent people become lovable as a reaction to fear and domineering ones elicit fear because they believe that love is impossible. Dependent types develop survival strategies around weakness, domineering types around aggression.

In contrast to the dependent types, who convert fear to love, the domineering ones protect themselves by overcompensating for their weakness, converting it to a semblance of strength. Thus behind the quest for power and prestige, the appearance of mastery and superiority, and the style of self-assured aggressiveness lies contempt for their own weakness. People of this type despise and feel humiliated by weakness and therefore demand that others unquestioningly accept their illusion of capability and strength. They must be admired as protection against their own feelings of insignificance; they must be obeyed as protection against their fear of being dominated. But, just as the dependent types deep down question the love that is their salvation, the domineering types are never fully convinced of the admiration and obedience they receive. This suspicion derives not only from the sense that their superiority is a bluff but also from a projection of their envy of others. They suspect that no one truly admires or submits to them and that expressions of admiration or subordination from others are simply masks for envy or hostility (Horney, 1937, pp. 162–87; 1945, p. 101; 1950a, pp. 189, 193, 311).

Horney regarded the conflicts of the dependent and domineering types to be the most central to modern neurosis. Especially as each represses the tendencies of the other, these types express what Horney called the central human conflict of the age: "the craving for affection and the craving for power and control" (Horney, 1937, p. 105).

The detached type attempts to evade the conflict between affection and ambition by withdrawing socially. Unlike the other two, this type is expressed primarily in negative terms as a desire to avoid, rather than to use, other people. The need is for utter independence, "not being influenced, coerced, tied, obligated" to others (Horney, 1945, p. 77). Independence is expressed by piling up possessions as a safeguard against all eventualities, jealously guarding one's privacy, restricting one's needs, resisting advice, schedules, competition, obligation, and demands for compliance (pp. 75–79; 1950a, p. 266). Internal needs are repressed through emotional detachment, renunciation of desire ("wishlessness"), an impersonal onlooker attitude toward oneself and others, a sense of one's superiority and unique significance in combination with a shrinking from and curtailing of life in resignation to the unalterable status quo (Horney, 1937, p. 99; 1945, pp. 74–79; 1950a, pp. 260–63). In seeking freedom from others, the detached individual attempts to evade the conflict between needing love and needing to dominate, between self-effacement and expansion. Physical and emotional isolation can create a sense that life is "easy, painless, and effortless" (Horney, 1950a, p. 264), as well as a feeling of inner integrity and sincerity. Detached people keep themselves "unsoiled and untarnished" by avoiding others (p. 280).

Horney saw these three neurotic "solutions" to basic anxiety and hostility as ideal types. As concepts, each one forms a pure configuration of motives, feelings, and behaviors uncontaminated by the others. The dependent and domineering types, for example, are diametric opposites, and the detached type opposes them both. As extremes they represent analytical concepts, not actual people, who display greater variety, complexity, and intermeshing of characteristics than the types suggest. But the analytic purity of the types permits greater theoretical insight and development.

Horney did not employ these types according to the methodology of classical sociological analysis. First, they are not used to build a theory of historical change (see Weber, 1971). Her concern was rather with understanding intrapsychic and interpersonal processes for purposes of healing. Second, while the types display conceptual clarity and focus, they are also extensively elaborated. This, too, is a reflection of Horney's clinical emphasis. A theorist concerned with economy and conceptual development would have pared down the details. As a therapist, however, Horney emphasized concrete examples. It is people's variety and complexity that makes them unique. Horney did not permit the theoretical imperative to overshadow human complexity.

Yet Horney's work does not lack theoretical depth or conceptual precision. Her writing is strong, clear, and straightforward, addressed to both the lay person and the expert. She introduced complexity and variation into her types in a way that was both cognizant of psychoanalytic tradition and committed to truth. Her attention to human reality lends her theoretical formulations verisimilitude and conceptual power. Consequently, her types suggest other possibilities for conceptual development. The varied applications of her types by scholars in fields from literary criticism to religious studies display this depth (see Paris, 1978; Cole, 1978).

Most important for my purpose, the theory and its types provide a conceptual basis for developing a social psychology of women. This extension of Horney's work is not simply another application; it is the unfolding of a central meaning in her theory. The key to that meaning is the pattern of female experience that Horney associated with the development of neurosis.

Girlhood Experience

The two categories of danger to which Horney implied children are exposed are devaluation and sexualization (Horney, 1937, pp. 80–84; 1939b, p. 82). Devaluation refers to the parents' lack of respect for the child as a unique and worthwhile human being. Sexualization "may consist in a gross sexual approach to the child; it may arise from sexually tinged caresses, or from an emotional hothouse atmosphere surrounding all members of the family or including some members and excluding others" (Horney, 1939b, p. 82). Sexualization is, in effect, a form of devaluation; the authentic needs of the child are subordinated to the self-absorbed purposes of the adult.

A child who is devalued may cling to a parent for reassurance. "Such a hanging on to a person out of sheer anxiety is easily confounded with love, and in the child's own mind seems like love. It does not necessarily take on sexual coloring, but may easily do so.... The resulting picture may look exactly like what Freud describes as the Oedipus complex: passionate clinging to one parent and jealousy toward the other" (Horney, 1939b, p. 83). But the reason for this clinging, according to Horney, has nothing to do with so-called incestuous desire on the part of the child. Rather, it is his or her anxious response to the parents' sexualizing and devaluing treatment. "I know of no case in which it was not neurotic parents who by terror and tenderness forced the child into these passionate attachments, with all the implications of possessiveness and jealousy described by Freud" (Horney, 1937, p. 84). The Oedipus complex is thus not the natural consequence of blocked instinct, but the neurotic outcome of the abuse of parental power.

While Horney assumed that these experiences affect children of both sexes, her discussions more often linked them to female socialization than to male. Horney repeatedly referred to the unfavored child, whose condition appears to encapsulate all the features of parental disregard and lack of affection (see Horney, 1937, pp. 80, 178, 249; 1945, p. 41; 1950a, p. 18). Being unfavored is not necessarily a result of being unwanted, although that too can be expressed and felt. It rather involves being considered less than valuable by parents. This may be expressed in outright abuse, but more often it is manifested more subtly. Many of Horney's examples describe a daughter who is less favored than her brother (for example, Horney, 1939b, p. 170; 1937, p. 164). Horney's adolescent diaries poignantly record her own response to feeling unloved and unappreciated: her anger and sense of rejection in response to her father's stern distance and control and her misery over her mother's preference for her older brother, Berndt (Horney, 1980). As a young woman of twenty-two Horney described to her future husband her mother's favoritism as well as her own vulnerability to it: "she silently overlooks my brother's meannesses, while at an unfriendly word from me she loses her temper. Incidentally, I am *really not* of a lovable nature, I mean even where it is not just a matter of fighting for a principle. A lack I am trying to get over but am not yet finished with" (p. 216).

The experience of Horney's patient Clare, described in *Self-Analysis* (1942), exemplifies the subtle pattern of female devaluation. "She was not badly treated or neglected in any coarse sense: she was sent to schools as good as those her brother attended, she received as many gifts as he did, she had music lessons with the same teacher, and in all material ways was treated as well. But in less tangible matters she received less than the brother, less tenderness, less interest in school marks, and in the thousand little daily experiences of a child, less concern when she was ill, less solicitude to have her around, less willingness to treat her as a confidante, less admiration for looks and accomplishments" (p. 49).

Horney regarded the devaluation of the daughter as more than an incidental fate; she asserted that it reflected a general cultural pattern of female inferiorization. Echoing her earlier critique of masculine civilization, she attacked Freud for dismissing the importance of the typical parental preference for sons. "How little weight Freud ascribed to cultural factors is evident also in his inclination to regard certain environmental influences as the incidental fate of the individual instead of recognizing the whole strength of cultural influences behind them. Thus, for example, Freud regards it as incidental that a brother in the family is preferred to the sister, whereas a preference for male children belongs to the pattern of patriarchal society. Here the objection might be raised that for the individual analysis it is irrelevant whether the preference be regarded in one way or the other, but this is not quite so. In reality, the preference for the brother is one of many factors impressing on the female child the feeling that she is inferior or less desirable" (Horney, 1939b, p. 170).

Horney's emphasis on the cultural pattern of preference for sons suggests that parents are disappointed with daughters whether or not there is an actual son who is favored in contrast. The family articulates broader cultural values, and daughters experience pervasive devaluation and a sense of inferiority. While individual cases indicate that parental devaluation is experienced by some males as well, that pattern of patriarchal society makes it a fundamentally female experience.

Horney's examples of the sexualization of children in families indicate that this too is a predominantly female experience. Sexualization includes brothers and fathers incestuously using their sisters and daughters or making sexual advances toward them, father flirtatiously treating a daughter and all other females as sexual playthings, or a mother whose identity derives from male admiration of her beauty (Horney, 1934, p. 194). Horney's examples suggest that the pattern of family sexualization of females creates an atmosphere in which girls' sexuality is presumed to be the fundamental aspect of their identity and the basis for male exploitation (pp. 194–213; I analyze this more fully in chapter 4).

Thus, I contend, Horney's discussion of the universal features of childhood that promote neurotic character structure is a presentation of predominantly female experience. Because that experience reflects generally accepted cultural values, the family devaluation and sexualization of daughters appear to be normal occurrences, independent of the intentions or foibles of particular parents. Individual parents may genuinely believe and report that they love their daughters at the same time that their behavior favors their sons. They may believe that in encouraging a daughter to see herself as a sex object they are treating her in a normal way. Indeed, by wanting "what is best" for their daughter, they may promote the very practices that devalue her. Individual circumstances may involve variation but not—except under unusual circumstances—reprieve. Thus, the implication of Horney's analysis is that to grow up female in this culture is to grow up neurotic.

But this is not exactly the intention of her analysis. Men are neurotic, too, as her discussions of the neurotic types indicate. Horney contended that each of the three types—domineering, dependent, and detached—can be found among men and women alike. Thus, her theory of development of the types should also reflect the childhood experience of both sexes. But on this point Horney was inconsistent. She employed the neurotic types as gender-neutral categories, yet she explained their development in terms of a predominantly female pattern of experience.

The contradiction between the typology and the theory is partially resolved by Horney's qualification of her claim that the neurotic types are gender-neutral. She conceded that the two primary types did tend to separate along gender lines: men tend more often to display the characteristics of the domineering type and women the dependent type (Horney, 1950a, p. 247). The detached type remains a secondary category, although Horney did link it more frequently to the drive for superiority, which she associated with the domineering type (for example, Horney, 1945, p. 79; see Symonds, 1973, p. 42).

The gender pattern of the types links the female experience undergirding the theory of neurotic development and the female characteristics of the dependent type. This link is underscored by Horney's explanations of the child's response to danger. In reaction to parental devaluation, the child develops an essentially submissive solution. The power of the parent is not challenged; it is instead solicited as a protective rather than an abusive force through the child's emphasis on his or her own weakness and need. The child, in effect, learns to identify with the aggressor and becomes pleasing, compliant, and affectionate as a means of securing safety. Hence fear is allayed by acquiescing to power, and hostility is turned back on the self, a self defined as bad in contrast to the now-admired parent.

Thus the basic neurotic solution to the anxiety created by childhood danger is compliant affection and repressed hostility, the solution of the dependent type. The theory did not explain the development of domineering or detached neurotic patterns as primary solutions. While repressed aspects of the other types always exist, Horney argued that one type predominates in the neurotic character structure. Her theory explains how compliant dependency emerges as a core neurotic type. But for hostile-domineering or detached types to emerge, the child would have to assume or be given power to express its hostility or independence vis à vis the parents. The theory does not explain how this might happen. In her emphasis on the child's basic anxiety and the solution of repressed hostility, Horney permits only one core neurotic solution, that of her dependent type.

Horney therefore seems to have left unexplained the development of the neurotic types that she associated with masculinity. When these types are presented in male examples, the men attempt to overcome basic anxiety by overpowering others or separating from them. But Horney did not explain developmentally why these solutions are employed or encouraged. Her failure to describe male development leaves a gap in understanding: one may see what the domineering male does, but one does not completely understand why (see Kelman, 1971, p. 23).

The domineering and detached types seem more intelligible when considered as secondary characteristics of the dependent type, Horney's concept of modern woman. Domination and detachment emerge in this type, as a protest against powerlessness, only after the core dependent character is formed. They are essentially attempts to claim power or establish restitution for past mistreatment. They remain represssed in the face of the dangerous parental power but appear later under social conditions in which the individual becomes able to exercise some power over others or independence from them.

My interpretation of Horney's theory of neurosis as a critical theory of female psychology is based on the idea that the dependent solution is the core neurotic pattern. The anger characteristic of the dominant type and the desire for social withdrawal common to the detached type are interpreted as repressed aspects of the core dependent character. This interpretive synthesis of Horney's three neurotic types elaborates her earlier concept of the feminine type as the sweetly compliant woman who brims with rage and longs for freedom from others' expectations. The feminine/dependent type is masculine civilization's stepchild; she has become the ideal object that her culture promotes. But the cost of her success is an inner conflict that alienates her from her real self.

4 | Sexualization

The theme of girlhood sexualization runs throughout Horney's work like a constant and familiar pain that is too evasive to examine closely. She seems to analyze it with averted eyes, perhaps out of fear of what she might discover. Or perhaps she was simply resigned to its utter facticity. Sexualization is one of the two themes of danger in childhood development and family life. One cannot undo it, for it is a matter of personal history.

Horney's treatment of girlhood sexualization—because it is evasive—seems much more personal than her analysis of the parallel theme of the frustration and humiliation of the devalued daughter. The devaluation of girls' abilities and ambitions is a publicly recognized problem, embedded in cultural values and social organization. One could speak of it in 1934 without blushing. Girlhood sexualization, however, is another matter. It is the secret that girls remember into adulthood but are reluctant to tell. This reluctance, which Horney shared, is at the heart of its personal meaning.

Horney's work contains isolated references to girlhood sexual encounters ranging from incest to sexually suggestive, intrusive, or controlling treatment—the wide range of experiences that I term sexualization (see MacKinnon, 1982). But Horney was less interested in identifying the experiences than in analyzing their consequences in adulthood, which include self-hatred, dependency, envy, fear, and disgust with the body. Her focus on adult suffering rather than causal childhood events was due not merely to her clinical interest but also to a reluctance to discuss that which culture and family had made secret. Horney mentioned the

unspeakable here and there, as an aside, an introspection, an isolated critique, a clinical description of a patient's childhood. But
she never drew the whole picture with confidence. One never sees
the same analytic power here that she employed with regard to the
neurotic types, for example. Instead, timidity seems to undercut
her theoretical acumen on this subject; yet the modern reader is
touched more deeply for the tentative connection the work makes
between the personal and the intellectual.

Horney's thoughts on sexualization are like pieces of a puzzle,
which at first seem scattered and unrelated. In gathering the frag-
ments, I will assemble them to describe a reality that was a secret
which merged with the routines of daily family living. Sexualization in middle-class late Victorian life appears at times to be an
anomaly—an extreme that is almost unbelievable—and at other
times it seems to be so normal that it is not even worth mentioning.
It is both: that is the difficulty in understanding it as a whole.

The Evidence

Early in the development of psychoanalysis, Freud was struck by
his female patients' reports of sexual exploitation by their fathers.
These reports led him to formulate a seduction theory, which postulated that paternal sexual abuse caused emotional disturbances
in adult women (Freud, 1896). Later, however, Freud came to
believe that these reports were fantasies. Not only did the events
themselves never occur, he argued, but the accusations were
expressions of an instinctual incestual desire. The women,
according to Freud, actually desired sexual union with their
fathers as children and continued to desire it unconsciously as
adults (Freud, 1925a, 1933a). This shift in position ultimately led
Freud to formulate the Oedipus theory, which postulates that all
children desire sexual union with the opposite-sex parent.

Feminist scholars have since argued convincingly that Freud,
not his patients, was engaging in wishful thinking. Florence Rush

(1977, 1980), among others, has documented the widespread sexual abuse of daughters. More recently, Jeffrey Masson (1984) has argued that Freud's reversal and his ultimate espousal of an instinctual incest wish can be explained in terms of his desire to exonerate his friend and colleague Wilhelm Fliess from blame for nearly killing a hysterical female patient of Freud in a surgical procedure. Rush, however, emphasizes that Freud's rejection of the evidence both reflected his disbelief that fathers could be so guilty and served to quell his disquieting ambivalence toward his own father (Rush, 1977, pp. 35–38). Following Catherine Clément, Jane Gallop (1982) extends the argument, showing how Freud's transformation of the original evidence into the drama of the Oedipal metaphor exonerates the father completely (pp. 143–45). The daughter's incestuous longing for her father became the basis for Freud's argument that the son desires his mother. But the mother—especially as represented by her lower-class surrogate, the nurse—is implicated in prompting this filial lust. The father, as the protector of what is rightfully his (his wife) and the object of his daughter's desires, is the one most removed from sexual responsibility (pp. 143–46).

The Real Danger

In the 1920s, when Horney began to struggle with the consequences of Freud's inversion of his female patients' reports, she did not have the benefit of this critical analysis. She attempted first to employ and then to adapt Freud's theoretical constructs, but her clinical practice undermined her attempts to find meaning in Freudian theory. The reports of her own patients took her back to the evidence, evidence that Horney was increasingly unwilling to dismiss in the name of instinctual incestuous longing.

In 1927 Horney published an essay entitled "The Masculinity Complex of Woman," in which she made her strongest assertion to that date of the veracity of the daughters' reports. Writing on a subject that was widely discussed in Weimar Germany—the reluctance of the new woman to accept her heterosexual femininity, defined in terms of traditional domesticity (see Grossmann, 1983b)—Horney asserted her own interpretation of the issue. She began with a recapitulation of the Freudian interpretation: "the development of girls normally proceeds in the following way. The desire for personal ownership of the penis switches over or merges into the desire for sexual unity with the man and the desire for a child. If the development takes this fortunate course, it is shown that the portions of the desires for masculinity which have been overcome in this way can be driven into sublimation" (Horney, 1927a, p. 148). But, Horney argued, this normal path to female heterosexual identity is fraught with many "restraints and disturbances in development," among which are "early sexual observation . . . especially in an environment in which normal sexual things are hidden from the child . . . they take on the character of the forbidden and the sinister for the child. According to our experience, this type of sexual observance is, without exception, understood in the sense that the mother has been raped" (p. 148).

This perception that sex places women in danger is exacerbated by what Horney called "typical fears which originate from Oedipus fantasies"—that is, fears of the father. These fears are expressed in dreams where, for example, "the father appears as a dog who wants to bite the child or as a lion. It surprises the daughter that the mother so calmly allows the lion to run around" (Horney, 1927a, p. 148). In another example, an agoraphobic girl who was her father's "darling" dreamed of him as death "which was behind the girl ready to grab her. Here, as so often, death and man, dying and sexuality are unconsciously equated." Horney noted that this girl was frightened and embarrassed to be alone with her father and that the phobia expressed the anxious concern, "Mother may not leave me alone with father."

Horney argued that these early fears sidetrack girls from the path to feminine heterosexual identity that Freud had defined. With this explanation Horney herself swerved from Freudian orthodoxy. Whereas Freud had claimed that in the case of the masculinity complex the girl's wish for the penis becomes the masculine woman's delusion that she has one (Freud, 1925b, p. 253), Horney contended that a woman's adoption of a masculine style identity is a protection against her fear of a sexually aggressive father. "Under the pressure of this fear, she is inclined not only to relinquish her father as a love object, but to escape from her feminine role altogether" (Horney, 1927a, p. 149; 1924). Thus, becoming like a man is her defense against men.

Horney explained a girl's escape into masculine traits and her rejection of a dangerous heterosexuality as an understandable defense rather than as a delusion. Along with her contention that these fears are typical, Horney's revision implies that the female masculinity complex is rational and normal and Freud's idea of the normal path to heterosexual femininity is irrational.

Horney sidestepped this radical implication of her critique, but her explanation of women's fear took her beyond Freudian orthodoxy. Recall Horney's struggle during the 1920s between her obedience to instinct theory and her growing conviction of the social and cultural causes of character development. Her explanation of the girl's fear of her father reflects this struggle. She claimed that the daughter's fear goes beyond the intimidation that boys and girls alike feel in the face of conflict with parents. Moreover, the girl's fear is neither imaginary nor the result of wishful thinking; rather, it reflects the girl's "real danger" (*realen Gefuhrdung*) of exposure to male sexual aggression (Horney, 1927a, p. 150).

But what is the source of this danger? At first Horney nodded to Freudian orthodoxy by suggesting it is determined by a girl's genital vulnerability to rape and the "primitive" phylogenetic experience "reflected from a time when the little girl was already very early exposed to the aggression of older men" (p. 150). The timeless determinant of biology and the fantastic memory of collective history thus serve to dilute the power of the concept of real danger: females will always be fearful of male sexual aggression regardless of the actual circumstances.

Yet Horney was edging toward locating causality in experience. She concluded her analysis with an observation that even she found "astonishing": "These fantasies occur with conviction so often that *it is a matter of real experience*" (Horney, 1927a, p. 150, emphasis added). Thus, despite the sidestepping, the bow to orthodoxy, the averted eyes, the new message came through: the girl's fear of male sexual aggression is based upon actual experience.[1]

Emotional Hothouse

In 1934, in "The Overvaluation of Love," Horney specified the real danger in concrete examples of "exaggerated early experience of sexual excitation" (p. 195) that were characteristic of the childhood of the feminine type.

> In one of these cases the mother was a particularly attractive woman, surrounded by a crowd of male acquaintances, and kept the father in a state of absolute dependence upon her. In another instance not only was the sister preferred, but the father had a love affair with a relative living in the house and in all

1. Freud, too, described anxiety associated with the Oedipal conflict. At first he attributed the anxiety to internal sources (1917, p. 395), but later he related Oedipal anxiety to "real danger" of external origin (1933b, pp. 85–88). However, for Freud, the real danger referred to the external circumstances surrounding the boy's castration fears. The boy fears castration because of his incestuous longings for his mother and hostility toward his father. This internal source of anxiety is merely exacerbated by the real threats of punishment, especially for masturbation; thus, for Freud, instinct, not real danger, is the primary cause of anxiety (pp. 85–86). Moreover, because girls do not fear castration, their fear is loss of the mother's love, which may be grounded in reality if the mother is indeed absent (p. 87). Contrary to Horney, Freud did not mention male sexual aggression in this connection, nor did he give causal primacy to the actual experience of real danger.

probability with other women. In yet another case the still young and unusually beautiful mother was the absolute center of attention on the part of the father as well as of the sons and the various men who frequented the house. In this last case there was the complicating factor . . . that the little girl from her fifth to her ninth year had had a sexually intimate relationship with a brother some years her senior, although the latter was the mother's favorite and had continued to be more closely tied to her than to his sister. On account of his mother, moreover, he suddenly broke off the relationship with his sister, at least as regards the sexual character, at the time of puberty. In still another case the father had made sexual advances to the patient from her fourth year, which became more outspoken in their character at the approach of puberty. At the same time he not only continued to be extremely dependent upon the mother, who received devotion on all sides, but was likewise very susceptible to the charms of other women, so that the girl got the impression of being merely her father's plaything, to be cast aside at his convenience or when grown-up women appeared on the scene.   (Horney, 1934, pp. 194–95)

Horney's examples indicate, first, that sexualization is not necessarily confined to or directly expressed in incest. Her examples show that it involves defining girls as essentially sexual beings and the treating of them in seductive and sexually suggestive ways. Incest is an extreme form of this general and universal treatment. Second, the sexualization usually hinges upon a power difference between the adult or older male and the young girl. It is therefore an expression of what Horney later called the confounding of "terror and tenderness" in adult sexual exploitation of children (Horney, 1937, p. 84). The girl's sexuality comes to derive its meaning from her powerlessness, and her powerlessness is confirmed in the sexualizing treatment. Third, the power difference between adult and child is compounded by the prerogative of gender, the socially sanctioned right of all males to sexualize all females, regardless of age or status. Finally, this male sexualization of females in what Horney later called an "emotional hothouse," the family (1939b, p. 82), has a chaotic quality. The marriage relationship is not the locus of commitment or the altar of sanctified intimacy. Moreover, the relationships between father and son and between mother and daughter are not governed by authority and role. Rather, the propriety and renunciations of the bourgeois family are cast to the wind as the sexuality of the adult couple is exploded as possibility onto all members of the household.

Sexuality and Power

The families in Horney's descriptions display a power shift that historians have associated with the period of modernity, a shift that appeared first in the sixteenth century and had established itself clearly by the mid-eighteenth century. The shift involved the triumph of the individual over the kin group, ambition over tradition, and the economic liberation of the son from the father (Stone, 1977; Tilly and Scott, 1978; Trumbeck, 1978). By the nineteenth century these changes had eroded the social and economic structure of traditional patriarchy and had cut off the middle-class family from its community supports (Mintz, 1983, p. 14). As a result, the family was exalted as the source of affection and order that stemmed the tide of corruption and chaos from the world outside. The mother's affection and the father's authority were the gendered poles of salvation that the middle-class family represented.

With these changes the father's authority within the middle-class family ceased to be patriarchal: he no longer controlled the destinies of his sons. Rather, he held power as a man and in his capacity as the family breadwinner (Mintz, 1983, p. 61). But this was a power that his sons were able to share—indeed, their education focused upon developing their independence and self-reliance so they could succeed in the individualistic world of wage-earning (pp. 62, 88). The son's developmental struggle was to free himself from the strong affective bonds of the cloistered family and establish himself as an autonomous individual. Growing up meant leaving the financial and emotional dependence of his childhood—a dependency associated with women—and asserting his manliness. Thus, according to Joseph Kett (1977), by the end of the nineteenth century "the word 'manliness' itself changed meaning, coming to signify less the opposite of childishness than the opposite of femininity" (p. 173).

This emphasis on gender distinction—the man's dominance as breadwinner and the woman's subordination as financial dependent—did not replace the father's traditional generational authority but created a shift within it. The importance attached to male autonomy and achievement meant that sons needed to assert their independence within the family structure itself while daughters—who were to be future wives and mothers—were expected to defer to male authority (Welter, 1973). Sons' power and independence were elevated while the subordination of all females was emphasized (Barker-Benfield, 1976, pp. 27–29; Poster, 1978, pp. 176–77; Ehrenreich and English, 1979).[2]

The isolated and affectively charged nineteenth-century middle-class family created a close quarters that, according to Michel Foucault (1978), was saturated with sexuality (p. 46). Paradoxically, this was the consequence of the new consciousness that associated middle-class identity with sexual repression. Considering itself superior to both the working classes and the aristocracy because of its sexually repressed respectability, the middle class exerted control upon itself. Nineteenth-century physicians,

2. On the authority of fathers and brothers over daughters and sisters, see Gorham, 1982, pp. 38–47, 201–02. Domination of young women by fathers and brothers was not unusual in the nineteenth century and forms an important theme in the middle-class daughter's struggle for autonomy. For examples, see Sklar, 1973; Strouse, 1980; Barker-Benfield, 1979.

purity writers, and sex experts contributed to a discourse that was designed to define acceptable sexual practices and to create techniques for sexual regulation (pp. 104–05).

Foucault argued that the equation of sexual repression with middle-class respectability fostered an obsession with control over anything that deviated from acceptable sexualtiy—that is, that of husband and wife. The definition of sexuality was narrowed to the behavior of the heterosexual couple, but universalized as the secret presumed to be desired by all. The control over those who deviated from "normal" sexuality—the hysterical woman, the masturbating child, the perverse adult—as well as the controls placed upon the reproductive couple created an elaborate apparatus that pervaded the middle-class family (Foucault, 1978, pp. 104–05). In this setting, power over another's sexuality became a sexual experience. Sexuality came to be experienced in terms of keeping one's own sexual secret and uncovering the secrets of others. Most important, sexual pleasure became an experience of power differences: "the pleasure that comes of exercising a power that questions, monitors, watches, spies, searches out, palpitates, brings to light; and on the other hand, the pleasure that kindles at having to evade this power, flee from it, fool it, or travesty it." This is the sexual pleasure associated with capture and seduction, predator and prey, aggression and vulnerability: "parents and children, adults and adolescents, educators and students, doctors and patient, the psychiatrist with his hysteric and his perverts, all have played this game continually since the nineteenth century" (p. 45).

Foucault's analysis implies that there is a sadomasochistic meaning to the power relations of surveillance and being observed, regulating and being controlled. This historical entwining of sexuality and power means that domination and submission became experiences of sexual pleasure. Unfortunately, Foucault did not extend the implications of his insight to an analysis of the gender-related power differences within the family. For him power is an aspect of constantly shifting relationships, never located solely in any one privileged group (see Weeks, 1981, pp. 4–11). He therefore glosses over the very real power differences between males and females in middle-class families and fails to recognize that the sadomasochistic pattern is built into family structure (cf. Plaza, 1981).

Sexuality, according to Foucault, was simultaneously repressed and incited for both sexes; the pervasive emphasis on regulation fostered a universal desire for transgression. Other historians have suggested that this conflict was experienced differently by men and women and that this difference in experience was rooted in the power structure of the middle-class family. Charles Rosenberg (1973), for example, argues that men were on the one hand incited by a belief that equated manliness with aggressive sexuality, and on the other repressed by the demand for sexual control. This opposition between the masculine ethos and the ideal of the Christian gentleman created a paradox of middle-class manliness that was rooted in conflicting gender and class expectations. All men were assumed to be driven by lust and thus had, in the words of one nineteenth-century physician, "an inherent need to gratify passions" (quoted p. 140). Yet, the Christian gentleman was expected to display the proper decorum and control of sexuality appropriate to his class, abstaining from sex before marriage and afterward placing his sexual behavior under the gentle control of his spiritually superior wife (p. 139).

The paradox of middle-class manliness was resolved in the double standard and the acceptance of prostitution as necessary vice. The ideology of the inherent prudishness of middle-class women and the sentimentalizing of motherhood preserved the image of respectable morality by requiring women's strict adherence to a code of absolute propriety (Cott, 1978). The acceptance of prostitution and the sexualization of "working girls" and servants permitted middle-class men to live up to the masculine ethos without tainting the virtue of their families (Weeks, 1981,

p. 30; Peiss, 1983, p. 778). In 1869 E. H. Lecky demonstrated this relationship succinctly in his argument for the necessity of the prostitute: "Herself the supreme type of vice, she is ultimately the most efficient guardian of virtue" (quoted in McHugh, 1980, p. 17).

The compartmentalization of women into those who were middle class and asexual and those who were poor and promiscuous was not so easily sustained. In the first place, it was contradicted by actual experience. Carl Degler argues that middle-class women were not the asexual angels and working-class women the sexually driven hoydens that the categories required (Degler, 1974; cf. Peiss, 1983, p. 75; DuBois and Gordon, 1983, p. 12). Concomitantly, men struggled to maintain the distinction with respect to their own behavior. Freud, for example, observed that impotence among "civilized" (that is, middle-class) men occurred because they were inhibited from feeling sexual desire for women they respected; they were able to feel sexual arousal only for women they debased. "Where they love they do not desire and where they desire they cannot love" (Freud, 1912, p. 183).

The conflict Freud described expresses men's difficulty in limiting themselves to the one acceptable outlet for sex—marriage. Because sexuality was debased, associated with animal instinct and brutishness as well as with lower-class degeneracy, a woman could not be both an object of sexual desire and spiritually pure. This distinction created difficulty for women as well as men. Young women of course experienced sexual urges with the onset of puberty, but these urges were repressed. But, unlike that of men, the sexual conflict of women itself was repressed because of the cultural presumption of their innocence. According to Peter Cominos (1972), the ideal of innocence required ignorance of sexuality, repression of any memory of childhood sexual experience, as well as denial of sexual feelings (pp. 157–58). Given the abyss between the categories of good woman and bad woman, this requirement for absolute innocence meant that girls were in perpetual danger of falling from grace. Every impulse, thought, or experience that so much as hinted at sexual meaning had to be suppressed. The girl who struggled with the impossibility of this feat had to convey a persona in which she at least appeared innocent. This posturing only reinforced the hostility that informed the absolute categories in the first place: the idea that respectable women were only pretending, that behind the façade they were "latently depraved" (p. 168).

The notion that within every good woman is a whore was the underlying theme of Victorian pornography (Marcus, 1964); it was paralleled in the fascination with fallen and evil women that captured the Victorian imagination (Auerbach, 1982), and, especially toward the end of the century, it was expressed in suspicion of middle-class young women (cf. Gorham, 1978, p. 356). It was assumed that "impure girls and women lost their virtue because delinquent parents, nurses, and governesses failed to cultivate their innocence and to check their inherited fallen nature. Their thoughts were allowed to become impure and their latent depravity, no longer thwarted, was affirmed" (Cominos, 1972, p. 166). Just as important was men's response to them. Girls "were either sexless ministering angels or sensuously oversexed temptresses of the devil; they were either aids to continence or incontinence" (p. 167). Thus, if a girl were treated in a sexually suggestive way, this would appear to her as proof of her own depravity.

But the conflict between the masculine ethos and the ideal of the Christian gentleman suggests that men's behavior toward middle-class women could not always adhere to the ideal of absolute respectability. Moreover, if all women were suspected of being latently depraved, then they were regarded on some level as sexual beings. Thus, a woman was not either angel or temptress, but "both a perpetual reproach and a perpetual temptation" (Christ, 1977, p. 162). Unmarried women especially were regarded as vulnerable to sexual depravity because they had not achieved the venerable status of wife and mother. A middle-class young woman was faced with the paradox that her innocence was suspect for its vulnerability to corruption (Davidoff, 1979, pp. 93–94). And she was also faced with the behavior of men who were excited by this possibility (S. Gilman, 1981).

Thus, the emphasis on female subordination, the eroticization of interpersonal power, and the gender differences in the simultaneous repression and incitement of sexuality contributed to a complex family dynamic in which daughters and sisters were treated in ways that were both sexually charged and repressed. It is this dynamic that underlies Horney's description of the family as an "emotional hothouse" in which women of the feminine type were sexualized as girls.

An example of this dynamic can be found in Jean Strouse's excellent biography of Alice James (Strouse, 1980). Although she was born a few generations earlier than the women Horney analyzed, Alice James too experienced the conflict between sexual incitement and respectability that historians have associated with the mid- to late nineteenth century. According to Strouse, the James family was a paragon of middle-class respectability (p. 130); indeed, they never spoke of sex at all (p. 54). Yet Alice was subject to much teasing and humiliation that were highly sexually charged. For example, when she was eight, her father's friend and frequent guest, William Makepeace Thackeray, turned to Alice suddenly and, according to Henry, Jr., "laid his hand on her little flounced person and exclaimed with ludicrous horror: 'Crinoline—I was suspecting it! So young and so depraved!'" (p. 52).

At age eight, of course, Alice did not know what depravity meant, but she did realize that she was being humiliated and that this had to do with her sex (Strouse, 1980, p. 52). No one, however, treated her in a more seductive way than her eldest brother, William, five years her senior. According to his biographer, "William had grown up with exalted ideals of chastity" (G. Allen, 1967, p. 212), ideals which he struggled to impose upon himself (p. 163). He went on to become a renowned philosopher and psychologist, rarely mentioning sex in his writing except in *The Prin-*

ciples of Psychology, vol. 2 (1981/1890), where he posited an "anti-sexual instinct" (p. 1053). James considered this natural repulsion to sexual contact with another to be more fundamental (that is, instinctual) than sexual desire. "This strongest passion of all [sex], so far from being the most 'irresistible,' may, on the contrary, be the hardest one to give rein to, and...individuals in whom the inhibiting influences are potent may pass through life and never find an occasion to have it gratified" (p. 1054); see Strouse, 1980, p. 54). James claimed that the anti-sexual instinct is stronger in women than in men; so too parental love, which he idealized as the "passionate devotion of a mother." "Condemning every danger, triumphing over every difficulty, outlasting all fatigue, woman's love is here invincibly superior to anything that man can show" (James, 1981/1890, vol. 2, p. 1056).

Despite his strict Christian gentlemanliness, William James treated his sister Alice in a seductively teasing and dominating manner. "He addressed courtly letters to her as 'you lovely babe,' 'Charmante Jeune Fille,' 'Perfidious child' and 'Cherie Charmante de Bal.' He referred constantly to her physical attributes and drew verbal portraits of her sensual, untutored, indulged feminine nature." He wrote to her, "a thousand thanks to the cherry lipped apricot nosed double chinned little Bal for her strongly dashed off letter, which inflamed the hearts of her lonely brothers with an intense longing to kiss and slap her cheeks" (Strouse, 1980, pp. 52–53). In 1859, when Alice was twelve, William composed a "sonnate" to her and "invited the family into the parlor to hear him sing it." In it he dreamed of "Sweet Alice," called her "my love," and implored, "I wished to join myself to thee/By matrimonial band." According to the song, Alice, "so very proud, but yet so fair," rejects William, who replies:

> Your childlike form, your golden hair
> I never more may see,
> But goaded on by dire despair
> I'll drown within the sea.

> Adieu to love! Adieu to life!
> Since I may not have thee,
> My Alice sweet, to be my wife,
> I'll drown me in the sea!   (p. 53)

Strouse reports that Alice was confused and embarrassed, and, although she eventually learned to tease back, she was nevertheless "titillated and frightened" by William's advances, which continued well into adulthood. "They put her on display before the family audience like a bright ornament, calling attention to her female body with mocking praise" (Strouse, 1980, p. 54). That body became "something alien, powerful, terrifying, and bad" (p. 119) when Alice had a nervous collapse at age nineteen, precipitated, according to Strouse, by her attempt to do intellectual work, to achieve the kind of personal authenticity that her father valued most highly and believed impossible for women to accomplish (pp. xiii, 45).

Alice and William James lived a few generations earlier than Horney's feminine type, but their relationship displays the tension between repression and incitement of sexuality that characterized the nineteenth century. Publicly, as well as in his writings, William appeared as the model of the Christian gentleman. Yet his treatment of his sister conveyed the conflict between the masculine ethos of sexual power and the middle-class imperative of repressive respectability. His sexual teasing of his sister and mocking praise of her body in jokes, songs, and letters is the ill-resolved compromise that permitted him both to assert his sexuality and to deny any serious intent. Joking objectification of another is, as Freud recognized, an attempt to relax sexual inhibitions in a socially acceptable way (Freud, 1905a). But the one objectified experiences not release but fear and alienation from her body. For Alice the sexualizing treatment brought her to regard her self as an external thing, "watching herself as object and learning to detach from the flushed confusions involved in also being the subject of the diversion" (Strouse, 1980, p. 55).

Compulsive Masculinity

William's sexualizing behavior—no matter how inhibited—was experienced as real danger by Alice James. In an essay entitled "The Dread of Woman" (1932a) Horney described men's sexualizing behavior from the perspective of the endangered female. She described male sexual conquest as a pervasive phenomenon, a kind of compulsive masculinity. Every man, she argued, suffers from an anxiety of inadequacy "that gives his general attitude toward woman a particular stamp" (p. 143). He devalues women as a way of elevating his own sense of superiority.

> In sexual life itself we see how the simple craving of love that drives men to women is very often overshadowed by their overwhelming inner compulsion to prove their manhood again and again to themselves and others. A man of this type in its more extreme form has therefore one interest only: to conquer. His aim is to have "possessed" many women . . . the most beautiful and most sought-after women. We find a remarkable mixture of this narcissistic overcompensation and of surviving anxiety in those men who, while wanting to make conquests, are very indignant with a woman who takes their intentions too seriously, or who cherish a lifelong gratitude to her if she spares them any further proof of their manhood.   (pp. 145–46)

The purpose of this compulsive masculinity is to establish self-esteem and affirm power through the sexual domination of women. Alluding to Freud, Horney found the same overcompensation in the sexual debasement of women. "If a man does not desire any woman who is his equal or even his superior—may it not be that he is protecting his threatened self-regard in accordance with that most useful principle of sour grapes? From the prostitute or the woman of easy virtue one need fear no rejection, and no demands in the sexual, ethical, or intellectual sphere. One can feel oneself the superior" (Horney, 1932a, p. 146).

But, unlike Freud, Horney did not explain this debasement in terms of a split between respect and sexual desire (Freud, 1912). According to her, the debasement of women occurs within the "craving of love that drives men to women" in all relationships, not just those with women of "easy virtue." Because of insecurity all men seek to prove their superiority through relationships with women. But the purpose is not to establish identity in a relationship with a particular woman; to the contrary, the proof of masculinity lies in the process of conquest itself. Thus, the realization of male identity is a never-ending pursuit in which proof is momentary and incomplete. Heterosexual conquest is the means—and women are the instruments along an endless path in the creation of male identity. In this pursuit, the man needs not only conquest of desirable women but also the conviction of female inferiority. This conviction is rooted in a cultural presumption: "the view that women are infantile and emotional creatures, and as such, incapable of responsibility and independence is the work of the masculine tendency to lower women's self-respect." This masculine principle asserts itself anew with each conquest. The narcissistic belief in his own superiority by virtue of being a male bolsters the "ever-precarious self-respect of the 'average man'" (Horney, 1932a, p. 146).

Later Horney reiterated this theme of compulsive masculinity in the narcissism of the domineering neurotic type (Horney, 1950a). "His pride . . . is invested in being the ideal lover and in being irresistible." But, "women who are easily available do not appeal to him. He must prove his mastery by conquering those who, for whatever reasons, are difficult to obtain. The conquest may consist in the consummation of the sexual act or he may aim at complete emotional surrender. When these aims are achieved his interest recedes" (p. 305). Here again is the theme of using women sexually and moving on, but in this revision the element of capturing the forbidden or seducing the inviolate is necessary to gratification. The purpose is not so much to assert one's masculinity with those who are already considered debased but to conquer sexually, and thus by implication to debase, the women who seem superior—that is, sexually unavailable or "pure." Thus, superiority is asserted in the act of revealing latent depravity beneath the superior façade, an act that is compulsively carried out over and over again.

The significance of Horney's analysis of compulsive masculinity lies in her assertion that it characterizes male anxiety and overcompensation in relationships wih all women. In 1932, she was still attempting to explain the behavior she observed in terms of the Freudian paradigm; thus, she posited that men are compulsively aggressive sexually because they are attempting to overcome the biologically determined genital inadequacy they felt as boys with regard to their mothers (Horney, 1932a, p. 145). In her later work she couched her understanding of the phenomenon in terms of anxiety and hostility within the neurotic character structure. But because her analysis of the development of neurotic conflict emphasized the experience of girls, her descriptions of male conflict lack a satisfactory theoretical base.

Horney's analysis of compulsive masculinity also lacks historical data about the social and economic conditions at the end of the nineteenth century that would have fostered male anxiety. Robert Wiebe has noted that during this period in America middle-class male identity was in jeopardy: the ideal of male autonomy was threatened by the expansion of industry, the centralization of business, and the creation of massive bureaucracies that fostered anonymity and required obedience (Wiebe, 1967). The middle-class man wanted to believe that he was the captain of his fate, but in reality he was struggling to keep from being submerged in vast social and economic systems that demanded his obedience and controlled his destiny (p. 12). It was also a time of feminist backlash against these male-created institutions and the economic symptoms of their degeneracy—the poverty, vice, and family decay associated with the working-class victims of industrial capitalism. The purity movement assaulted male sexual privilege and excesses through attacks on prostitution, drunkenness, and incest (Pivar, 1973; Walkowitz, 1980; L. Gordon, 1976; Weeks,

1981). In this context many men felt that male identity itself was under attack (Filene, 1974, pp. 68–94).

Although the purity agitators protested the degeneracy of the world outside the family, several historians have interpreted their reform activities as, in part, a projection of anxieties and sexual tensions within middle-class households (See Weeks, 1981, p. 31; DuBois and Gordon, 1983; Wohl, 1978). In the final decades of the nineteenth century many attempted to shake off the hypocrisy associated with sexual repression in what Peter Cominos (1963) has termed the "revolt against respectability" (p. 248). In America, sex radicals and free-love feminists advocated personal freedom, which they saw as being destroyed by conventional marriage and family responsibilities (Sears, 1977; Leach, 1980; DuBois and Gordon, 1983). Within marriage, sexual pleasure was beginning to be presented in manuals as desirable and independent of procreation (M. Gordon, 1971, p. 58). While social and economic conditions were generating anxiety over masculine identity and autonomy, the growing impetus to sexual liberation was providing a new avenue for masculine assertion and revolt as well as new anxieties and tensions (Cominos, 1963, p. 250). Thus, if the feminine type experienced chaos and sexualization as a child within her middle-class family, she encountered there male family members whose compulsive masculinity was similarly historically situated.

The Sexual Horde

Horney's description of male anxiety and overcompensating sexual conquest extended her earlier notion of "real danger." In her 1927 essay she took male sexual aggression to be the real family danger to girls; in her 1932 and 1950 analyses compulsive masculinity is identified as the behavior that made this danger a continuous reality. Together they explain the girlhood sexual experiences described in "The Overvaluation of Love" (1934): the female danger, the male sexual prerogative, the family chaos.

Horney's portrait of these sexually charged households stands in contrast to the civilized authority and family order that is presumed in Freud's notion of the middle-class family (Poster, 1978, pp. 1–41); indeed, the example of the feminine type's sexualized childhood appears to be drawn from the kind of kin relations that Freud had associated with "primitive" eras.

In *Totem and Taboo* (1913) Freud created a myth of a primitive horde of people where all women—mothers and daughters alike—were the sexual property of the father, until the sons killed and devoured him and took the women for themselves (pp. 140–42). This act of patricidal cannibalism and the claiming of the tribal women actually accomplished the Oedipal wishes that, according to Freud, all males instinctively have: to eliminate the father as a rival and to sexually possess the mother. However, in cannibalizing the father (literally incorporating him), the sons identified with him and out of remorse recreated his rules against patricide and incest (p. 143). All sons, according to Freud, experience these desires and their consequences in the Oedipus complex. Their hostility toward the father is not actually carried out, but the desire to destroy him as their competitor for the mother clashes with the affection they feel for him. Remorse leads them to identify with him and internalize the rules against instinctual patricide and incest. This forms the foundation of guilt, renunciation, the superego, and civilized life (Freud, 1917, 1924). Thus, through the myth of civilizing the primal horde, Freud sought to establish that, as the mechanism for internalizing the father's authority, the Oedipus complex is the guardian of family order and the apotheosis of patriarchy.

However, the portrait of childhood sexualization that emerges from Horney's references shows households, not under the influence of patriarchal authority and renunciation of impulse, but as the setting for male sexual conquest. According to her picture, the late nineteenth-century family *was* the primal horde: fathers and sons were competitors and colleagues—in effect, brothers—in pursuit of the family women. All females are in real danger, protected neither by the father's power nor by his internalized authority in the consciences of his sons. Indeed, the father's right to conquest is the problem itself; it has become democratized as filial prerogative.[3]

Sexualized Girlhood

The portrait of the family as a horde of sexually conquering men and women in perpetual danger of rape appears as a nightmare of hysterical imagination. How is it to be reconciled with the self-conscious portrait that late nineteenth-century middle-class society drew of itself: the authoritative but kindly paterfamilias governing his family, who in their renunciation of sexual urges are paragons of harmony and respectability? The sexual horde, I suggest, does not compete with the respectable model; rather it intersects it in two ways. First, as Foucault (1978) implied in his idea of the historical entwining of sexuality and power, the exercise of power within the family became a sexual experience. Control over a daughter's social behavior, authoritative solicitude for her safety, articulation of the ideals for which she should strive, surveillance of her activities: all these assertions of power are highly sexually charged. They all pivot on her sexual identity, requiring innocence and suspecting depravity. Evading and submitting to power also have sexual meaning. In her submission to the respectability required of her, the daughter complies to sexual control and therefore sexualizes her goodness. Thus, the horde of sexually aggressive men and women in danger is not the image projected by the middle-class

3. Ricoeur (1970) interprets *Totem and Taboo* as the transformation of war into law, the creation of social order. Horney's description of the sexual chaos of middle-class households implies what both Freud and Ricoeur obscure: the disorder within the order (see Swan, 1974). Horney's descriptions suggest that the disorder is sustained by the practices of masculine civilization in which females remain objects of male sexual conquest and control. This extends Rubin's argument that the exchange of women is premised on female oppression (Rubin, 1975) to the notion that male collegial competition for women is the "civilized" disorder that sets the conditions of female danger. For a perceptive analysis of the trivialization of this phenomenon as "playful woman-sharing" in the films of the 1940s, see Wolfenstein and Leites (1950).

family; it is rather the sexual secret of the family hierarchy, an order premised on male domination and female submission.

Second, the symbol of the sexual horde mirrors the respectable ideal as its repressed underside. Auerbach's (1982) analysis of the Victorian fascination with fallen, sexual, dangerous, and depraved women, Gorham's (1982) and Cominos's (1972) analyses of the good girl/bad girl dichotomy, and Charles Rosenberg's (1973) descriptions of male ambivalence together suggest the sexually charged but repressed heterosocial relationships of the middle class. If a daughter or sister is defined as both mysteriously sexual and respectably pure the attitudes of male family members toward her would, like that of Willaim James toward Alice, reflect that ambivalence in inhibited sexualization. This is the behavior that flirts with the bounds of propriety, behavior that Judith Herman (1981) has recently identified with seductive fathers: sexual teasing, joking, innuendo, flirtation, courting, sexually tinged concern with a girl's appearance, accidental exhibition, caresses, and spying (pp. 109–25). Through this behavior seductive fathers treat daughters as sexualized objects but deny responsibility for doing so. Horney associated such behavior with the compulsive need to assert male identity through endless sexual conquest, but the conquest is inhibited and denied. "We find a remarkable mixture of this narcissistic overcompensation and of surviving anxiety in those men who, while wanting to make conquests, are very indignant with a woman who takes their intentions too seriously" (Horney, 1932a, p. 146).

Sexual dominance simultaneously asserted and denied trivializes the sexualizing experience itself by the pretense that it is unintentional and one of the routines of everyday life. It is understandable that in this setting girls experienced themselves as both debased and powerless and that, as Freud discovered, many actually identified with prostitutes and servants, the women considered most debased and least powerful. Freud recognized that this identification had a grounding in reality. "There is tragic justice in the circumstance that the family head's stooping to a maidservant is atoned for by his daughter's self-abasement" (Freud, 1985, p. 241). Unfortunately, Freud did not recognize that the daughter's self-debasement was not necessarily a surrogate atonement for her father's treatment of another woman. As in the case of his patient Dora (Freud, 1905a), the middle-class daughter's identification with serving women reflected her own sexualization, which led her to "the unconscious belief that femininity, bondage and debasement were synonymous" (Ramas, 1980, p. 502).

It is, I suggest, the very common occurrence of female sexualization and exercise of male power that blinded Freud to the real danger in the setting in which incest occurs. Jeffrey Masson overlooks this historical context in his recent interpretation of Freud's reversal of the seduction theory (Masson, 1984). By focusing on Freud's original linking of his patients' hysteria with actual sexual abuse and incest, Masson skims over the wider reality that all girls were sexualized within the middle-class family as an everyday exercise of power. Thus, hysterical symptoms such as Dora's (Freud, 1905a) can be interpreted as a psychological response to the more general exercise of eroticized power and not just as the outcome of incest (cf. Marcus, 1984; Ramas, 1980). Her father's use of her to provide amorous diversion for Herr K. (the husband of his lover) is indeed sexualization but not incest. His indignant protest that he had not pandered his daughter, that she had been guilty of exaggeration (Freud, 1905a, p. 34) denies the reality of her experience. By siding with him and explaining Dora's hysterical symptoms as expressions of her incestuous longing for her father (p. 56), Freud was discounting the causal significance of her sexualizing treatment by her father and Herr K.[4] If Freud had been aware of the wider pattern of men's seductive treatment and sexualized control over daughters, he might have been able to explain the frequency of hysterical symptoms such as Dora's without pos-

4. The case of Dora has generated a considerable number of secondary analyses. Some have recently been collected in Bernheimer and Kahane (1985), which includes a good bibliography on Dora scholarship.

tulating universal internal processes. Without this awareness, he was left with the discrepancy between the frequency of hysteria in his women patients and his growing conviction that not all hysterical symptoms could be the product of actual incest (Freud, 1985, p. 264).

Had Freud seriously considered this family landscape of sexualization, he would have had to question the behavior of all men, including himself and his father (Freud, 1985, pp. 264, 268), as well as the moral integrity of the "civilized" middle-class family. I suggest that Freud did not see this sexualizing landscape—or saw it only hazily—not simply because of his own moral commitments to middle-class respectability but also because the sexualizing experiences were trivialized and absorbed into everyday life as unimportant events that hysterical daughters were likely to exaggerate. In a context where female sexualization was mystified, Freud eventually had little difficulty convincing himself that his patients' reports of sexual abuse were dreams of events that never occurred and desires for that which could not be.

Furtive, fragmentary, yet part of everyday family life, the sexualization of girls seems commonplace yet so elusive, routine yet undefined. To speak of it invites disbelief. To call it sexual aggression sounds hysterical, delusional. To identify it as the "real danger" appears an over-reaction. How does one speak of something that fades from scrutiny, denies its own existence, or pretends that it is something else at the same time that it merges with the routines of daily living? No wonder Horney turned from the difficult task of telling the daughter's secret to the somewhat easier one of analyzing its effects.

The Sexualization of Fear

The feminine type grew up fearing compulsive masculinity and reached adulthood in an era when the sexualization of women had become public. The equation of female liberation with the overcoming of heterosexual inhibitions, the sexual harassment of working women, the portrayal of women's bodies as playthings, the increasing emphasis upon the loosening of sexual inhibition all extended the young woman's earlier sexualizing experiences (see chapter 1). Childhood may have taught her to focus on the desires and pleasures of men, to regard herself as an instrument of male demands, and to compete with and envy all other women in the process. If as an adult she encountered a world that saw her as a sexual object, she was well prepared to meet that demand. Indeed, as a result of her childhood sexualization, she embraced it compulsively.

Underlying the feminine type's compulsive heterosexuality is not desire but fear. The terror of childhood sexualization (Horney, 1937, p. 84) is the context out of which basic anxiety and basic hostility emerge. In a dangerous situation the child's response is realistic fear and hostility toward the aggressive adult. But because of the power differences between adult and child, the child will deny her own hostility, converting protest into admiration. When the adult's abusive and exploitative behavior is sexual, the child does not dare to oppose it. Instead, through the reversal of her hostility, she develops the belief that her exploiter is good and that she deserves to be used by him. Identifying with her aggressor requires her to regard herself as contemptible. This is Horney's description of the submissive survival solution (pp. 257–80).[5]

This is a solution not simply to exploitation but to *sexual* exploitation: the paradoxical confounding of terror and tenderness. The young girl is exploited through apparent affection. She is used and controlled by being treated as if she were loved and admired. Hence, her solution is not simply her belief that she deserves what she gets. She is compliant in the concrete reality of *sexual* submission. By giving in, she renders her own sexuality compliant, passive. This is accomplished both through the rever-

5. According to Masson, Ferenczi first referred to this identification with the sexual aggressor in a paper delivered before the International Psycho-Analytic Congress in 1932 (Masson, 1984, p. 148; Ferenczi, 1984).

sal of hostility (her degraded sexuality in the hands of her powerful master) and through her attempt to escape the conditions she
fears. Her realistic fear is converted into love and admiration or,
more precisely, into a strategy of rendering herself lovable to her
sexualizer. "If you love me, you will not hurt me" (Horney, 1937,
p. 96) is the struggle for safety underlying her attempts to become
desirable.

Thus, compliance (the conversion of hostility into admiring
submission) and seductiveness (the conversion of fear into desirability) combine in a submissive identity informed by sexuality.
Horney's analysis shows that the behavior associated with
women's masochism has nothing to do with an instinctual sexual
wish, as Deutsch (1930), following Freud, had argued. It is primarily, according to Horney, a response of the powerless to the
aggression of the powerful. Submission is expressed sexually only
when the aggression itself is sexual and demands sexual compliance. The victim's submission then *becomes* sexual and her
attempt to be treated nonaggressively becomes sexual seductiveness. Horney's distinction between submission and sexuality
illuminates the issues of power, fear, hostility, and striving for
safety that lie behind the solution of sexual submission (Horney,
1939b, p. 113).[6]

Horney implied that sexual exploitation of girls lies behind the
sexual submission and seductiveness of adult females. While submission is a passive attempt to gain safety, seductiveness presents
the appearance of desire with the underlying goal of safety. Thus it
is not desire that informs seductiveness but the strategy to make
oneself desirable and to find safety in being chosen.

But to be chosen is to be sexually used. Why is seductiveness a
safety strategy if it leads to being used sexually? Horney's later

6. At first Horney called the submissive solution *masochism* (Horney, 1937),
but later rejected the term (Horney, 1945). See my discussion of morbid dependency in chapter 6.

work provides one answer to this question: seductiveness can be interpreted as a form of submission. If a woman is resigned to the inevitability of sexualization, seductive behavior can be a manipulative strategy to avoid force or brutality. It is like a weaker animal's baring its neck to a stronger one, an invitation that pleads for restraint. By being seductive a woman indicates willing submission that suggests the lack of need for force. She is trying to elicit tenderness and safety (Horney, 1937, pp. 96–97).

In "The Overvaluation of Love" (1934) Horney offered two other explanations for seductive behavior. First, she noticed that the women of the feminine type had an "excess of sexual desire" (p. 202), which derived from their fear of being abnormal and their belief that the proof of normality was in being sexualized by men. The need to attract men—expressed both in prostitution fantasies and in the desire to marry—was closely linked to the wish to overcome this fear. Like compulsive masculinity, female seductiveness is a sexual overcompensation for feelings of inadequacy. But whereas Horney explained men's overvaluing of love as a compensation for anxiety over performance, she explained women's seductiveness as a response to inadequacy of appearance. Thus, the feminine type is seductive in order to be chosen, not to exert the power of choice. Being chosen is evidence that she is normal—that is, attractive to men—and proof that she is not the worthless and ugly creature she fears herself to be (pp. 196–97).

Seductive behavior that invites male attention is also suffused with hostility toward other women. Indeed for the feminine type, capturing the attention and love of men is a triumphant victory over other women with whom she feels herself in constant competition. Horney linked this destructive rivalry to childhood experiences of sexualization in which all females in a household were objects of male evaluation and sexual objectification (Horney, 1934, pp. 191–96). The mother was much hated as a rival, but the feminine type's hatred of her mother went beyond the envy directed at sisters or other women who were the sexual favorites of men. Horney found great hostility directed toward mothers in sexual fantasies. These destructive wishes, she posited, expressed the daughter's fear that the same type of injury might befall her (pp. 198–200). Although Horney did not probe the source of the daughter's intense hostility toward her mother, Judith Herman (1981) has claimed that all sexualized daughters and victims of incest feel bitter toward their mothers for failing to protect them (pp. 112–14, 123).

Horney found that hostility toward men also lurks within seductiveness. While the feminine type is dependent upon the admiration and love of men she is profoundly fearful of that dependence. "The fear of dependence is . . . a profound fear of the disappointments and humiliations that they expect to result from falling in love, humiliations that they have themselves experienced in childhood and would like subsequently to pass on to others. The original experience that has thus left behind it such a strong feeling of vulnerability was presumably caused by a man, but the resultant behavior is directed almost equally toward men and women" (Horney, 1934, p. 206). This hostility can be expressed as a desire to make the other person more dependent on her than she is on him or her. When directed toward men, hostility is expressed as "deep-seated desire for revenge . . . the desire is to get the better of a man, to cast him aside, to reject him just as she herself once felt cast aside and rejected" (p. 206). This can sometimes take the form of desiring ever-new relationships as proof of erotic superiority, paralleling the man's pursuit of compulsive masculinity, but differing in the desire to be chosen and eventually to cause the man to become dependent, rather than in the wish to exact his total emotional submission before casting him aside (p. 205).

But, perhaps most fundamental, the feminine type's defensive seductiveness expresses hostility directed back toward herself. In this reversal, she identifies with the sexualizer in self-contempt.

To be chosen is to be confirmed in degradation. Horney suggests that the adult submissive solution originates in the degradation experienced in childhood sexualization. Adult self-contempt is not a repetition of the childhood experience but its consequence. The reversal of the hostility that the earlier experience produced creates a sense of self that is fundamentally degraded, worthless, defective. It also produces an indiscriminate admiration for aggressors, in particular a need to admire all men, who are perceived as potential aggressors. The woman's submission is thus the expression of a fundamental feeling of worthlessness combined with a striving to merge with absolute power: "to be at once everything and nothing" (Horney, 1937, p. 276) and to be "putty in the master's hands" (p. 268). Seductive behavior, then, manifests the wish to be chosen as a means of simultaneously confirming and vicariously overcoming fundamental worthlessness.

The sense of worthlessness is reconfirmed in every sexualizing encounter. Compulsive masculinity as the endless sexualization of females calls out a corresponding female seductiveness that searches for identity in the gaze, the evaluation, and the choices of men. This is the compulsive heterosexuality that Horney found in the feminine type (Horney, 1934, p. 202). Ironically, the compulsion simultaneously expresses a woman's degradation and her identity. Every sexualizing encounter confirms this self, reminding the woman that she has been chosen, but only because she is considered powerless, a sexual object, and therefore degraded: hence her competition with and envy of other women; hence her need to be chosen over other women and her fear of being left alone, unchosen, without identity; hence her belief that the married woman and the prostitute both represent normal femininity (Horney, 1934, pp. 195, 203; 1942, pp. 190–246).

The feminine type's sexualization as a girl led her to believe that she was a despicable being beneath her façade as a respectable person. This self-contemptuous sense of being a fraud is expressed in her diary by seventeen-year-old Karen Horney:

The depraved fable, that is me. In my own imagination I am a strumpet! In my own imagination there is no spot on me that has not been kissed by a burning mouth. In my own imagination there is no depravity I have not tasted, to the dregs.

And in reality ... !

But not even the tips of my fingers have been kissed. But there is nothing in the world more immaculate than I. I have committed mental sins, which are the worst because they destroy and do not create—because they are a sin against holy life!

Perhaps I am the saddest fable of them all.   (Horney, 1980, p. 64)

In 1910, seven years after Horney had written these words, Karl Abraham, her psychoanalyst, told her that she had a "wish to throw myself away, prostitute myself—give myself to any man at random" (Horney, 1980, p. 242). Only after considerable torment and with a deep sense of failure did she terminate this unsuccessful analysis (pp. 258–71). Thus began her long journey through the science that turned women's sexualization into an inherent female wish, the science that "discovered" the essential whore within the apparent virgin.[7] Not until she was almost fifty did Horney work her way back to the truth of the matter, to the daughter's secret and to the primacy of women's experience.

Horney did not expand her personal teenage fable to a cultural one, but she did develop an understanding of contemporary femininity that begins with the fable's reality in the sexualizing experience of females. Her theoretical work suggests a powerful alternative to the Oedipus myth—not another myth or fable but the concept of the *real danger* of male sexual aggression. Implied in this concept is the idea of the sexualization of male power and female fear. Horney demonstrated that sexualization was a pervasive fact of family life in the childhood of her feminine type. The

7. In a 1907 essay Abraham argued that children who are sexually abused have often provoked the attacking adult by behaving in a sexually teasing manner (Abraham, 1927/1907).

struggles of the adult woman of this type suggest that the twentieth-century imperative to release sexual inhibitions was not a
true liberation for women but, rather, an imperative that touched
on hidden experiences of fear, anger, and shame.

5 | Devaluation

Although Horney's discussions of devaluation are relatively brief, they do not display the reticence characteristic of her analysis of girlhood sexualization. She linked female devaluation with a patriarchal pattern of preference for males and an ideology of male superiority (Horney, 1939b, p. 170). Her writings on development describe the social relations that result from this pattern, which convey "in the thousand little daily experiences of a child" (Horney, 1942, p 49) that the girl is unworthy of genuine affection or respect. The areas of experience Horney enumerated—everyday tasks, school work, health, aspirations—are those through which a child derives a sense of worth as an active human being in our culture. The child who is not encouraged in these areas, whose capabilities and aspirations are not respected or valued, soon feels that what she does—and therefore who she is—is worthless (Horney, 1937, pp. 80–81; 1942, p. 49; 1945, p. 41).

The gender pattern of devaluation is well known to contemporary students of childhood socialization. During the past twenty years, social scientists have studied and analyzed extensively the "little daily experiences" that devalue girls' activities in contrast to those of boys (Lott, 1981, pp. 17–76)—for example, constraining a girl's freedom, ignoring her achievements, paying less attention to her activities, and ridiculing or discouraging her aspirations. All are ways of devaluing anything that detracts from the girl's sexualized femininity. If the girl learns from her sexualization that she is an object to be used for the purposes and pleasures of men, she learns that lesson again from the devaluation of her attempts to be a self-directed person. Sexualization and devaluation are parts of the same process. This is a dialectic that Horney implied and Simone de Beauvoir later made explicit. "In woman," writes Beauvoir, "there is from the beginning a conflict between her autonomous existence and her objective self . . . she is taught that to please she must try to please, she must make herself object; she should therefore renounce her autonomy. She is treated like a live doll and refused liberty" (Beauvoir, 1952, p. 316).

To be an object rather than a subject means that the girl is denied choice, intention, and the freedom to transform her situation according to her vision. With no independent basis for judgment or action, she is at the mercy of others. They become not only the source of her actions but also the standard for evaluating them. Her self-worth is dependent upon their opinions; their desire becomes her own because, lacking judgment of her own, her overwhelming need is to be judged favorably by them.

Upon what basis is a woman or girl in our culture judged? The effects of her devaluation return full circle to the conditions of her sexualization. She is valued first as a sexually attractive being, an object that is chosen for its sexual desirability. "It is understandable that the care of her physical appearance should become for the young girl a real obsession. . . . Be they princesses or shepherdesses, [girls] must always be pretty in order to obtain love and happiness" (Beauvoir, 1952, p. 328). Horney found this concern with sexualized appearance in her patients' anguish over their physical imperfections, their obsessive attention to clothes, and their unremitting need to have all men find them attractive (Horney, 1934).

The message a girl receives through devaluation underscores the degradation of her sexualization. Her sexualized being is dependent upon her absence of will, her objectification, and her powerlessness. Her submission to sexualization is not only a strategy of safety but also a confirmation of her utter selflessness. Conversely, the devaluation of her aspirations and capabilities is not simply a destruction of will; it is a reinforcement that she is nothing more than a sex object. Every devaluing experience is, in effect, a confirmation of the female's sexual subordination, and every sexualizing encounter deepens her sense of a lack of self.

Horney's own experience as a daughter supplied the source for some of her observations. Although she was an enthusiastic and gifted student, her father at first refused financial support for her to attend the Gymnasium. After Karen, her mother, and her brother repeatedly pleaded in her behalf, they awaited her father's answer, as this diary entry of fifteen-year-old Karen records: "Why can't Father make up his mind a little faster? He, who has flung out thousands for my stepbrother Enoch, who is both stupid and bad, first turns every additional penny he is to spend for me ten times in his fingers.... He would like me to stay at home now, so we could dismiss our maid and I could do her work. He brings me almost to the point of cursing my good gifts" (Horney, 1980, p. 26). Eventually Danielsen conceded after Karen and her mother promised in writing "that after graduation he need do nothing for me" (p. 27).

Sonni's intercession is the one instance recorded in Horney's diary of her mother's opposing her father's power. It is also the one recorded occasion where Sonni appears to have acted genuinely on her daughter's behalf. The rest of the diary paints a very different picture of the relationship between mother and daughter; it is one in which a depressed mother looks to her daughter for consolation. This expectation that a daughter nurture a parent conveys another component of female devaluation—one that Horney did not explore in her work but that she certainly lived. The rest of this chapter explores this nurturing imperative as the epitome of female devaluation. I will elaborate the idea through examples of girls' nurturing parents (including Horney and her mother) and an analysis of the developmental consequences of this nurturing reversal.

The Nuturing Imperative

The expectation that women care for others is not unique to Western culture. Women nurturing their young appears as a universal motif (Rich, 1976; Dinnerstein, 1976; Neumann, 1963). However, the idea that women should give emotional and physical sustenance to adult men is not universal. In Western industrial countries it is expresssed in a concept of the motherly wife who became idealized in the nineteenth-century domestic cult and was extended in the twentieth-century romanticized marriage (see chapter 1). That all women should develop the selfless capacity to meet the emotional needs of men has been reflected in expectations of daughters from the cheerfully attentive "sunbeam" of the nineteenth century (Gorham, 1982, pp. 37–50) to the "mother's little helper" of the twentieth (Weitzman, 1979, pp. 14–17; Caplan, 1981, pp. 42–43).

Recently feminists have examined the consequences of the nurturing imperative on the psychology of women. Nancy Chodorow (1978) has posited that the capacity to nurture others is developed in women as an aspect of their relational identity. This identity expresses a need to affiliate with others which emerges from the contemporary structure of parenting. Chodorow's theory rests upon the pivotal but unproven assumption that a mother will naturally identify more closely with her daughter because she is of the same gender. The structure of parenting in contemporary Western industrial society—women expected to care for children and men absent from domestic responsibility—encourages this tendency for mothers to experience themselves as continuous with their daughters, keeping them in a close relationship longer and more intensely than sons (p. 189). As a result, daughters never experience the frustration of primary love that Chodorow assumes is necessary to achieve separation from the mother (p. 69); instead, they experience themselves to be continuous with their mothers, later with other people, and eventually with their own daughters, hence repeating the pattern.

Chodorow assumes that, in contrast, a mother experiences a son as a "male opposite" and pushes him into an Oedipal conflict which fosters his separation from her and promotes his sense of separateness from others (Chodorow, 1978, pp. 107–10). "As long as women mother, we can expect that a girl's preoedipal period will be longer than that of a boy and that women, more than men, will be...open to and preoccupied with those very relational issues that go into mothering—feelings of primary identification, lack of separateness or differentiation, ego and body-ego boundary issues and love not under the sway of the reality principle" (p. 110). Chodorow deduces that girls grow up with a strong need to affiliate with others; they have "a basis for 'empathy' built into their primary definition of self in a way that boys do not. Girls emerge with a stronger basis for experiencing another's needs or feelings as one's own" (p. 167). Thus, the nurturing imperative becomes embedded in the female psyche—and not in the male—as a fundamental need to relate to others and to care for them.

Chodorow has contributed to our understanding of the socialization of gender by emphasizing that gender does not merely reflect the prevailing social definitions but is developed through social interaction. However, although she identifies a characteristic of female identity that many women recognize, I find Chodorow's explanation for its development problematic both theoretically and empirically.[1] By drawing from Horney's life and work as well as from the writings of later psychologists of women, I will attempt to construct an alternative explanation, positing that the development of a woman's need to nurture others is a consequence of the historical changes (identified in chapter 1) which created male entitlement to nurturing.

1. For an elaboration of this critique see Westkott, 1978.

Male Entitlement

A gap in Chodorow's analysis is the explanatory significance of the cultural expectation that women should nurture men, not just children. While she refers to male desire for female nurturing in terms of an ambivalent longing for a pre-oedipal oneness with the mother, she identifies this need merely as a psychological consequence of the structure of parenting rather than as a culturally embedded entitlement that defines the heterosexual bond as well as parenting (see Lorber et al., 1981). In contrast, Jean Baker Miller has identified the cultural expectation for women unilaterally to care for men as one which devalues both women and the socially necessary practice of caring for others (J. Miller, 1976, pp. 21–24). Because women are expected to nurture men, and not vice versa, women's psyches have become organized around the principle that they exist to serve others'—especially men's—needs. Miller concludes that as a result women cannot permit themselves to feel that their actions are for themselves, and thus they translate their own intentions into doing for others (pp. 61–63). From this perspective, the female nurturing disposition derives not so much from the structure of parenting as from the culturally sanctioned view that men are entitled to nurturing by women. The issue shifts from one that assumes men's psychological incapacity to nurture (because they are reared by women) to the expectation that men deserve women's care and attention. It also shifts from the psychological need of the mother to the nurturing responsibilities of the wife. Mothers turn to other women and to their own children to fulfill their emotional needs, not simply because men are not there for them, as Chodorow argues, but because men *are* there—too much so—demanding to be cared for.

Chodorow's explanation, grounded in men's absence from modern family life, misses the impact of men's *presence*. This presence, as a demand to be taken care of, sets the stage for family psycho dynamics and social relations. As both Juliet Mitchell (1974) and

Adrienne Rich (1976) note, male-defined purposes pervade family life even in men's absence. "My father's wishes, but my mother carried them out" (Rich, 1976, p. 224). Paula Caplan (1981) notes that the demand that the woman nurture her husband as well as her children can lead to her dependence on her daughter to help her with her nurturing responsibilities—the daughter is taught both to curtail her own nurturing needs (p. 28) and to take care of the male family members herself (pp. 76–78).

Men's expectation that daughters and sisters owe them emotional and physical caretaking may be expressed sexually (p. 78). Studies of incest have supported this argument by finding that many incestuous fathers are searching for unconditional love and unquestioning validation (for example, Meiselman, 1978). Judith Herman (1981) suggests that this is also true of seductive fathers (pp. 109–25). In both cases, the men exert power and control within their marriage, rigidly requiring obedience from wives and children. At the same time, they turn to their daughters for admiration and sexualized affirmation. This tendency is exacerbated if their wives, for whatever reasons, are unable to provide all the nurturing the husbands require (which may, indeed, be endless). "The father, like the children, is presumed to be entitled to the mother's love, nurturance, and care. In fact, his dependent needs actually supersede those of the children, for if the mother fails to provide the accustomed attentions, it is taken for granted that some other female must be found to take her place" (p. 46).

But turning to a daughter for love, sexual excitement or gratification, submissive caretaking, and validation is a reversal of the parent-child roles that reflects the cultural ideology of male entitlement to female nurturing. The daughter is idolized as the all-giving source of love and care. The fact that she is powerless to refuse secures the father unlimited access to her nurturance. "The reality, that she is the child and he the adult, becomes quite immaterial to him . . . he seeks repeated reassurance that she will never refuse or frustrate him" (Herman, 1981, p. 87). Dominating a daughter through sexual aggression not only realizes a father's longing for unconditional nurturing but also allows him to express his "unlimited" sexual power.

Hence, in the sexualized daughter the conflicting male entitlements for sexual satisfaction and maternal caretaking are resolved (see chapter 1; cf. Swan, 1985). Domination through sexualization is unfettered by opposition. A father's sexual pleasure does not have to consider the needs of the other. Indeed, the very violation of the needs of the child contributes to the sexual pleasure (Herman, 1981, p. 87). At the same time, the daughter is in her very powerlessness accessible to him; in her dependence upon him, she cannot refuse him; and in her naive but defensive "love" of him, she gives him the unconditional love and validation he craves. He is both the uncontested and dominant sexual predator and the eternally beloved and cared-for son. Like the good-hearted whore that many sexually victimized daughters fantasize themselves to be (and some become) (pp. 4, 30, 98–99), the sexualized daughter is the realization of competing male demands. In submitting to and nurturing her father, she resolves the conflict between his needs for sexual power and nurturance. With his daughter, a seductively domineering father can find the pleasures that others seek from prostitutes: "You experience the masculine dream, as seductive as it is absurd, of being coddled by women like a baby and at the same time commanding them like a pascha" (A. Miller, 1981, p. 89).

The nurturing reversal is not limited to incest or explicit seductive treatment. Horney's contemporary, Virginia Woolf, recorded in both memoir and fiction her own experience of her father's demands for care and validation. When her mother, the embodiment of the nurturing imperative, died unexpectedly when Virginia was a girl, she, her older sister Vanessa and her stepsister Stella took on the responsibilities of the household. This included caring for their brothers and father, Leslie Stephen, assuaging his grief, and grimly bearing his never-ending demands (Woolf, 1976).

During these unhappy times, when the daughters themselves needed solace for the loss of their mother, they were required to put aside their own grief to nurture their father. The father's feeling of being personally wronged by his wife's death and by Stella's death soon after that pervaded the household as a cloying presence that demanded pity from the young women. In her description of a regular ritual of going over the weekly household accounts with her father, Virginia Woolf wrote:

> The books were presented. Silence. He was putting on his glasses. He had read the figures. Down came his fist on the account book. There was a roar. His vein filled. His face flushed. Then he shouted, "I am ruined." Then he beat his breast. He went through an extraordinary dramatization of self-pity, anger and despair. He was ruined—dying ... tortured by the wanton extravagance of Vanessa and Sophie. "And you stand there like a block of stone. Don't you pity me? Haven't you a word to say to me?" and so on. Vanessa stood by his side absolutely dumb. He flung at her all of the phrases—about shooting Niagara and so on—that came handy. She remained static. Another attitude was adopted. With a deep groan he picked up his pen and with ostentatiously trembling fingers he wrote out the cheque. This was wearily tossed to Vanessa. Slowly and with many groans of the pen, the account books were put away. Then he sank into his chair and sat with his head on his breast. And then at last, after glancing at a book, he would look up and say plaintively, "And what are you doing this afternoon, Ginny?"
>
> Never have I felt such rage and such frustration. For not a word of my feeling could be expressed.   (Woolf, 1976, pp. 124–25)

Woolf brilliantly portrayed the demanding, self-pitying Leslie Stephen in the character of Mr. Ramsay in her novel *To the Lighthouse*. She expressed also her own feeling of vulnerability to and anger against her father's presumption of entitlement to nur-

turance in the character of Lily, a friend of the Ramsay family who
was treated like an older daughter. In this scene, the family have
returned to their summer home after Mrs. Ramsay's death. Lily is
concentrating on a painting, trying to complete it, while Mr. Ramsay's presence—though in the background—is dominating.

> She sat her clean canvas firmly upon the easel as a barrier, frail,
> but she hoped sufficiently substantial to ward off Mr. Ramsay
> and his exactingness. She did her best to look, when his back
> was turned, at her picture; that line there, that mass there. But it
> was out of the question. Let him be fifty feet away, let him not
> even speak to you, let him not even see you, he permeated, he
> prevailed, he imposed himself. He changed everything. She
> could not see the colour; could not see the lines; even with his
> back turned to her, she could only think, But he'll be down on
> me in a moment, demanding—something she felt she could not
> give him. She rejected one brush; she chose another. . . . She
> fidgeted. . . . That man took. She, on the other hand, would be
> forced to give. Mrs. Ramsay had given. Giving, giving, giving,
> she had died—and had left all this. Really, she was angry with
> Mrs. Ramsay. With the brush slightly trembling in her fingers
> she looked at the hedge, the step, the wall. It was all Mrs. Ram-
> say's doing. She was dead.   (Woolf, 1955/1927, p. 223)

Lily was angry that she had to be available to attend to the
demands of the self-absorbed Mr. Ramsay. But she also felt responsible to those demands and chided herself for occasionally resisting them. "His immense self pity, his demand for sympathy
poured and spread itself in pools at her feet, and all she did, miserable sinner that she was, was to draw her skirts a little closer
around her ankles, lest she should get wet. In complete silence she
stood there, grasping her paint brush" (Woolf, 1955/1927, p. 228).

Lily's anger was directed not against the intrusive Ramsay but
against herself for not responding to him as she felt she should
have and for feeling drawn to respond when she would rather

ignore him and finish her painting. She resented Mrs. Ramsay for dying and thus not being available as a buffer against his expectations. But even the mother's presence does not eliminate the pressure upon a daughter that a father who feels entitled to her nurturing can exert. Virginia Woolf felt it deeply as a child. So did her contemporary Alice Foley, who recorded the following memory of her father in her diary:

> Taking me on his knee, and enveloping me in rough arms and beery breath, he had a habit of posing painful propositions. "Now," he said, "suppose we three, you and I and your mother, were together in a small boat on a lake; it suddenly capsizes and you can save one of us; which shall it be?" Deep in my infant consciousness I knew that if ever such a trial arose, the rescued parent would be mother. But I pitied father, for I sensed a secret yearning, so I hugged him closely, crying, "Both, both, I would save both." Yet, he was never satisfied and continued to press and pester, and on going to bed the conflict turned into nightmarish struggle in the water by an upturned boat. Vainly I would try to reach mother, but was forever frustrated by father's frantic arms closing round me. I would awaken in a sweat of anguish desperately relieved to find myself safe in bed, but always dumbly aware of a tragic dilemma that lay beyond my youthful comprehension of solution.   (Foley, 1982, p. 105)

Daughters saving their parents—whether from hypothetical swirling waters or from the day-to-day whirlpool of parental needs—forms the developmental bedrock of the female nurturing imperative. Essential to its meaning is the presumption of male entitlement to female nurturance. It is this entitlement that led Leslie Stephen upon his wife's death to expect the weight of his needs for care to be carried by his grieving daughters. Karen Horney's father also apparently expected, and her mother struggled to provide, unconditional validation. But while attempting to meet the needs of her husband, her own needs went unmet. In her

own unhappiness and in her middle-class sense of propriety—
that personal problems were a private affair—Karen's mother
neglected her daughter's needs and expected her nurturance and
admiration. Horney's relationship with her mother suggests that
the development of a need to care for others is not a structural
issue of mothers identifying with their daughters who then
develop "permeable" ego boundaries (Chodorow, 1978, p. 169) but
the result of parent-child relations premised on the cultural belief
that all females should be nurturant.

Mother and Daughter

What stands out in Horney's description of her relationship to her
mother is her feeling of responsibility for her. She identified with
Sonni's unhappiness in her marriage and expressed a protective,
nurturing attitude toward "poor little mutti" (Horney, 1980, p. 42).
She felt responsible for her mother, yet powerless to help her; the
resulting frustration caused her to reproach herself for her own
moments of happiness. "For things are bad at home, and mutti, my
all, is so ill and unhappy. Oh, how I would love to help her and
cheer her up. If only she had, as I do, some sort of school or other
means of distraction" (p. 45). Later, young Karen protected herself
against such self-reproach. Like Clare in Self-Analysis, Horney
developed a "compulsion to give first importance to her mother's
needs in order to avoid becoming the object of even a vague resentment" (Horney, 1942, p. 200). Her diaries record a self-protective
shrinking and denial of her own emotional needs as those of her
unhappy mother consumed her attention. Although she found a
redeeming outlet in school work, she nevertheless left her mother
in the morning "with tears in my eyes" (Horney, 1980, p. 45).

On one level, Horney's admiring concern for her mother, her
"all," can be understood as a reaction formation to her feelings of
rejection by Sonni. The mother's preference for Karen's older
brother, her absorption in her unhappy marriage, her restriction

and rigid control of Karen and her friendships all suggest a relationship in which Karen felt devalued, unloved for who she was. She spoke of her mother in her diary as her "beloved" (Horney, 1980, p. 17), yet wrote that she herself is unloved (p. 30) and, later, in a letter to her future husband, that she felt herself to be unlovable (p. 216). When Horney was twenty-one she stated that her mother "is a person one *has* to love" (pp. 180–81).

But more is going on here than a reversal of the child's hostility. As Horney later realized, Sonni was struggling with a conflict between dependency and hostility (Horney, 1980, p. 260). Her marriage made her miserable, yet she clung to it with all the symptoms that Horney later associated with morbid dependency. Sonni's repressed hostility was somatized in illness, evident in her depression, and expressed in her complaints. But it was also apparently released through her narcissistic and domineering claims upon her daughter. Her demands for blind admiration and obedience expressed her own expansive drives for perfection. She required her daughter's complicity in validating her idealized self-image as the perfect mother. The more miserable she was in her marriage and the more she despised her real self, the more Sonni demanded that her daughter believe this lie. After she had started psychoanalytic therapy and began to understand her mother's conflicts, Horney realized their influence on her. At age twenty-five, Horney wrote of her mother, "She has to be first everywhere, uses every available means to put herself in the foreground, make herself interesting: hence her craze for giving presents, her grand bearing, her desire to command in the house; hence her having managed to make me, even up to my eighteenth or nineteenth year, look upon her as perfection itself" (p. 251).

Sonni's demands to be seen as perfect were imposed on those around her. In a letter of 1906 to her future husband, Karen wrote, "Sonni operates with the word 'healthy' a great deal. That is all well and good, but it involves a disregard of everything that goes beyond a certain borderline. . . . Generally speaking: she is not free from the mistake, frequent enough, to be sure, of setting up a norm meant for everybody" (Horney, 1980, p. 180). The perfectionist norm was especially imposed upon her daughter, whose behavior was expected to mirror the mother's ideal image of a woman of her class (p. 100). Like the patient Clare's mother, Sonni demanded her daughter's perfection at the same time she criticized her slightest flaws (Horney, 1942, pp. 49–50). Evidently Horney took the perfectionist standard and the charges of failure as evidence of her inferiority; as a girl and young woman she thought of herself as clumsy, ugly, and unlovable (Horney, 1980, pp. 21, 103, 216, 251).

This kind of projection is consistent with Chodorow's argument for the endurance of mother-daughter identification (Chodorow, 1978, p. 177). Sonni's criticisms of Karen are also consistent with Chodorow's analysis of the ambivalence of that identification in adolescence (pp. 130–40). But Sonni's projection was not the source of Karen Horney's need to nurture others. That need developed as the consequence of her mother's need for nurturance, not from her mother's identification with her. In identification the daughter was projected as the mother's conflicting idealized and despised selves, to use the terminology that Horney later created. But the mother also looked to her daughter for nurturing, and it was in this aspect of their relationship that the daughter's own need to nurture developed.

Horney defended her mother against her father's criticisms, took on her judgments of other people, commiserated with her unhappy plight, listened to her complaints, and looked for ways to make her happy (Horney, 1980, pp. 13–14). In nurturing her mother Horney denied her own need for mothering and repressed her real self. Her nurturing, however intense and emotionally involved, was nevertheless powerless to make any real changes in her mother's life. Sonni's misery was rooted in her own powerlessness in her marriage, in her dependence on a husband whom she did not love, and in her lack of the self-esteem that would have enabled her to confront these issues. Her myriad complaints, which Karen took to heart, were in effect "help-rejecting" (Frank et al., 1952): the daughter was used as a sounding board for problems that the mother would not solve. The daughter absorbed these problems, made them her own, and took the one action that she had the power to take: she held her own needs and happiness in check. If she could not actually solve her mother's problems, at least she could protect herself from being accused of exacerbating them. By denying her own needs, by minimizing her own expansive wishes, by deadening her longings, Horney made her mother's emotional life the center of her own and protected herself out of fear of resentment.

Like the poet Louise Bogan, writing about her own mother, Horney's "earliest instinct was to protect—to take care of, to endure" (Bogan, 1978, p. 62). In protecting her mother, Horney developed a precocious strength, but a strength that seemed valid to her only when used for someone else. In caring for her mother, she denied her own compelling emotional needs and desires. And in enduring, she resigned herself to powerlessness, to pain, to help-rejecting complaints. Thus young Horney became the under-nurtured nurturer, the female altruist.[2]

Female Altruism

Female altruism is the characterological need to care for others. It emerges, I argue, not out of an extended attachment between mother and daughter but out of the parents' need for nurturing. The mother turns to her daughter not because they are of the same gender but because the culturally rooted nurturing imperative presumes that all females are to nurture others. This, I suggest, does not lead to the daughter's extended stay in the so-called pre-

2. Of course, Horney became more. Her absorption in her schoolwork and her ambition provided a release as well as an opportunity to triumph—in a field in which she translated her nurturing tendencies into helping others.

oedipal nest, but to the mother's devaluation of the daughter's needs, expressed in her imposing her own needs to be nurtured. In this respect a mother's identification with her daughter as a female is important only to the extent that she has internalized the cultural assumption that daughters are of less value than sons, that their needs are less important, and that they exist to serve the needs of others, including those of the mother.

In the context of these assumptions, the daughter's own need for nurturing is viewed as a troublesome annoyance. Caplan (1981) argues that mothers who are themselves overburdened with family nurturing responsibilities and have been undernurtured as daughters will regard their own daughters' needs as least important and most troublesome. They will convey to their daughters the necessity to hold their needs in check as a way of helping their mothers and gaining love (p. 77). Citing evidence from Belotti (1975), Caplan implies that it is daughters, not sons, who are shoved from the pre-oedipal nest: mothers wean daughters earlier, are less tolerant of fussiness in their eating, begin their toilet training earlier, and require of them greater self-control and cleanliness (Caplan, 1981, p. 28). Girls are required to grow up more quickly and to make fewer demands on others for care.

Learning to hold back the need to be taken care of is not simply a way of avoiding resentment and gaining a semblance of love; it is also a means of protecting the mother's weakness (Caplan, 1981, p. 18). Like Karen Horney's protection of her "poor little *mutti*," the daughter who shrinks from her own desires makes her mother's needs her own. She becomes the selfless caretaker that her mother has been deprived of and thus desires. "Insofar as the daughter tries to meet those needs, to that extent will her own needs for nurturance go unmet. Thus, the daughter grows up feeling inadequately nurtured. When she becomes a mother, she will have unmet needs and may turn to her own daughter, hoping the daughter will meet them" (p. 17).

But why does a daughter become her mother's nurturer if this means her own needs for nurturing go unmet? The answer to this question lies not, I suggest, in extended mother-daughter identification but in the fear and anger that Horney identifies with the development of the devalued child. Experiencing devaluation of her own needs, the child will fear loss of safety, well-being, and love and will be angry at those who deny her true self. Because in the face of parental power the child's fear wins out over her anger, she will defensively turn her anger against herself and will admire the devaluing adults, endowing them with idealized virtues and behaving as they demand in order to hide her own feeling of worthlessness. Thus admiring obedience procures safety by destroying the subjective basis of judgment (Horney, 1937).

This parental use of children has been the concern of psychoanalyst Alice Miller, whose work extends Horney's in some illuminating ways. Miller does not refer to Horney, although she does cite D. W. Winnicott, whose analysis of child development is built on concepts of the real and idealized selves that resemble Horney's categories.[3] Indeed, Miller's work can be read as an interpretation of Winnicott that illuminates some of Horney's ideas implied by Winnicott's analysis.

In Miller's *Prisoners of Childhood, or The Drama of the Gifted Child* (1981), "gifted" refers to the idea of the child as a gift to the parents. It means becoming what the parents unconsciously need the child to be (which can include being "gifted" in the more conventional sense of the term). But for the child to give herself as a gift to her parents she must deny her true self; she thus identifies

3. See, for example, D. W. Winnicott, "Ego Distortion of True and False Self" and "The Theory of Parent-Infant Relationship," in *The Maturational Processes and the Facilitating Environment* (1965). Winnicott analyzes many of the dynamics Horney identified between the real and idealized selves, although his explanation for the development of the false self abstracts the mother-child relationship from the cultural contexts that inform Horney's theory. For Winnicott the cause of the split lies in the "not-good-enough mother," the mother who does not meet the infant's inherent need for "omnipotence." See "Ego Distortion," p. 145.

with the idealized self, the gift, the fulfillment of the parents' needs (A. Miller, 1981, p. 8; cf. Horney, 1937, p. 181). As a result, the child grows up feeling that her true self is unlovable and that only by becoming what they expect her to be can she feel needed, safe, accepted. "Later, these children not only become mothers (confidantes, comforters, advisors, supporters) of their own mothers, but also take over the responsibility for their siblings and eventually develop a special sensitivity to unconscious signals manifesting the needs of others" (A. Miller, 1981, pp. 8–9). Their altruism is rooted in dependency—they feel loved only if they are needed; they have a self only as a reflection of and response to someone else's needs.

Like Horney, Miller identifies the inability to feel certain emotions, especially "negative" emotions of jealousy, anger, and hostility, as a consequence of early adaptation to parental neediness (A. Miller, 981, p. 9) and also as a result of the parents' inability to accept the child's negative feelings as legitimate. This is implied when Horney speaks of the child's shift from realistic criticism to false admiration (Horney, 1942, pp. 50–51). While both Horney and Miller maintain that this reversal, which creates the idealized self, is an attempt to gain safety, they also imply that the strategem protects the parents from the child's anger (Horney, 1937, pp. 247–48; A. Miller, 1981, p. 16). If, indeed, the parents cannot cope with the child's anger (for treating the child unfairly, abusively, and so on), then in turning her hostility into admiration the child is not only protecting herself from reprisals and punishment but also protecting her parents. The repression of anger therefore results in self-contempt and in the conviction that one's anger is powerfully destructive, especially to those whose love is desired. It might also result in the unconscious suspicion that those powerful others on whom one is dependent are weak and that their rules and entitlements are so rigidly guarded and upheld to protect them from the annihilating anger of the child. The child would then fear her own anger not simply because it might jeopardize the love of the powerful adults but also because it might destroy them (A. Miller, 1981, p. 18). Thus, the child's nurturing of the parent protects the parent from the child's true feelings and her independent judgment. She becomes what her parents—and, later, others—wish her to be both to protect herself from the loss of their compensatory "love" and to protect them from her murderous rage.

Miller, like Horney does not systematically analyze this process in terms of gender differences. Yet her work leaves open the possibility of interpreting this "gifting" adaptation in gender terms. In *For Your Own Good* (1983), Miller emphasizes that the problem for the child lies less in the original devaluation or abuse than in the parental demand that the child's retaliatory anger be repressed. "The greatest cruelty that can be inflicted on children is to refuse to let them express their anger and suffering except at the risk of losing their parents' love and affection" (p. 106). Parental control is not only a defense against the expression of a child's anger but also a release of hostility and contempt. The original devaluation is confounded with the demand for loving obedience, a sadistic insistence upon the child's sweet acquiescence to suffering. Miller noted that parents who most clearly display this behavior had a certain ideal in mind for their children: "they wanted their children to be good, responsive, well-behaved, agreeable, undemanding, considerate, unselfish, self-controlled, grateful, neither willful nor headstrong nor defiant, and above all meek" (p. 65). In short, feminine.

Although Miller does not identify these qualities as stereotypically feminine, they clearly suggest this pattern. Moreoever, disallowing anger as unladylike, which others have identified in female socialization (for example, Fox, 1977; Lott, 1981, p. 49), constitutes in Miller's terms "the greatest cruelty" to the child. The result is self-contemptuous altruism. The idea that boys are entitled to express expansive, angry, or "negative" feelings while girls are denied this expression thus appears to have far more devastating consequences than are readily apparent. This is not to say that boys are not abused, treated unfairly, or narcissistically used by parents or that parents who treat their sons in this way allow a boy's hostile criticism. The point is rather that the normal definition of femininity as sweetly well-behaved and the normal patterns of female family socialization that devalues female needs make this a pattern predominant for girls and women.

This pattern is manifested in the role reversal between mother and daughter, in which the undernurtured mother looks to her own daughter for reinforcement, care, and validation; and in the father-daughter role reversal, in which expectations for emotional validation and sexualizing aggression—expressed in the extreme in incest—secures unconditional access to the powerless but giving daughther. Hence, the practice in which girls are "protected" by being kept close to home, "out of harm's way," and controlled by parental supervision (Fox, 1977; Hoffman, 1977) should not be confused with parental nurturing. From this perspective, keeping daughters close to home is the obverse of parental nurturing; it is the means by which daughters' lives are limited in order to meet the parents' needs (Caplan, 1981, p. 29).

Beyond these injuries and even more devastating is the demand that they be denied through sweet compliance (A. Miller, 1983, p. 106; Horney, 1937, pp. 84–85). Even if the experience of devaluation and sexualization is relatively mild, the demand for "good girl" behavior (acquiescent, sweet, courteous, thoughtful, kind, cheerful, obedient) closes off realistic criticism and the self-defending expression of hostility for injuries received. It is this feminine behavior, demanded overtly and subtly, that forms the foundation of the idealized self and sustains the conviction of utter worthlessness. All this goodness serves only to sustain the rage at being undernurtured, a rage that is also feared.

Female altruism, from this perspective, is a contradiction in which the undernurtured nurterer gives what she does not have in order to be "loved" by those who have disregard or even contempt for her true self and needs. It is a precocious and in some ways spurious strength that denies the self and attributes greatest importance to the needs of others. Consequently, the woman or girl needs to "affiliate" with others in order to validate that she is who she should be, her idealized nurturant self.

Ironically, this female dependency is the developmental consequence of the historically created adult male dependence on women's physical and emotional caretaking (described in chapter 1). The nurturing imperative reflects men's needs and sets the stage for the unfolding of family relations. The demand for female care, backed by a family hierarchy that assumes male superiority, sets the social foundation of women's powerless responsibility. Daughters—those with least power and lowest status—are burdened with the caretaking that others require. This nurturing reversal— the epitome of female devaluation—assumes that girls are least important and that their own needs are inconsequential.

The devaluation is all the more insidious when it is conveyed through normal patterns of socialization. Indeed, there is usually no malicious intent on the part of parents whose behavior denies a daughter's real self. Their behavior merely reflects the unconscious acceptance of female inferiority that Horney claimed permeated masculine civilization. Thus, whether it is motivated by malice or good intentions, "conveyed brutally or delicately," cultural devaluation of women seeps into all relations. It is the reality that infests the most proper as well as the most explicitly abusive relationships. The inevitable consequence is that "a girl is exposed from birth onward to the suggestion . . . of her inferiority" (Horney, 1926, p. 69).

Responsibility for Others

The idea of female altruism explains Carol Gilligan's findings on the differences in male and female morality (Gilligan, 1982). According to Gilligan, male definitions of morality refer to the application of abstract principles that protect the rights of individuals (pp. 21, 104). Women, on the other hand, associate moral behavior with obligation, sacrifice, and inhibitions against hurting others. They are reluctant to make moral judgments about other people and perceive a conflict between power and care (pp. 64–66). They see their own moral imperative in terms of responsibility: "the need for response . . . arises from the recognition that others are counting on you and that you are in a position to help" (p. 54). In short, they define their moral responsibility in terms of caring for others. This is the "different voice" of women that Gilligan hears. But the underlying message in that voice is essential to its meaning. That message is the degree to which caring for others is entwined with issues of power. Gilligan implies this when she notes that some women fear they will lose their compassion for others if they empower themselves (p. 97). She also observes that women see their obligations to others in terms of their dependence upon them. "The moral ideal is not cooperation or interdependence but rather the fulfillment of an obligation, the repayment of a debt, by giving to others without taking anything for oneself" (p. 139). Hence, this female voice of moral responsibility is an expression of a contradiction of powerless responsibility, a duty to care for others out of subordination to them.

Gilligan's concern is not with explaining the developmental origins of this powerlessness that suffuses the female morality of care. In this respect, one of her references to Freud is illuminating, although she herself does not extend his observation. In his first essay on female sexuality, Freud remarked "that for women the level of what is ethically normal is different from what it is in men. Their superego is never so inexorable, so impersonal, so independent of its emotional origins as we require it to be in men" (Freud, 1925b, p. 257; Gilligan, 1982, p. 7). The implication is that the moral judgment of girls and women is linked much more closely to their relationship with their parents, while the authority behind male moral judgment is derived from abstract rules and values. Unlike men, women personalize authority through their continuing internal identification or morality with their parents. Obedience and duty are confounded with love and attachment. This personalization of authority explains Gilligan's observation that women tend to make a moral judgment not because it follows some abstract hierarchy of "rightness" or implements a universal truth but because of its consequences for others to whom one is responsible (Gilligan, 1982, p. 21).

It is not necessary to turn to Freudian theory to explain Freud's observation. When combined with Gilligan's findings on the fundamental importance of care to women, the idea of a parentally rooted, personalized morality ties in with the idea of female responsibility to others. That responsibility involves not only a sense of connectedness to others but also subordination to them. It is not simply caring for others but giving to them as an act of deference, of selfless renunciation. It is understandable, therefore, to find women in Gilligan's study articulating their struggle "between personal integrity and loyalty in family relationships" (Gilligan, 1982, p. 138). In example after example, the conflict is between a young woman's seeking to act for herself and the obligations of the dutiful daughter. In adult women this conflict is expressed in terms of not wanting to act selfishly, not wanting to hurt others, being afraid of making any moral judgment, feeling that others are counting on one (pp. 64–66, 97–100, 138–39). In short, the different voice of female morality is the voice of female altruism.

But female altruism is hardly the ideal that Gilligan implies this different morality to be. As I have attempted to demonstrate, female altruism is rooted in premature renunciation of needs, deprivation, reversal of nurturing roles, conversion of anger into compliance and of self-assertion into caring for others. Female altruism is loaded with unresolved issues of basic anxiety and hostility: fear of the power of others, of abandonment, of one's own hostility and that of others. In this respect, caring for others as an expression of selflessness is a peace offering to devaluing authority. It is self-protection through self-denial. If one is ultimately responsible for the happiness of everyone else, then everyone else is assumed to be superior to and thus threatening to oneself. Thus one's moral responsibility is to respond to a needy world: balancing everyone's needs in the complex web of obligations in which one finds oneself. Don't make anyone angry. Try not to rob Peter to pay Paul, but convince Peter of Paul's needs in a way that does not make him feel angry or deprived. The female altruist is not only the selfless caretaker of others but also the great mediator of this vast web of competing needs. Thus the moral paralysis that keeps her from taking a stand which would favor one person over another. This is the underside of her affiliation.

Despite her tendency to idealize this female caretaking, Gilligan is aware of the quivering in the different voice and of the need to get beyond the condition in which morality is tied to "dependence on others and equated with responsibility to care for them" (Gilligan, 1982, p. 139). The ability to go beyond the conundrum of dependent responsibility will come, according to Gilligan, when a woman is capable of fearless assertion. "When assertion no longer seems dangerous, the concept of relationship changes from a bond of continuing dependence to a dynamic of interdependence. Then the notion of care expands from the paralyzing injunction not to hurt others to an injunction to act responsively toward self and others and thus to sustain connection" (p. 149). Gilligan has identified an important point, but she leaves unexplained why assertion "seems dangerous" to women in the first place. The explanation, I argue, lies in female altruism, in which caring for others and being subordinated to them are entwined. If assertion no longer seems dangerous, then the very basis of dependency—the conversion of anger into admiring compliance as a means of warding off fear—must be undone. This is not accomplished by stiffening the upper lip and forcing oneself into idealized independence, as some would have it (for example,

Dowling, 1981; Gilbert and Webster, 1982). Nor is it done by the vague transformation of dependence into "interdependence" that Gilligan offers. Rather, one must work through the dependency itself, as well as the underlying rage.

6 | Dependency

Dependency is, on the one hand, a characterological solution to childhood sexualization. It involves submission as confirmation of a degraded sense of self, the need to merge with a powerful other, and attraction to intimate relationships as salvation. Dependency is also, as we have seen, the consequence of childhood experiences of devaluation. It is the response of the female altruist who needs the appreciation of others to assure herself that she is not the contemptible and selfish person she fears she is. Together the experiences of sexualization and devaluation foster the development of a dependent character structure that is dominated by the idealized self.

The Idealized Self

Dependency is based on an underlying feeling of worthlessness, which is experienced as hatred of one's body, suppression of genuine feeling, and contempt for the unique qualities that form one's real self. The feelings of worthlessness refer to a total lack of acceptance of who one actually is physically, emotionally, and spiritually. This hatred of the actual self leads to cultivation of the imaginary idealized, or "proud" self that the dependent individual believes she should be (Horney, 1950a, pp. 17–39). Hatred of the actual self expresses contempt for one's unique, real characteristics; the substitute proud self is the idealization of stereotypical and abstract ones.

The idealized self is the key to the internalization of culturally prescribed femininity. Horney interpreted the idealized self as a reaction formation to experiences of sexualization and devaluation. Turning her anger back on herself and identifying with and idealizing those who sexualize and devalue her, the dependent type confirms the worthlessness that her childhood experiences imparted and idealizes the characteristics demanded by her oppressor. But these idealized characteristics of seductive and nurturant femininity are not simply the consequences of a psychological reaction; they are also culturally prescribed expectations for female behavior. The psychological reaction is compulsive adoption of the very behavior that the powerful devaluers expect; what they expect reflects masculine civilization's definition of the feminine. Horney implied this connection in her various references to cultural expectations for female behavior (see Horney, 1939b, pp. 114–15) but she did not explicitly link the cultural expectations with the psychological reaction. The female idealized self is an inner critic that demands ideal appearance, perfect understanding, and selfless caretaking. These behaviors, as we saw in chapter 1, are the historically created, culturally defined expectations for girls and women. The psychological reaction formation transforms the cultural ideals into internal "shoulds." Through this mechanism, compulsory femininity becomes compulsively pursued.

Although Horney did not make explicit the process by which the cultural becomes the psychological, her explanation of the development of the idealized self implies it. Her idea of the defensive reaction that gives rise to the idealized self parallels Freud's idea of the development of the superego in the Oedipus complex (although the idealized self as internalized social control and grandiose self-image more closely approximates a combination of Freud's superego and ego ideal; see Horney, 1945, p. 99). However, because Horney did not posit a sequence in the unfolding of human development (for example, oral, anal, genital stages), she defined no normative period in childhood in which the reaction formation occurs. Indeed, according to her, the reaction that forms the idealized self would not occur if healthy conditions exist; when the defensive reaction does occur, it constitutes an arrest in the developmental process that creates psychic alienation, not a maturing differentiation of the psyche. The idealized self is not an internal regulator of immoral behavior; it is rather an arrogant and coercive intruder that is created as a defense against rage, which is a response to unnecessary conditions of sexualization and devaluation. The shoulds that constitute the idealized self are not genuine moral ideals required for maintaining civilized life, but externalized abstractions and "the neurotic counterfeit of normal moral strivings" (Horney, 1950a, p. 73).

In contrast to the grandiose abstractions of the idealized self, authentic moral behavior is the domain of the real self and its capacity for choice and responsibility. Horney derived her concept of the real self from William James's notion of the spiritual self (Horney, 1939a, p. 130; James, 1981/1890, vol. 1, pp. 279–302). For James, however, the spiritual self—as inner subjective being—is one of several normal constituents of the self. In addition to the spiritual self, he identified the social self, which refers to one's consciousness of the regard of others (pp. 281–82). The idealized social self, which James termed the "potential social self," refers to what the self should be according to cultural values. "This self is the true, the intimate, the ultimate, the permanent Me which I seek" (p. 301). Although James contended that one's spiritual self, as the central active core, takes precedence over concern for social regard, he nevertheless affirmed, as Horney did not, the importance of the social self, expecially of its idealization, for moral behavior.

Many of Horney's American contemporaries shared James's belief in the importance of a constituent of the self that embodies social expectations and ideals. Building on James, Charles Horton Cooley (1964/1902) coined the concept of the "looking-glass self" to refer to the idea that the self emerges from social interchange as a reflection of the reactions of others. George Herbert Mead extended James's categories in his concepts of the "I" and the "Me." The "Me" is the social component of the self, referring to the expectations that others have and impart—through roles, manners, habits, rules—for one's behavior. The "I," on the other hand, refers to the freedom to choose; it is the creative capacity that makes one more than the social roles one holds (Mead, 1962/1934, pp. 172–78). Although Mead argued that both the Me and the I are necessary for socially responsible and innovative behavior, he gave precedence to the social component, the Me. Not only are the highest human values realized through participation in the community (that is, through the Me) (p. 310), but the Me is the benign source of social direction of behavior (p. 255).

Horney's colleague Harry Stack Sullivan shared her idea that internalized social control—as the socialized component of the self—arises from negative childhood experiences. He too interpreted the resultant socialized character formation (the *self-system*) as the developing child's attempt to find interpersonal security and avoid anxiety (Sullivan, 1953, pp. 158–71). At times Sullivan gave this social adaptation positive value (for example, Sullivan, 1940, p. 57), but generally he regarded it as an unfortunate but necessary defense. Paralleling Adler (1956) more than Horney, Sullivan argued that the defensive self-system is inevitable because the social context necessary for healthy development "has never been approximated and at the present moment looks as though it never will be" (Sullivan, 1953, p. 169). The self-system is the unfortunate result of conditions to which Sullivan resigned himself. In this he paralleled Freud, who argued that internalized social control is unpleasant but necessary. However, for Freud inner control (by the superego) was necessary to maintain civilization against the inevitable antisocial drives of the individual (Freud, 1930), whereas for Sullivan the socialized component was a necessary personal defense inevitably arising from inadequate parenting.

Horney neither idealized inner social control nor resigned herself to it. For her the social component of the self was not a humanizing beneficence, an unfortunate inevitability, or a civilizing necessity, but an alienating intruder. Rather than providing inner regulation that promotes ethical behavior and controls aggression, the idealized self is the Frankenstein Monster (Horney, 1950a, p. 367) that destroys the capacity for choice, undermines responsibility, and creates rage. Horney's rejection of the theoretical arguments for inner social control is existential. In this respect the moral component of her theory is closer to that of Kierkegaard, Nietzsche, Rank, and Fromm, from whom she drew some of her ideas.[1] Horney's theory and her therapy converge in the ontology of human choice. The creation of the idealized self is a flight into safety that denies choice by adapting to the external world and its prescribed patterns for behavior. The therapeutic journey is the release from dictates of pride and the recovery of the real self as the locus of choice. The real self is foremost a consciousness of oneself as a being capable of choice. This includes the recognition that external prescriptions are neither inevitable determinants nor absolute ideals. It is the awareness that one's future is the consequence of one's freedom to act in the world.

When Horney's existential psychology is linked to her psychology of women, one sees a perspective similar to Simone de Beauvoir's. Like Beauvoir, Horney recognized that the cultural definition of the ideal feminine self is the annihilation of the real self. The feminine type, or the Other, to use Beauvoir's term, is a being distinguished by absence of choice (Beauvoir, 1952, p. xxiv). She is required to attempt constantly and fatalistically to achieve the internalized ideal of femininity. Her existence is not one of life

1. Horney drew upon the existentialist ideas of Kierkegaard, especially *The Sickness Unto Death* (1941). She also referred to Nietzsche's concepts, especially resentment (Nietzsche, 1967), but was critical of his concept of the will to power, calling it a neurotic striving rather than a positive human capacity (Horney, 1937, p. 186). In *New Ways in Psychoanalysis* (1939a) she referred to Rank's *Will Therapy* (1972/1936). References to Fromm's early work, especially *Escape from Freedom* (1941) and "Individual and Social Origins of Neurosis" (1944), appear throughout Horney's books.

creating itself but one of death. The goal is already established; she has only to try to merge with it and judge herself accordingly. She approaches life as a predetermined fate, as the predictable unfolding of her death. In rejecting the choicelessness of femininity, both Horney and Beauvoir affirm the freedom of women to create themselves and their futures. However, unlike Beauvoir, Horney did not locate this human capacity for transcendence in inherited male patterns of domination, violence, and control (Beauvoir, 1952, pp. 72–73, 792–93). Indeed, for Horney, the traditionally male values celebrating risk-taking in violence and history-making in the triumphant success over others represents a "search for glory" that fosters self-pride, undermines self-acceptance, breeds egocentric use of others, and encourages unreflective adulation of authority (Horney, 1937, pp. 284–86; 1950a). The liberation of the feminine type from the compulsion to be loved by men lies not in emulating their historically created pattern of domination but in abjuring all such fictitious values (Horney, 1950a, p. 364).

Horney's position suggests that there is something self-serving in Freud's and her American colleagues' deference to civilizing control. Celebrating or even accepting the laws and customs of civilization is different for one who has the freedom to create them and is valued by them than for one who has and is not. The male theorists' acceptance of the necessity of social control confirms the world in which men—especially particular races and classes of men—are valued. Their celebration of civilized life applauds a community in which their social selves are positively reflected. Horney's refusal to espouse social adaptation implies a criticism of a masculine civilization that denies women freedom. Her insistence that the socialized self is a monster is thus "disloyal to civilization" (Rich, 1979).

As the intruder from masculine civilization, the proud idealized self opposes women's freedom of choice—both as the capacity of the real self and as actual behavior. But trying to mold one's behavior to the imagined ideals of the proud self is "willing the impossible" (Horney, 1952b, p. 7) because the ideals are so grandiose and because, on the level of the real self, one's heart simply isn't in it. Within this alienated structure, actual behavior is doomed to failure.

Shame

Shame, according to Horney, results from the experience of continually failing to make one's behavior, feelings, or thoughts live up to the claims of the proud self. It is essentially unconscious but is felt as a fundamental failure of being (Horney, 1950a, p. 97),[2] as an underlying, constant feeling that one is irremediably defective. Because the shamed person has a deep, unconscious belief that she can never be salvaged, her unconscious solution is to hide this belief with a mask of its opposite, the proud self. But this only adds to the anxiety that requires the mask in the first place, because the idealized self is a constant reminder of her imperfections. "The best way to describe the situation is in terms of two people. There is the unique, ideal person; and there is an omnipresent stranger (the actual self), always interfering, disturbing, embarrassing... wanting to make an indelible impression on somebody.... [Her] hands shake or... [she] stammers or blushes.... The desired sylph-like slenderness is never attained because, compulsively,... [she] eats too much. The actual, empirical self becomes the offensive stranger to whom the idealized self happens to be tied, and the latter turns against this stranger with hate and contempt. The actual self becomes the victim of the proud idealized self" (pp. 111–12).[3]

The proud self is the unconscious substitute for genuine self-

2. Others have analyzed this aspect of shame. For example, see Herbert Morris, 1976, pp. 59–63; Wurmser, 1981; Lynd, 1958; Piers and Singer, 1971; Erikson, 1950; Sartre, 1966, pp. 340–493. Helen Block Lewis links shame to "field dependency" (the extent to which one depends on one's environment for self-perception), which she finds to be greater among women than among men (1971, pp. 130, 137, 144–64).
3. Because I am here interpreting Horney's work specifically as a social psychology of women, I substitute the female pronoun for her male pronouns.

esteem (Horney, 1945, pp. 99–100). It displays all the characteristics that the despised self would like to have but does not. The
more deeply a woman feels that she is worthless and contemptible, the more unrealistically perfectionist is her idealized
self-image, and the more desperately she will cling to it as the only
positive component of her being. Unfortunately, this very idealized image, which she regards as her salvation, is the internal
critic that deepens her self-contempt. The gap between the proud,
idealized self-image and the despised self widens as the need for
perfection creates claims impossible to realize in actual behavior.

Even if the feminine type momentarily achieves perfection—in
just the right gesture, beautiful appearance, or altruistic attitude—
she cannot sustain the pride she feels as an ongoing basis for self-
acceptance. Because her actual behavior and feelings keep intrud-
ing upon her ability to meet the standards of the ideal, they wound
her pride and hurl her back "into the abyss of self-contempt"
(Horney, 1950a, p. 102). She "wavers in ... [her] self-valuation
between feeling great and feeling worthless" (Horney, 1937,
p. 225). This psychic seesawing between shame and pride can be
experienced in dramatic swings from depression to elation. The
individual "wavers ... between self-adoration and self-contempt,
between ... [her] idealized image and ... [her] despised image,
with no solid middle ground to fall back on" (Horney, 1945,
p. 112).

Frequently the pain of this vacillation is dulled through a low-
level depression that Horney called "living in a fog." This inner
haziness walls off "awareness of pride and self-hate, triumph and
defeat, hurts, illusions." The hazy protection against self-
awareness is not uniform or entirely predictable. "The fog ... may
lift at times and at others becomes impenetrable. Then feelings of
unreality may result. All of a sudden some hurts, some loss, some
work of art may penetrate and elicit a response. Some areas may be
relatively free, like a relation to nature or music" (Horney, 1952b,
p. 3). The blurring of one's feelings and thought creates a feeling of
inner emptiness. Frequently these feelings are somatized; a grow-

ing feeling of emptiness can lead, for example, to compulsive eating (Horney, 1945, p. 117). However, as recent works on eating disorders have shown (for example, Sours, 1980; Andersen, 1985), this only exacerbates the problem, since gaining weight violates the idealized feminine self-image, strengthens self-contempt, and thus increases the need to haze over one's feelings, resulting once again in a sense of emptiness.

Living in a fog exacerbates the self-distrust that underlies the experience of shame. As a mask for worthlessness and a substitute for genuine self-esteem, the idealized self represents externally defined ideals of femininity. The internalized cultural standard imposes itself as a "should" while it erodes the independent basis of judgment, the real self. The individual attempting to live up to the shoulds of the idealized self is left without an internal basis for judging her success or failure. She must instead evaluate herself by the responses she receives from others. The more she hazes over her inner life, the more she comes to depend upon the judgmental mirror that other people provide.

This is the characterological core of dependency, the desperate, fearful clinging that Horney identified in her concept of modern femininty. Some of its overt manifestations—coy helplessness, self-subordinating devotion, seductive weakness—convey a dimension of manipulation that belies the motivational source. The need is absolute, desperate, and irrational. Its core is an unconscious sense of oneself as utterly worthless and despicable. Others are needed, not to quell some superficial insecurity, but to confirm constantly that one has a self and that that self is lovable. This fundamental need is manifested in the mechanism of externalized living as well as in the relationships of dependent altruism and morbid dependency.

Externalized Living

The most elementary characteristic of dependency is externalized living, living in the eyes of others, constantly seeking outside affirmation that one is one's idealized self (Horney, 1945, p. 16). This attention to the response of others should not be confused with normal communication. The concern with others' responses is not a mechanism for confirming whether or not one is understood; rather, the concern is with seeing how one is being judged. And because of the overwhelming need to be judged favorably, thus confirming the illusion that one is one's proud self, one's behavior will be directed toward impressing others.

Hence one's awareness of others is both retrospective and anticipatory. The dependent feminine type watches herself being watched (to see how she is judged) and also is alert to all the nuances and standards of judgment. What this group admires, what that person believes in, what these people value, what the standards of appropriate appearance and behavior are: these become objects of intense study because they help to define the subtleties of the ideal image itself. The femine type must not only read the subtleties of responses that tell her how well she measures up but must also be a serious student of the details of the ideal that tells her how to measure up. "Vigilant observation of others becomes a supreme necessity and is cherished as a precious asset" (Horney, 1952b, p. 4).

Because the feminine type must create herself anew for each situation, she becomes aware of the social contextual shifts that require changes in her behavior, appearance, even feelings. She creates a self, including make-believe feelings (Horney, 1950a, p. 83), for each situation. "Chameleonlike, [such women] always play some role in life without knowing that they do it and, like good actors, produce feelings that go with the roles" (p. 165). Horney described this self that depends on external affirmation as phony; Helene Deutsch (1942) termed it the "as if" personality, and, more recently, others have described it as the "female imposter phenomenon" (Clance and Imes, 1978). This is not a trivial or superficially based other-directedness, nor is it a strategy for manipulating others as an end in itself. While the behavior indicates a concern with creating a positive effect upon each audience, its purpose is compensatory. Beneath the mask of superficial adaptability and engaging affection is the open wound of self-contempt.

Dependence upon the favorable response of others underscores the absence of independent judgment or feelings. The internal critic that is constantly offended by one's actual behavior has no judgmental basis within the self. Informed by externally defined standards, it is a critic without a position. Its function is to hide worthlessness and to condemn behavior that reveals imperfections, but the basis of that condemnation shifts according to changes in standards and audience. Regardless of changes in content, the nature of the idealized image gives the experience of shame a static quality. One always is coming up short regardless of the ideal to which one is attempting to conform.

In externalized living "the expectations of others . . . have the same compulsory character as . . . [one's] own 'shoulds'." In giving others power over her self, the dependent type shifts the emphasis "from *being* to *appearing*. What counts . . . is proper behavior, proper functioning, physical looks—in short, . . . the impression . . . [one] makes on others" (Horney, 1952b, p. 4). For the feminine type the concern with creating a good impression through physical appearance is heightened by the cultural emphasis upon women as sexualized objects. Horney noted that, for women, "The question 'Am I attractive?' is inseparable from another one, 'Am I lovable?'" (Horney, 1950a, p. 138). She found that for many women, the answer to the latter is dependent upon the answer to the former. A woman's attractiveness, reflected in the eyes of those who behold her, in effect, indicates her value as a lovable and worthwhile human being. She curries the admiration of others by creating, through cosmetics, clothes, and so on, the appearance that conforms with the cultural ideal.

However, these attempts serve as a painful reminder of her failure, for the cultural standard is an abstraction. "Even though by common acclaim she may be a beauty, she still is not the *absolute* beauty—such as never was and never will be. And so she may focus on her imperfections—a scar, a wrist not slender enough, or hair not naturally wavy—and run herself down on this score, sometimes to the extent of hating to look at a mirror" (Horney, 1950a, 138). Her very dependence upon having her appearance judged by and mirrored in the look of others heightens her shame. The abstract standard that defines her own critical, idealized self-image reminds her of her imperfections. Whether the eyes that judge her reflect admiration or criticism is not always clear; the look does not always reveal the verdict. "Men's stares flatter and hurt her simultaneously; she wants only what she shows to be seen; eyes are always too penetrating" (Beauvoir, 1952, p. 392). Because her sexualized appearance is her only source of feelings of self-worth, her physical imperfections are grounds for self-contempt and proof of her worthlessness. The very gaze that reflects her beauty becomes in the grasp of her critical, idealized self-image the judgmental look in which she is undressed, exposed, and condemned. If in her dependence she needs the reflection of others, in her anxiety "she shuns the enveloping gaze" (p. 425).

Thus, the very social confirmation that the feminine type needs creates the danger that the mask of pride will be pulled back and the despised self exposed. The person who feels shame intrapsychically always feels herself at risk of being humiliated if others see through the idealized façade to the contemptible core. Consequently, she puts even more effort into making her mask impenetrable, controlled, and devoid of spontaneity. But the effort is always undermined by actual behavior, which is never perfect enough and always endangers the self through exposure. When she falls short she is ashamed of her performance, which may be unconsciously expressed in, for example, blushing. But the blushing itself causes further embarrassment. Hence, she fears not only having her imperfections exposed but also having her shame exposed. Her fear of blushing expresses her fear of being humiliated for feeling ashamed (Horney, 1945, pp. 148–50).

In "The New Dress" (1944) Virginia Woolf captured these conflicts between dependency on the approval of others and fear of their criticism, and between proud desire for spectacular success and conviction of one's wretchedness. Mabel attends a party in a new dress with the hope of inspiring admiration from all. This is her fantasy when she first tries on the dress. "Suffused with light, she sprang into existence. Rid of cares and wrinkles, what she had dreamed herself was there—a beautiful woman" (p. 50). But the dress, an inexpensive copy of the romantic styles of an earlier era, too obviously deviates from present fashion, and Mabel is too shy and insecure to pull off her fantasy of the beautiful style setter. As soon as she steps into the party, Mabel's insecurity and self-depreciation overtake her as she thinks, "Oh these men, oh these women, all were thinking—'What's Mabel wearing? What a fright she looks! What a hideous new dress!'—their eyelids flickering as they came up and then their lids shutting rather tight" (p. 47). In her shame she craves some approving glance, some admiring word; when none is forthcoming she attributes the conventional party chatter to intentional hostility. "One word of praise, one word of affection from Charles would have made all the difference to her at the moment. If he had only said, 'Mabel, you're looking charming tonight!' it would have changed her life. . . . Charles said nothing of the kind, of course. He was malice itself. He always saw through one, especially if one were feeling particularly mean, paltry, or feeble-minded" (pp. 51–52). Mabel's shame is heightened by her humiliation, her anxious belief that Charles can see through to her wretched discomfort. Excoriating herself for being so "paltry" and "so utterly dependent on other people's opinions" (p. 51), Mabel flees the party, thanking the hostess for the lovely time and cursing to herself, "Lies, lies, lies!" (p. 57).

Woolf's portrayal of these feelings and needs from the protagonist's point of view exemplifies the painful conflict that Horney identified: the imaginary triumph of the idealized self versus the actual failure, the need for others' approval and the fear of their criticism, the desire for acceptance and the self-sabotaging belief in one's inferiority. Mabel's inner struggle reflects the self-destructive consequences of identifying inner shoulds with the judgments of others in externalized living.

Dependent Altruism

The ways of seeking approval in the eyes of others are not limited to enhancing physical attractiveness. A second component of the feminine type's idealized self is the complex of "lovable" qualities associated with altruism: "unselfishness, goodness, generosity, humility, saintliness, nobility, sympathy" (Horney, 1950a, p. 222). Doing for others, caring for them, making their needs the source of one's motives, complying with their demands are idealized and imposed as shoulds. The altruistic behavior is not an end in itself, however; its purpose is to win the affection, help, and approval of others. Like the concern with physical appearance, the cultivation of cheerful and unselfish goodness toward others is compulsively pursued as a means of warding off anxiety over underlying self-hatred.

This feeling of worthlessness distinguishes dependent altruism from authentic affection for others. Genuine affection has no end other than itself; care is offered freely as an expression of love. The dependent altruist, on the other hand, needs to care for others to bolster her self-esteem; in effect, she seeks out the neediness of others and uses it to accomplish this purpose (Horney, 1937, pp. 109–12). The altruist's purposes are egocentric: she seeks to overcome her own feelings of worthlessness by creating a self— that is, living up to the dictates of the idealized self—in order to gain affirming approval from others.

This approval, of course, is forthcoming largely because

altruism is encouraged by culturally sanctioned expectations for female selflessness (see chapter 5). But the need for others' grateful appreciation—like all externalized living—works as a psychological mechanism to reinforce the cultural pattern. The idealized self sets high expectations for sweet compliance and imposes rigid restriction against self-assertion. The dependent altruist outwardly scorns ambition, acclaim, and privilege. She suppresses any display of presumptiveness, selfishness, or hostility. She must be modest, self-effacing, understanding, and forgiving (Horney, 1950a, pp. 216–19). By minimizing herself she accords others importance, which she believes will bring her admiring gratitude and protection.

The need for social confirmation that one is one's idealized self extends beyond the more obvious nurturant behaviors to an indiscriminate craving for the company and confirmation of others, no matter who they may be (Horney, 1950a, pp. 226–28). Being disliked or criticized by anyone is taken as a sign of worthlessness. Because the dependent person has no independent basis of judgment, she cannot form her own idea of whose opinion is valuable. Everyone is superior to her; therefore she must be liked by everyone, no matter how contradictory this demand might be. Beyond this, the judgment of those with public acclaim or reputation matters most, for their good opinion represents validation by many others. Paradoxically, however, affirming smiles from the mighty invoke competitive hostility. Her dependency upon admiration is suffused with rivalry with all others, because nothing short of absolute superiority will quell the underlying sense of degradation (p. 30). The dependent one seeks validation from the very individuals who invoke her fears of inferiority. This kind of dependency, especially if it occurs in an intimate relationship, may lead to conflict between her need for validation by successful others and her envy of their success.

Dependency is also expressed in an inability to be alone. Interaction with others is the sole confirmation that one has a self. The dependent type can "see herself only in the reflected light of others" (Horney, 1942, p. 240); alone she feels as if she were a shadowy illusion, a figure without substance (Horney, 1945, pp. 116–17). Because of her underlying feeling of worthlessness, she seeks social confirmation of her worth; she "is worth as much as . . . [she] is liked, needed, wanted or loved." Cut off from this social validation, she feels cut off from life. If her self-contempt is especially acute, "feeling lost may grow into a nameless terror, and it is exactly at this point that the need for others becomes frantic." Finally, being alone is felt as rejection, "proof of being unwanted and unliked and . . . therefore a disgrace to be kept secret" (Horney, 1950a, p. 227). Thus, being alone means both the loss of identity and the proof of being despicable.

To ward off the indignity and escape the terrifying loss of self that being alone can invoke, the dependent one may seek out the company of others with a compulsiveness that disregards their needs for privacy. This clinging reveals the egocentric purposes of dependent altruism. The need for others, felt to be so overwhelming, becomes a claim upon them. "The needs for love, affection, understanding, sympathy, or help turn into: 'I am entitled to love, affection, understanding, sympathy'" (Horney, 1950a, p. 229). The claims upon others are most often unconscious, but they nevertheless lend to the dependent type's endearing helpfulness an underlying expectation for reciprocity. If others do not respond to her altruism with sufficient gratitude or reciprocate with adequate affection, she will suffer resentful injury. But no amount of confirmation from others can compensate for the lack of genuine care in childhood or the present feelings of worthlessness. Thus, the dependent altruist is frequently in a state of self-pity, feeling unappreciated, unloved, and exploited. The suffering is real and, indeed, reinforced by her need always to defer to others; but it is also her justification for making claims upon them. Only by exaggerating her suffering can she feel entitled to the affection she craves. (p. 229).

Thus the dependent altruist gives to others the care that she craves but cannot give to herself. The gratitude that she expects in return is both a paltry substitute for satisfaction of her real needs and a recompense to the idealized self, which thrives on social approval and erodes genuine self-acceptance.

Morbid Dependency

If in altruism the dependent type needs others to confirm the goodness that her idealized self demands, in morbid dependency she seeks to abolish those inner demands by submerging herself in another. Horney's interest in the subject of morbid dependency is evident in her analysis of the feminine type (Horney, 1934). In *Self Analysis* (1942) she presented a lengthy discussion of the morbid dependency of the patient Clare, and in *Neurosis and Human Growth* (1950a) she devoted a chapter to the topic. In her earlier books (1937, 1939b) Horney had begun to develop her understanding of the subject in her analysis of masochism.

Horney claimed that morbid dependency is found frequently among contemporary women (Horney, 1939b, p. 190; 1950a, p. 247). The morbidly dependent woman is the feminine type who overvalues love. But it is not love per se that she craves; it is the safety and powerful identity that a loving partner can provide. Because of the intensity of her basic anxiety, the feminine type searches for another person who appears to have the strength and self-sufficiency she lacks. She "is naturally attracted by a person of the same or opposite sex who impresses [her] as stronger or superior" (Horney, 1950a, p. 243). She is drawn to the type of individual who openly flaunts power or superiority as a means of impressing others or who disparages and humiliates others to bolster his or her self-esteem. In other words, the morbidly dependent woman is attracted to domineering partners, because she believes that they will provide the safety that she craves.

Clare, for example, was compulsively attached to Peter (Horney,

1942). The attachment, however, derived less from a genuine appreciation for Peter as a person than from her deeply felt need to be protected by him. Peter, in fact, was not a particularly attractive person. "But he could not help playing the role of one who was always right, always superior, always generous—and he had feet of clay. He was wrapped up in himself, and when he yielded to her wishes it was not because of love and generosity but because of his own weakness. Finally, in his dealing with her there was much subtle cruelty" (p. 217). Clare was unable to see Peter's domineering use of her because she needed him desperately for a feeling of well-being. Any disinterest or active disengagement on his part aroused her fear of being left alone. "If Peter was late, if he did not telephone, if he was preoccupied with other matters than herself, if he was withdrawn, if he was tense or irritated, if he was not sexually interested in her—always the same dread of desertion was touched off" (pp. 208–09).

Clare's desperate clinging to Peter went beyond her need for protection against a hostile world. More subtle was her dependency on him to take control of her life, to accept responsibility for guessing her wishes and magically fulfilling them. "She demanded to be cared for in such a way that she should not have to make up her mind as to what is right or wrong, should not have to take the initiative, should not have to be responsible for herself, should not have to solve external difficulties" (Horney, 1942, p. 215). By placing her fate in Peter's hands, Clare was expressing a wish for a real self, not her own but someone else's that she believed was superior.

Horney had earlier described this desire to merge with another as masochism (1937, 1939b). "The masochistic way of coping with the situation [basic anxiety] is to thrust oneself on the mercy of someone. By submerging his own individuality entirely and by merging with the partner the masochistic person gains a certain reassurance" (1939b, p. 253). The reassurance is not simply protection against outside dangers; it is also a feeling of having a surrogate self and being released from inner conflicts. The most central conflict is generated by anxiety and hostility, between wanting to disappear into the "security of unobtrusiveness" (Horney, 1939b, p. 254) and longing for omnipotence, a conflict between self-contempt and grandiosity. By merging with a domineering other, the dependent type reconciles these desires "to be at once everything and nothing" (Horney, 1937, p. 276). By becoming putty in the master's hands (p. 268), she loses the self in something greater (p. 270). She ceases to be an active agent, yet is still the focus of her partner's power. This temporary oblivion (p. 279) is a flight from universal hostility by means of submission to someone overwhelmingly powerful and potentially destructive.

Later Horney abandoned the term *masochism*, although she elaborated the ideas that she had associated with it. "Since the term and the concept behind it are misleading, it is better to steer away from it and describe instead the elements involved" (Horney, 1945, pp. 214–15). Horney may have found the term misleading in part because of its association with the Freudian definition of women as instinctually masochistic (Freud, 1933a; Deutsch, 1930; Caplan, 1985). Freud's definition preserves assumptions about instinct, women, and suffering that Horney rejected and thus distorts the explanation of the behavior that Horney sought to understand. Horney rejected the term, but maintained her definition of it as the desire to merge with a powerful other. She associated this longing and the behavior it generates with morbid dependency and located their roots in the developmental experiences of the dependent or self-effacing type (Horney, 1950a, pp. 240n, 258).

The morbidly dependent feminine type places herself in the same danger in an intimate relationship that she fears from the world in general. Her dependency upon her partner is experienced as a matter of life and death, and she complies with humiliation so as not to lose the superior other. The compliance reflects not simply clinging but destruction of her independent will as a condition of merger. Because she needs to merge with the other as an ideal object, she panics at the thought of losing him. Such a loss would mean the loss of the self, a kind of death. Thus, "the partner becomes the sole center of her existence. Everything revolves around him. Her mood depends upon whether his attitude toward her is more positive or negative. She does not dare make any plans lest she might miss a call or an evening with him. Her thoughts are centered on understanding or helping him. Her endeavors are directed toward measuring up to what she feels he expects. She has but one fear—that of antagonizing and losing him" (Horney, 1950a, p. 247). She attempts to preserve the relationship at all costs, including accepting blame for all its problems (Horney, 1942, p. 201).

But if the dependent type merges with a partner who is domineering then she is clinging to one who fears her dependence on him and is repulsed by her need for assurance of love. Contemptuous of any weakness in himself, he despises her weakness. He believes that love is impossible and therefore considers her professions of love hypocritical. He believes that her dependence on him is based on a lie and is likely to dissolve. Any assertion of strength on her part thus strengthens his need to break her will. Yet her submission to his brutality repulses him. His abuse arouses the anxiety that causes her to cling to him. Her forgiveness wounds his pride. He "senses her feeling morally superior and feels provoked to tear down the pretenses involved." And so the cycle is perpetuated in a "cat-and-mouse play attracting and repulsing, binding and withdrawing" (Horney, 1950a, pp. 248–49). This cycle of abuse that others have since described (for example, L. Walker, 1979) is indeed morbid, for its consequence can be the dependent woman's emotional and physical destruction.

Clare gradually worked through her morbid dependency on Peter and resolved the eventual loss of that relationship. In the process she realized that by being dependent she avoided having to find her own center of gravity, her real self. "The dependent relationship had so completely fulfilled its function of allowing her to cope with life without having to rely on herself that it had robbed her of any real incentive to abandon the small-girlism ... entailed in her compulsive modesty. In fact, the dependency had not only perpetuated her weakness by stifling her incentive to become more self-reliant but it had actually created an interest in remaining helpless. If she remained humble and self-effacing all happiness, all triumph would be hers. Any attempt at greater self-reliance and greater self-assertion was bound to jeopardize these expectations of heaven on earth. This finding, incidentally, sheds light on the panic she felt at her first steps toward asserting her opinions and wishes. The compulsive modesty had not only given her the sheltering cloak of inconspicuousness, but it had also been the indispensable basis for her expectations of 'love'" (Horney. 1942, pp. 237–38).

Horney recognized that in analyzing the desire for love and the need for affection, she was touching upon longings which many people, including Horney herself, saw as normal aspects of being human (Horney, 1937, pp. 103, 115, 131). By exposing the underside of these needs she was not playing the cynic, for she believed that authentic care for others and mutual love in intimate relationships are possible (Horney, 1945, pp. 241–42). Rather, her analysis of dependent, caring, and self-sacrificing behavior derived from her early concern that in masculine civilization women learn to overvalue "love" as the most important source of their identity and their primary goal in life (Horney, 1934, 1939b).

7 | Anger

Whether she was describing the vindictiveness of the dependent type (Horney, 1934, 1948), the self-destructive masochism of the morbidly dependent partner (Horney, 1950a), or the begrudging envy of the perpetual caretaker (Horney, 1937, p. 182), Horney was perceptively attuned to the ways in which dependency and anger interlock in the character structure of the feminine type. Indeed, the idealized attributes that she associated with dependency—cheerful acquiescence and selfless attention to others—rest upon the volcanic foundation of repressed rage.

In seeking safety by turning her hostility against herself and attempting to live up to an imaginary ideal, the feminine type internalized anger as a child and preserved it as an inner experience in her adult life. Inner anger is maintained in two ways. First, the idealized self continually assaults actual behavior through relentless demands for self-effacement, compliant altruism, and physical beauty. The feminine type who lives under the dictatorship of the idealized self constantly accuses herself of failure to achieve perfection. And, because the proud self is utterly perfectionistic, she also ridicules her efforts to realize that ideal, for example, saying to herself, "How ridiculous! Ugly duckling, trying to look pretty!" (Horney, 1950a, p. 132). Because the idealized self also demands modesty, the feminine type cannot allow herself to feel pride even when she does what she should. Instead, she belittles her accomplishments and shirks praise. "Thus a person, after having taken good care of a sick relative may think or say: 'that's the least I could do!'" (p. 133). Anger toward the self is also expressed in crushing enjoyment, frustrating one's own wishes, and withholding money, time, or physical pleasure (pp. 141–45). This stinginess is grounded in the lesson of female altruism: doing anything for oneself is selfish and contemptible. Repressing desire and gratification is an attempt to protect oneself from inner criticism as well as from the hostile resentment of others. But because one is never perfectly selfless and because one's appearance never matches the ideal, one is constantly angry at oneself—ashamed—for failure.

The dependent character structure preserves anger in yet another way. For this type self-assertion is alway suffused with anger, experienced as a dangerous expression of being (Horney, 1942; 1950a, p. 219). This suggests that the child's original repression of anger, an authentic expression of the real self, results in an unconscious confounding of the real self with anger. Anger, the dangerous emotion that threatened the child's safety, remains the buried and terrifying force of the real self's authentic but repressed being. I suspect that this is why Horney found the real self so vehemently opposed by the idealized self (1950a, p. 112). It is not just that the real self falls short of the abstract ideal, but that it preserves a rage that the ideal of sweet femininity cannot permit. The real self as a repressed possibility represents more than anger, but because anger is the feeling that required the real self to go into hiding in the first place, it predominates as the terrifying secret of one's being. This is why the release of anger is experienced by the dependent type as a momentous and self-threatening expression of her fundamental being, and conversely why shaking off the shoulds of perfectionism touches deep anger in the real self's striving for assertion (Horney, 1942; 1950a, p. 219).

The feminine type's psyche is the scene of a hostile struggle between the real self and the combined forces of the idealized self and self-hatred (Horney termed these the "pride system"). Horney (1950a) called this the "central inner conflict" (p. 112), the battle between what one could be (the real self) and what one should be (the idealized self) and fears she is (self-hatred). The attempt to release the real self (and to change) is attacked by hostile demands of pride and self-defeating feelings of worthlessness. It is no wonder that the person suffering from inner rage feels abused. She *is* abused. While this condition may have originated in response to others, it becomes internalized as a continuing aspect of her character (Horney, 1951).[1]

Anger is not confined to the embattled psyche, however—equally important is the hostility that the feminine type feels toward others. In *The Neurotic Personality of Our Time* (1937), Horney interpreted the anger of the dependent type as a reaction to dependency itself; the feminine type feels hostile toward the very individuals on whom she believes she must rely. Especially in intimate relationships this conflict is expressed both as a wish for the other to take charge of her life and protect her and as resentment of the power that the other exerts over her. In an intriguing foreshadowing of Janice Radway's recent interpretation of contemporary romance novels as female fantasies of cruelly heroic men who magically become kindhearted partners (Radway, 1984), Horney wrote that what dependent women "secretly look for is the hero, the super-strong man, who at the same time is so weak that he will bend to all their wishes without hesitation" (Horney, 1937, p. 170). This contradictory wish for a partner of domineering strength and unconditional acquiescence expresses the needs of dependency as well as the resistance to it. For Horney the resistance is more than a wish for male kindness; it is also a desire for revenge against men by reversing the gendered power relationship (pp. 197–200).

Thus anger at those on whom one is dependent is not confined to resentment at being dependent but can also be expressed in a desire for retribution for past humiliation and deprivation. For

1. See Helen Block Lewis (1976) for an analysis of depression as a consequence of this dynamic in which anger is directed at the self.

example, reaction to shame brought on by degrading sexualiza-tion can be felt unconsciously as hostility toward all men as potential sexual aggressors (Horney, 1937, pp. 199–200). But, because the idealized self demands sexual attractiveness, this unconscious hatred is harbored simultaneously with exaggerated admiration for men (p. 201). Similarly, beneath the attempts to live up to the idealized image of the perfect mother can lie deep hos-tility toward having to give unconditionally to others when one feels herself to be deprived (p. 182). This may be expressed in a desire to deprive one's children, out of envy of them, by withhold-ing possessions or denying them pleasure (pp. 182–83). It can also be expressed in the neediness that forms the nurturing reversal (see chapter 5) in the behavior of a "mother who acts according to the belief that the child exists to give her satisfaction" (p. 181). Because anger violates the idealized image of self-effacing femi-ninity and loving motherhood, it is never expressed directly but becomes suffused with attempts to live up to perfectionist expec-tations. Thus, seething within the feminie type's sweet com-pliance to men is a rage to triumph over them. And beneath the proclamation of unbounded love and dedication to children lie the begrudging envy and anger that form what Adrienne Rich has called "the heart of maternal darkness" (Rich, 1976, pp. 256–80); Horney, 1937, p. 182).

Horney later elaborated on the idea that anger toward others is a projection of inner conflict (Horney, 1945; 1950a; 1951). For the feminine type this means that inner hostility is experienced as if it originated from outside herself. The externalization of inner abuse mirrors the process of externalized living. Dependent individuals embrace and internalize the expectations and judgments of others and experience themselves as living "out there" exposed to and under the power of others. The abuse one actually directs toward oneself is therefore experienced as a consequence of perpetually trying to meet others' expectations, a consequence of their power. Because dependent individuals are so vulnerable to others' opinions of them, any criticism, disinterest, or disagreement will be experienced as a major assault (Horney, 1951). Thus, the feeling of victimization combined with oversensitivity to anything other than unconditional affirmation creates a "pervasive experience of being the victim—a feeling which in its extent and intensity goes beyond, and is out of proportion to, actual provocations and may become a way of experiencing life" (p. 6).

The experience of victimization is real and infuriating. The dependent one dwells upon incidents in which others were unfair, demanding, ungrateful, deceitful (Horney, 1951, p. 5). Her sense is that she is always the innocent victim; her own goodness and fairness (her idealized image) contrast sharply with the inconsiderate treatment she receives from others. She perceives life and its unfairness as something that "happens to me" (p. 7). Externalizing abuse thus preserves one's idealized self and keeps repressed the feelings of anger associated with the real self. But by accepting herself as a passive recipient of wrongdoing, the dependent one blurs her perception of actual situations. Because others are seen as more powerful, as the locus of her self-judgment and the source of her abuse, she tends to admire and defer to them at the same time that she resents them (p. 8).

The ambivalence of admiring resentment befogs the capacity to interpet interpersonal relations. The feminine type is never certain how she is being treated. She tends to exaggerate superficial wrongs and minimize actual abuse. Because she depends upon the approval of those who may treat her badly, she undermines her ability to respond to external conditions that are, indeed, abusive. In such circumstances she shuffles "between accusations and self-recriminations" (Horney, 1937, p. 256) without knowing whether she is right in criticizing others. She knows that her feelings of being abused are not always realistic, and this awareness weakens her ability to grasp the truth of the situation. She has difficulty in recognizing whether she has been "really wronged," and this prevents her from "taking a firm stand when necessary" (p. 257).

The feminine type does not wish to be victimized; she does not encourage it or cause it to happen. Horney was emphatic on the point that suffering is not the desired goal (see Horney, 1937, p. 280). The issue is rather that the dependent character structure—formed in childhood in response to angering conditions—perpetuates victimization inwardly in order to appease others. By embracing the false ideal of sweet femininity, the feminine type denies her anger but remains churning with rage. By trying to avoid victimization she feels herself the perpetual victim and becomes vulnerable to actual abuse.

The feminine type may be too unsure of herself, too dependent, and too terrified to express her anger directly in situations that are indeed angering, but she does release it. Its expression, however, is condemned by the idealized self and it must therefore be released in "safe" or passive-aggressive ways. Horney's examples of the interpersonal release of anger form a continuum according to the strength of the inhibition against its direct expression. At one extreme is the self-destructive solution: because of the severe injunction against expressing hostility, anger is directed toward the self, which identifies with the hostile partner. The self becomes its own object for abuse by merging with the power and triumph of the abusing other. Hostility is thus denied but experienced vicariously (Horney, 1937, pp. 256–80; 1939b, pp. 250–70; 1950a, pp. 239–58). A less severe form of self-abusive hostility occurs in the various forms of physical and emotional suffering. Somatizing hostility into physical illness and accident-prone behavior or expressing it in general discontent are other ways of treating the self abusively. But here the effect is not to identify with a hostile other but to cause others to feel guilty for one's unhappiness. This externalization of feeling abused can release hostility: reproachful martyrdom blames others and excuses oneself for one's miserable plight (Horney, 1951). It is also safe because one's irritability and suffering appear justified by external conditions such as the unfairness of the world, the unappreciativeness of others, the inconsiderateness of strangers. Suffering does not appear to violate the dependent one's idealized self-image of selflessness, compliance, and responsibility for others (Horney, 1951, pp. 8–9; 1950a, pp. 229–36).

Beyond these self-destructive expressions of inner hostility are the forms of release that occur simultaneously with fulfilling the shoulds of the idealized self. These demands, it will be recalled, oppose the true, repressed feelings of the real self that interfere with living up to the perfectionist image. On a deeper level, the level of the real self, one's heart simply is not into living up to the dictates of the proud self. Anger at its demands continually threatens to undermine one's sincerest efforts to become perfectly feminine. Thus, one's feminine attributes are experienced as slightly insincere, and their expression in concrete behavior is suffused with hostility, revenge, and rage.

Repressed hostility seeps into the very acts of care, compliance, and selflessness that oppose it. It is expressed in self-pity when others do not fully appreciate one's generosity or attentiveness (Horney, 1950a, pp. 230, 241) and in the vague but constant feelings of depression that accompany self-sacrificing dependency in an intimate relationship (Horney, 1942, pp. 190–246). It is in the grinding resentment and begrudging envy of those for whom one is supposed to be unceasingly responsible (Horney, 1937, p. 182). And it is expressed in the apparently unintentional forgetfulness, disregard, and frustration of others whom one is supposed to be helping and admiring (Horney, 1948, p. 4).

Horney's most extensive and perspicacious analysis of the expression of anger is in her concept of vindictiveness (Horney, 1948; 1950a). Vindictiveness is "retribution for injury done" (Horney, 1950a, p. 201). It goes hand in hand with feeling abused, for it requires that "injuries received, whether ancient or recent," be treasured and kept alive. Vindictiveness is revenge against individuals from the past but it is expressed toward others in the present. It also forms an attitude toward the future in the expression of vindictive triumph.

Vindictive Triumph

Vindictive triumph is an example of less inhibited hostility that still finds "safe" expression. Most often linked with a compulsive drive for career success, vindictive triumph is a striving to overcome, outshine, and rise above all others by achieving public acclaim. It is lodged in the desire to humiliate others, to make them feel the shame, envy, and self-contempt that plague the vindictive one. It is a relatively safe expression of hostility because it manifests as achievement rather than as a punitive and destructive desire to defeat. Moreover, it is reinforced by a cultural ideology that presumes competition to be a natural social process, ambition to be a healthy striving, and envy to be a fact of life. Vindictive triumph receives its greatest legitimation, and thus its aura of safety, from the apotheosis of middle-class career ambition in industrial-capitalist societies (Horney, 1948; 1950a, pp. 197–213).

Horney did not, however, derive all ambition and success from vindictiveness. Healthy, as opposed to neurotic, ambition encourages the development of the potentials of the real self. Healthy striving is rooted in basic honesty and commitment to the content of one's work. Neurotic ambition, in contrast, is a search for glory that "springs from the need to actualize the idealized self" (Horney, 1950a, pp. 37–38). The proud, idealized self is an aspect of externalized living and thus seeks to attain only the *image* of success. Public validation and acclaim, not content or process, is the motivation. In searching for glory, the vindictive one is disinterested in and, indeed, scorns the slow, laborious process of achievement. "He does not want to climb a mountain; he wants to be on the peak" (p. 38).

This image conveys the compulsiveness and wishful thinking that Horney identified with the vindictive search for glory. The desire is for unlimited and absolute success; nothing short of being on top will satisfy the excessive demands of the idealized self. Moreover, the accomplishment must be effortless, not only because the effort itself is intrinsically unappealing, but also because it is humiliation. The vindictive one simply deserves to be at the top; indicating ambition threatens to expose his or her deep-seated envy and insatiable need. Moreover, to try and then fail to achieve one's desire is a humiliation that the vindictive one cannot risk. The absence of effort is therefore considered a further confirmation of the vindictive one's innate superiority (Horney, 1950a, pp. 34–38). Others may not recognize this superiority now; but through wishful thinking, living in a triumphant future, the vindictive one "'"lives for the 'day of reckoning'"' (p. 203) in which his or her infinite greatness will be revealed and all others will be put to shame.

The wish for future triumph reflects back on present dispositions. The vindictive one is extremely competitive, cannot tolerate anyone who is superior in any way, and finds strategies—obvious and subtle—to drag down all rivals. Envy inevitably affects interpersonal relations. The vindictive one attempts to humiliate and exploit rivals (especially those with public recognition) and demands blind admiration and devotion from those of "lesser status." He or she sees all others as either superior or inferior, successes or failures, worthwhile or insignificant. This perceptual dualism reflects the absolute abyss between the neurotic's idealized, proud self and the despised real self. Others are treated with "contemptuous disregard" (Horney, 1950a, p. 200) so that the proud self can confirm its own superiority. Beneath this façade of disdain, however, is the feeling that *all* others are superior and the fear that they will hurt and humiliate. Hence, the vindictive one is always on guard, armoring the self with righteousness as a defense against both self-loathing and the hostility that others are assumed to have. In addition, he or she flees the perceived superiority and hostility of others by developing an image of invulnerability and independence. This too is a defense against feelings of humiliating weakness (pp. 197–213).

Vindictive Triumph and the Feminine Type

But what happens when a dependent type seeks the release of hostility in vindictive triumph? What is the consequence of pitting altruism and self-effacement against self-assertion and the ambitious drive for revenge? Which inhibition and which striving will prevail? This is the same conflict that Horney described in "The Overvaluation of Love" (1934). It was the conflict of the feminine type, which surfaced later in Horney's work as the central conflict of the age: the striving for affection versus ambition. Couched in her earlier formulation, it establishes Horney's concept of the conflict of modern women.

At first Horney's 1934 analysis of women's conflict appears to recapitulate the terms of the debate on the masculinity complex (see Fliegel, 1973). To Freud (1925b), ambitious women were deluded in their belief that they were like men, neurotic in their inability to accept their natural inferiority. Horney argued that preference for the masculine role expresses a girl's identification with her father, which arises from Oedipal disappointments (Horney, 1924) and from fear of his sexuality (Horney, 1927). In this early debate with Freud, Horney accepted the widely held notion that ambition was masculine and that ambition in women expressed homosexuality (Horney, 1926, p. 53; cf. Smith-Rosenberg, 1985, p. 265).

In "The Overvaluation of Love" Horney changed her position and refined the debate. First she differentiated between women's desire to find satisfaction in work, even work formerly identified with male roles, and an exaggerated need for public recognition. Horney regarded the former as a normal wish for self-assertion and responsibility and the latter as a compulsive need to rise above all others (Horney, 1934, pp. 183–85). By this distinction she legitimated women's career goals by separating them from the "masculinity complex" and from the overcompensating desire for revenge that she later termed vindictive triumph and that Adler had earlier associated with women's "masculine protest" (Adler, 1917, pp. 99–100).

Horney also disassociated homosexuality from both the desire to find satisfaction in work and the vindictive urge for public acclaim. Indeed, in a bold reversal of the earlier equation of female assertion and ambition with lesbianism, Horney connected the exaggerated need for public recognition with a heterosexual pattern of behavior. The feminine type overvalues both the love of men and their models of success. Her desire for vindictive triumph in both love and work is grounded in male identification and in a belief in the superiority of men. On the one hand she strives to find security in the arms of a man, to merge with the powerful and superior man, to attain a feeling of self-worth, and to humiliate other women in her victory. On the other hand is the desire to emulate men by triumphing in the professional world, where few women receive admission, much less acclaim. This, of course, does not eliminate the possibility that lesbians may identify with male images of career triumph; but in linking the compulsion to be loved by men with the desire to emulate them, Horney emphasized that the problem is not women's sexual identity but masculine civilization's overvaluation of men.

Horney's later analysis of vindictive triumph is an elaboration of the feminine type's overvaluation of both love and success. Fantasies of triumph in romantic and professional spheres compete because the requirements for success in each are opposed: how can a woman be both lovable and ambitious if the former requires being deferential to others and the latter necessitates triumphing over them? Some women, according to Horney, attempt to solve the problem by compartmentalizing these objectives. "In their love life they may tend toward a morbid dependency while in their career they may show all the earmarks of neurotic ambition and a need for triumph. These latter trends are usually suppressed but sufficiently alive to allow them a measure of productivity—or at least of success. In theoretical terms they have tried to relegate their self-effacing trends to their love life and their expansive drives to their work. In actual fact so neat a division is not feasible. And it will become apparent in analysis that, roughly, a drive for mastery also operates in their love relations, as do self-abnegating trends in their careers—with the result that they have become increasingly unhappy" (Horney, 1950a, p. 354).

When the compartmentalization breaks down, love and work are infused with the characteristics reserved for the other. Work is made difficult by the vindictive drives. Because it is the vision of success rather than the content or the process that is compelling, the work itself becomes uninteresting. This attitude undermines the effort necessary for success. When success is not forthcoming, defeatism sets in and confirms the underlying self-contempt. The romantic solution of a dependent relationship appears to promise salvation, but it only further erodes belief in one's personal capabilities (Horney, 1934, pp. 207–13).

The romantic solution is a false one in another respect: it cannot provide the happiness and self-esteem that are sought. In the first place, the competition and perfectionist visions that characterize the search for glory in the professional sphere inform the desire for love as well. For the feminine type, having the most beautiful, sexually desirable appearance, capturing the most successful and attractive man, or being desired by all men are the triumphant fantasies in which other women are immediately put to shame. But like the fantasy of immediate and absolute career success, the vision of heterosexual triumph is easily shaken by details of imperfect reality. A woman's own body shames her in its imperfections; no suitor is ever perfect or successful enough; and the intentions and stares of men are never admiring enough. The insatiable quality of vindictive triumph asserts itself here, and so does the abstraction. It is not the quality of the relationship that matters but only the fact that a relationship exists. The lack of discrimination with regard to career success is paralleled in the drive for heterosexual success. Just as the career activity is subordinate to the success it brings, so the quality of the relationship is secondary to the fact of its existence. Both are publicly validated triumphs of idealized self-images. Consequently, Horney argued, modern women who chase the twin phantoms of emulating men and being desirable to them hover unhappily between these goals. "They think that they can be happy only through love, whereas, constituted as they are, they never can be, while on the other hand they have an ever-diminishing faith in the worth of their abilities" (Horney, 1934, p. 212).

In her later work, Horney expanded upon this modern female conflict (Horney, 1947a, 1950a). Work, she argued, is inhibited not only by vindictive motives but also by dependent inhibitions against expansive behavior and success. If ambition presses for achievement, self-doubt and self-criticism undermine it. If success requires increasing responsibility and supervision of others, insecurity renders the assumption of responsibility ineffectual. If accomplishment requires working alone, the nurturing imperative, which validates only work that is done for others, calls it selfish (Horney, 1950a, pp. 316–24). And if the idea of success is highly perfectionistic, the hope of achieving it is attacked by self-defeating attention to the minutest flaws. Such women "are pushed into an almost hopeless battle in which they struggle for perfection while at the same time they beat themselves down. In addition the demands for excelling are reinforced from a peculiar source. Their taboos on ambition and pride make them feel 'guilty' if they reach out for personal achievements, and only the ultimate attainment is a redemption for this guilt. ('If you are not the perfect musician, you had better scrub floors.')" (p. 317).

The Elusive Type

When this "conflict between expansive and self-effacing drives is close to the surface," the mood swings are more dramatic: elation at any sign of success alternates with despair and murderous rage (Horney, 1950a, p. 318). This pattern is also evident when the two drives conflict in personal relationships. Rooted in the tension between anxiety and hostility, the opposed strivings for dependency and vindictive revenge threaten and exacerbate each other. The adaptive defenses of dependency stifle the release of hostility, undermine self-esteem by adopting the appearance of softness, and permit others to triumph over the self through criticism, exploitation, or success. Indeed, the compliance necessary for dependency creates conditions that heighten the feelings of being abused; hostility is increased, but the inhibitions of dependency forbid its release. On the other hand, release of hostility in the vindictive abuse of others arouses anxiety over abandonment and loss of love. Behavior is thus modified, infused with opposing messages of neediness and affection, directed at safe (less powerful) others, or expressed in helplessness and envy toward those on whom the dependent-hostile one is dependent. Behavior and feelings may then seesaw between insecurity and hostility, alluring compliance and explosive rage, helplessness and fury over feeling humiliated or disrespected by another (Horney, 1937, p. 225; 1950a, pp. 233–34).

The conflict begins to inform all areas of life: compliance, vindictiveness, helplessness, rage, seductiveness, envy, suffering, ambition, and self-effacement all compete and interact. The result is psychic confusion. "Patients inclined toward this kind of defense often resemble those characters in fairy tales who when pursued turn into fish; if not safe in this guise, they turn into deer; if the hunter catches up with them they fly away as birds. You can never pin them down to any statement; they deny having said it or assure you they did not mean it that way. They have a bewildering capacity to becloud issues. . . . They are vicious one moment, sympathetic the next; at times overconsiderate, ruthlessly inconsiderate at others; domineering in some respects, self-effacing in others. They reach out for a dominating partner, only to change to a 'doormat,' then back to the former variety. After treating someone badly, they will be overcome by remorse, attempt to make amends, then feel like a 'sucker' and turn to being abusive all over again. Nothing is quite real to them" (Horney, 1945, pp. 138–39).

When the inhibitions of compliant and alluring dependency form a unifying idealized image, behavior is criticized from a single position. The content of the demands may shift with audience, fashion, and so on, but the basic imperative remains tied to the demands and inhibitions of dependency. When the two competing sets of neurotic drives are evenly matched, however, the patient lacks the "customary unifying procedures" (Horney, 1945, p. 139) that prevail when one solution predominates. In particular, the idealized image—for all its self-destructive and alienating characteristics—is never firmly established as an integrated proud self. Or, perhaps more accurately, the two sets of idealized demands compete for ascendency. The intrapsychic conflict is therefore greatly intensified. Behavior is simultaneously incited and inhibited, validated and punished. Inhibitions that foster dependency are upheld and bitterly denounced at the same time. If the denunciation is strong enough, the inhibitions will be temporarily rejected. Indignant rage may be the response; but the rage is not only a release of hostile strivings but also a severe violation of dependent inhibitions. It is no wonder that Horney found that this conflict produces behavior most difficult to pin down. She designated those who hover between dependency and hostility as "elusive" (p. 138) and interpreted their switching from one side of the contradiction to the other as both a sign of inner turmoil and a strategy to ward off detection by others. In effect, this "aversion to any transparency" serves both sets of demands: on the one hand, it

wards off the humiliation of being exposed, which is feared by the
dependent type; on the other hand, it satisfies the vindictive
desire to frustrate others' attempts to help or understand (p. 139).
The conflict also expresses a simultaneous fear of failure, or
humiliation, and of success, which may expose one to the hostile
envy of others (Horney, 1937, pp. 210–16).[2]

While Horney regarded the conflict between affection and
ambition as central to her time, she spent very little time analyzing the battle of these two strivings in the elusive type, apparently
because in her clinical observation one trend or the other usually
predominated (Horney, 1945, p. 43). Her emphasis on the dependent type reflects the problems characteristic of her women
patients, who typically had inhibitions against expressing hostility. This is certainly evident in "The Overvaluation of Love," in
which the women described emphasized the romantic over the
professional image. Their needs for dependency appear greater
than those for retaliation (Horney, 1934, p. 211).

The romantic solution was, of course, the socially expected one
for women in 1934. As Kessler-Harris (1982) has shown, American
women flocked into the labor force in the 1920s, but their career
success was limited by male control of female professions and by

2. The symptoms that Horney identified in the conflict between dependency
and vindictiveness, especially in the elusive personality, bear a strong
resemblance to the symptoms of the borderline personality disorder. However,
the description of the borderline personality is derived from object-relations
theory, which postdates Horney's work, and its explanation emphasizes early
mother-infant interaction as the foundation for the development of ego strength
and relatedness. As the term suggests, borderline at first implied a condition on
the border between neurosis and psychosis. It is now generally recognized as a
distinct diagnostic category.
The literature on the borderline syndrome is voluminous. Major theoretical
works include M. A. Mahler (1968, 1971); Heinz Kohut (1971); O. F. Kernberg
(1975, 1984); J. F. Masterson (1976, 1981); R. R. Grinker et al. (1968); Peter
Hartocollis, ed. (1977). Although clinical evidence shows that both males and
females present borderline symptoms, few researchers of the disorder have
explored gender differences—but see Haakene (1983); Kimsey and Arnold
(1977); Kaplan (1983).

gender segregation of the workplace (pp. 229–36). During the 1930s, the number of women who were wage-earners continued to climb slowly, but this was in part the result of gender segregation: women could be hired more cheaply than men during the economic depression (pp. 258–72). Women lost ground in traditionally female professions such as teaching, social work, accounting, and librarianship (p. 260). Moreover, despite the devaluation of the nineteenth-century cult of spiritual motherhood, women were still expected to marry and have children—the legacy of romanticized marriage promoted the romantic solution as women's primary goal in life (pp. 253–55; Fass, 1977, p. 82). Thus, if the feminine type opted for affection over ambition, the reason lay as much in masculine civilization's promotion of female economic dependency (Horney, 1934, p. 183) as it did in psychological inhibition.

In contrast, one could interpret the stance of the elusive one, who claims equally the desires for affection and ambition, as an implicitly feminist critique of the separation of spheres that promotes female deference and economic dependency. By rejecting the feminine type's acquiescence to the romantic ideal, the elusive one would claim the right to both love and work—in contemporary parlance, "to have it all." Unfortunately, according to Horney's analysis, the elusive one's potentially feminist revolt would be a caricature of feminism in vindictive triumph. She does not wish to release her real self or to challenge the social and economic structures that keep women in their place. Instead, she seeks individual retribution for her wounded pride by becoming the triumphant exception to the constraints endured by all others. As a caricature of the feminist, she would revel in her triumph over ordinary women. This is the rage for uniqueness and superiority that Horney found informing the competitive search for glory (Horney, 1950a, pp. 17–39) and that Rosabeth Moss Kanter has found in the "queen bee" who denies the structural conditions of her tokenism (Kanter, 1977, p. 230). Ironically, the elusive one's triumph would actually flatten her individuality, for it would require merging with the proud dictates of the idealized selves, defined externally. Thus, her triumph is not the realization of the unique but the proud imitation of stereotypical ideals. Trying to live up to these ideals only increases alienation from the real self and exacerbates rage, promoting ever-renewed attempts to find in acclaim the public redemption for private pain.

8 | Detachment

If the strivings for affection and ambition are equally strong, as in the case of the elusive character, the individual is caught in a raging inner battle and exhibits constantly vascillating, contradictory behavior. Detachment is a resolution that represses both the desire to comply to others and the compulsion to overpower them. A numbing of the feeling of conflict, it is an attempt to immobilize both strivings by withdrawing socially, resisting obligation or advice, guarding one's privacy, and resigning oneself to presumably unalterable conditions. Behind the detachment, the resignation, and the deadening of feeling, however, is the continuing reality of the competing domineering and dependent solutions of a conflicted pride system. Thus, the detached solution is "no true solution, because the compulsive cravings for closeness, as well as for aggressive domination, exploitation, and excelling, remain, and they keep harassing if not paralyzing their carrier" (Horney, 1945, p. 95).

Because the domineering and dependent strivings are still experienced as demands, the detached individual is sensitive to feelings of inner coercion. The solution of evading and denying the inner dictates is projected outward as an avoidance of obligation or expectations for behavior. All interaction with others is experienced as coercive. Privacy, self-sufficiency, and the sanctity of one's personal thoughts are carefully guarded. Engagement with others is undertaken but guarded against through resignation, an absence of vitality, or an intellectualized, superior stance. Behind this self-protective estrangement is a longing for freedom from expectations—from oneself as well as from other people (Horney, 1950a, pp. 274–80).

Detachment does not create a proud self so much as it attempts to avoid all claims for perfection. As a type, therefore, it is qualitatively different from both dependent and domineering types. By rejecting the externalized living of both the overvaluation of love and the compulsion for ambition, the detached individual implies a critique of the other two neurotic solutions. Mirroring the revolt of the elusive one who wants it all, the rebellion of detachment strives for freedom from all other-directedness. However, neither the elusive nor the detached type realizes its protest in a resolution of the inner conflict, thus releasing the real self and transforming their behavior. Rather, they resign themselves to characterological conflict: the elusive individual embraces it in conflicting visions of triumph, while the detached one denies it in a fantasy of freedom.

Nevertheless, in its opposition to the compulsive pursuit of both love and ambition, detachment suggests that at some level of consciousness the self opposes externalized living. Horney implied this possibility in her discussion of the ways detachment can combine with either dependent or domineering solutions to create a conflict in which one fulfills the shoulds of the idealized self but simultaneously sabotages one's efforts. Fulfilling nurturing expectations with emotional aloofness or procrastinating in carrying out career-enhancing activities are examples of this simultaneous submission and resistance. Undermining one's actions through detachment differs from the ways repressed dependency interferes with ambitious pursuits or anger sabotages nurturing. The detached individual desires not to lean on others or rage against them but to avoid them.

The combination of detachment and dominance has been identified as a stereotypical characteristic of masculinity (Symonds, 1973, p. 42). Barbara Ehrenreich (1983) argues that since the 1950s men have employed detachment as a rebellion against the responsibilities associated with their dominant role as the breadwinner. Their attempts to reject the responsibilities and emotional involvement of marriage represent a struggle to protect their privacy, freedom, independence, and disposable income from women. The shrinking of opportunities for ruggedly individualistic achievement, the conflicting corporate virtues of cooperation and ambition, the devaluation of homemaking, and the unmasking of the idealized nuclear family are the changes that Ehrenreich identifies with the years after 1950. These changes in public and private life (which began much earlier in the century) challenged the traditional means by which men strove for affection and achievement. Men came to believe that love led to financial and emotional entrapment and work required conformity with inadequate rewards. Ehrenreich implies that, even for those who accepted the role of breadwinner, the conflicts surrounding male identity promoted emotional—if not physical—detachment.

If the real male rebels—Ehrenreich identifies them with the authentic Beats—rejected both work and marriage, the vast majority of men became "subdued rebels" (Horney, 1950a, p. 283). Ehrenreich calls them "gray flannel rebels" (Ehrenreich, 1983, p. 29), men resigned to life. They fulfill the roles of husband, father, breadwinner, responsible worker, but with little enthusiasm. They resolve their unfulfilled and conflicting strivings for affection and ambition by renouncing both. They ask only to be left alone, to keep their obligations and duties to the barest minimum, to be free from others' emotional needs. And in this retreat from others, they retreat from themselves: from wishes, feelings, and hope. Horney noted that this "resignation implies settling for a peace which is merely the absence of conflicts ... a process of shrinking, of restricting, of curtailing life and growth ... life without pain or friction but also without zest" (Horney, 1950a, p. 260).

Although Ehrenreich contends that the male rebellion could be a protest "against a system of social control that operates to make men unquestioning and obedient servants" (Ehrenreich, 1983,

p. 170), she concludes that it has been coopted into self-absorbed consumerism. "The common drift, from *Playboy* through the counterculture of the sixties and the psychological reevaluation of masculinity in the seventies, has been to legitimate a consumerist personality *for men*.... And, if this movement has had a sustaining sense of indignation, it has more often been directed against women than against the corporate manipulaters of tastes and dictators of the work routine" (p. 171). Just as the female elusive whose desire to have it all implies a feminist critique of her conflicting roles (chapter 7), the male rebel questions an economic system premised on men's ambition and breadwinning. However, in both instances the rebellion is sidetracked into individualism, the former in vindictive triumph and the latter in self-absorbed materialism. Horney described the latter form of detachment as "shallow living," a cynical and mindlessly egocentric consumption of things and "fun." "This may superficially look like a zest for living, in contrast to a basic characteristic of resignation—a not wanting. But the motive force here is not a reaching out for enjoyment but the necessity to push down a gnawing feeling of futility by means of distracting pleasures" (Horney, 1950a, p. 286).

Detached Femininity

Detachment can also combine with feminine dependency (Horney, 1950a, p. 278). When it does, fantasies of escape, isolation, and independence may emerge as an imaginative alternative to feminine altruism. As Horney noted, self-sacrificing and self-effacing dependence on others both creates and represses anger, which may be channeled into domineering behaviors, such as striving for vindictive triumph. Another response is to reject the traps of both compassion and success by imagining a different world, or a place of freedom within the world, but separated from it (Westkott, 1977). Visions of absolute, protective separation convey a longing to be free of the conditions that trigger the inner necessity to care for others. This can be a wish to escape from the demands of others in order to avoid guilt for not giving enough, for feeling resentful, for wanting to consider one's own needs, or for any other conscious or unconscious resistance to the imperative to place others' needs above one's own. Such fantasies of detachment are appealing not only because they negate unpleasant reality but also because they suggest a kind of guiltless sincerity and integrity (Horney, 1950a, p. 280). Underlying them is the belief that only a radical social break can silence the shoulds and melt the bonds of self-denying attachment. Attending to one's own needs free of self-recrimination is possible only if there are no others. The vulnerability to feminine altruism would remain, but the imagined solution is momentarily free of it.

Horney also suggested that detachment can combine with rather than negate altruism. In these instances a woman complies with the demands of others but detaches herself emotionally and intellectually from these activities. Marxists have identified this separation of consciousness from activity with the routinization of alienated labor (Lukacs, 1971, pp. 83–109). One "may go through the motions of complying with the wishes of others but sabotage them in spirit, without in the least being aware of doing so" (Horney, 1950a, p. 278). Daydreaming and emotional aloofness are examples of the silent resistance of withdrawing while meeting other's needs (p. 279. It can also be expressed on a more conscious level—for example, by a woman who meets the demands for her domestic presence while immersing herself in needlework (Mann, 1980). The sabotage produced by detachment is different from that arising from anger in that it expresses a desire for freedom rather than a wish for revenge. This reaction, which psychiatrists term *dissociation* (English and Finch, 1954, pp. 180–90), separates one's mental processes from one's activities and can serve as a defense against anxiety.

This aloofness places detachment in a curious relationship with externalized living. "Reading" other people is essential to knowing how to respond to them, but detachment interferes with perceptiveness. These conflicting attitudes may be compartmentalized—for example, by detaching from those on whom one is less dependent or who are less powerful and "reading" those whose power and judgment are most important. However, like all compartmentalization, this distinction is too neat. The externalization and detachment flow into one another, conflict, and add to the emptiness and clouding of feeling that Horney identified with inner paucity. Both the externalized dependence and the detachment would be immobilized: the person would be neither here nor not here. In the extreme, it would be as if she were suspended in time and place. But befogged suspension is not the only way that these defenses interact. Horney implies another method in her description of the onlooker phenomenon.

The Onlooker

The onlooker replicates externalized living in her attention to others, their behavior, and their judgments. Horney described this as a "ubiquitous and prominent attitude" of the detached person. She lives as if she "were sitting in the orchestra and observing a drama acted on the stage, and a drama which is most of the time not too exciting at that" (Horney, 1950a, p. 261). But whereas in dependency a person reads others to know how to act and feel— as if she were on stage too—in detachment she disengages from the drama. Others are the objects of intellectual curiosity, not the source of influence. But the careful observation of others can serve both detached and dependent purposes and can allow both moving into and moving away from the drama. It also reinforces the dependent one's self-minimizing disengagement from actual involvement in the risks of life. The astute observer is protected against joining the potentially dangerous fray, especially if she has been taught that she can never succeed in it anyway.

Protectionist measures (such as domestication, keeping girls "out of harm's way") reinforce psychological attitudes (the astute observation of others, especially those more powerful) to create an onlooker, detached from life. They can also create, according to Horney, an estranged, observant attitude toward oneself. Horney's diary contains an example of this when she was refused permission to join a class in animal dissection in medical school. With prescience and wit, she commented, "*Et voilà* a substitute: I shall take myself to pieces. That will probably be more difficult, but also more interesting. What shall I begin with?" (Horney, 1980, p. 58). The statement suggests not only her future profession but also the ability that she displayed very early to take herself as well as others "to pieces." Her sense of ironic detachment from herself, and in this instance from her feelings in response to being excluded from the class, becomes a defensive stance. By intellectualizing her situation, she observes her vicissitudes and foibles, and those of others, and masks her feelings, especially from herself. In this alienation from herself, she becomes her own object for critical observation. But the eyes that judge her are her own. To extend Horney's metaphor of the theater, it is as if she were both in the audience and on stage, observing herself and others on stage from the vantage point of the nonparticipant. There is, as Horney notes, a stance of superiority in this position, the purity of one whose integrity is unsullied by engagement, involvement, or effort (Horney, 1945, p. 79). To the extent that one does engage in life, one's behavior can be assessed with ironic detachment.

When the onlooking attitude occurs in women, it may be more than a consequence of structural restriction or a psychological defense against dependency. It may also convey the practice of fetishizing women as objects to be looked at. Critical observation of herself and others may be the way a woman looks at herself being looked at. She becomes the omniscient observer of her own sexualization, the voyeur of the voyeurs of her unintentionally exhibited body. As a spectator she rises above the trivialization that she cannot otherwise avoid. She creates an idealized, disembodied self, a desexualized, immaterial commentator on life who records wittily and caustically her own pretensions as well as the judgments and foibles of others.

Virginia Woolf recognized this stance in herself—it was part of her genius for capturing meaningful detail. Resigning herself to the demands of her socially ambitious half-brother, George Duckworth, Woolf recalled, "I must obey, because he had force of age, of wealth, of tradition behind him. But even while I obeyed I asked, 'How could anyone believe what he believed?' There was a spectator in me who, while I squirmed at his criticism and deferred to it, yet remained cool, critical, observant" (Woolf, 1976, pp. 132–33). This is the critical onlooker who, when she was sexualized as a child, alienated herself from her exploited body and observed herself and her abuser (pp. 68–69). It is the witty young woman who complied with men's demands to become the idealized image they needed her to be. Yet her compliance is observed with critical, ironic detachment. She is the dutiful stepsister and daughter but she rebels while she complies; she rises above domination, her superiority lodged in stinging, demystifying, revealing observation and judgment.

Woolf's detached observation of her own sexual abuse corresponds to the attitude of "frozen watchfulness" that clinicians have found in children who have been abused (Helfer, McKinney, and Kempe, 1976). Frozen watchfulness expresses a generalized fear of others and the need to be alert to their motives and behaviors. A sexualizing experience does not have to be violent or physically abusive to promote such an attitutde. Jean Strouse reports that, in response to her brother's sexual teasing and control, Alice James became an onlooker, observing herself as an object and learning "to detach from the flushed confusions involved in also being the subject of the diversion" (Strouse, 1980, p. 55). Later in life, Alice employed this self-estrangement as a coping mechanism. "Detachment enabled her to submit and resist at the same time. It was as if she ceded her body to the 'feminine' principle of frailty and submission, while cultivating with her mind a 'masculine' strength and indifference to pain" (p. 125).

Both Virginia Woolf and Alice James found a position of superiority in the detachment that enabled them to take a critical perspective on the world (Garnett, 1985, pp. 19–23, 110; Strouse, 1980, p. 55). But their critical aloofness was inseparable from their powerlessness, submission, and their identities as sexualized objects. Indeed, their submission to male power was itself sexually defined.

Woolf, was forced to act as an attractive and charming accomplice to half-brother George's forays into society and was required to pass his perfectionist, self-serving test of her appearance. "He looked me up and down as if [I] were a horse turned into a ring. Then the sullen look came over him; a look in which one traced not merely aesthetic disapproval, but something that went deeper; morally, socially, he scented some kind of insurrection; of defiance of social standards. I was condemned from many more points of view than I can analyze as I stood there, conscious of those criticisms; and conscious too of fear, of shame and of despair" (Woolf, 1976, p. 130). The emphasis in this passage on her self-conscious compliance suggests that, as an observer of others, the detached woman is very much an onlooker with regard to herself (see Berger, 1972, pp. 46–47). Furthermore, as Woolf's autobiographical observations reveal, as a critical spectator of life, the detached woman is also self-critical. Because she is very much on stage, under the judgmental gaze of others, a woman does not escape the criticism she directs toward that drama. Therefore, despite the superiority of the position of detachment, her observant criticism lacks arrogance. She remains very much a part of the scene that she rises above, takes "to pieces," and judges.

That the person who perceives and judges a situation is simultaneously in the situation observing and judging herself suggests the limits of detachment. No pretense to objective, unattached intelligence (Mannheim, 1936, p. 155) or superior judgment can emerge from a sense of being a part of the very object world one judges. Women's consciousness of being looked at, of being obtrusive, of being the intruder in the male-defined world of work, play, and politics denies the illusion of detachment or the pretension of pure judgment. As a sex object, a woman stands out; she cannot avoid it. But, as Horney argued, in her devaluation by masculine civilization a woman is also an outsider. Her alienation from masculine civilization is defined by her visualized presence in it, by being taken as a fetish by others and therefore by herself. The alienation is also defined by her marginality, by the lack of power, influence, or will that is accorded her. She is detached even when she is engaged, because she is the other, the outsider, the intruder. She is of necesssity an onlooker even as a participant. Together her experience of standing out and being disregarded, her obtrusive objectness and her trivialization, form an experience of alienation that informs perceptions and judgments. She is the outsider who, like Horney and Woolf, can see through the pretensions of others. Yet, like Woolf's image of the horse in the ring, she is too obtrusive to hide from judgment. If she takes others to pieces, she must dissect herself as well.

The critical possibilities and the limits of female detachment are portrayed in the character of Kate Brown in Doris Lessing's *The Summer before the Dark* (1973). Ostensibly this novel is about a forty-five-year-old Englishwoman coming to terms with the inevitability of aging, but on a deeper level it concerns the birth of her real self. Kate for the first time in her life is on her own. Her four children, now young adults, have plans that take them away from home, and her husband, Michael, who is something of a philanderer, has scheduled a business trip to America. He encourages Kate to work as a translator for a conference on world hunger. Kate agrees and sets herself on a path of self-discovery that takes her to Istanbul, Spain, and back alone to London.

But character more than geography is the focus of the journey.

When she is first introduced, Kate is the epitome of dependent femininity. Once a beautiful young woman, she has cultivated the appearance that she believed she should have: "her appearance was choice, all exquisite tact, for it was appropriate for this middle-class suburb and in it as her husband's wife. And, of course, as the mother of her children. The dress came off a rail marked *Jolie Madame*, and was becoming and discreet. She wore shoes and stockings. Her hair—and now we reach the place where most energy had gone into choice—was done in large soft waves around a face where a few freckles had been allowed to remain on the bridge of her nose and her upper cheeks. Her husband always said he liked them there. The hair was reddish—not too dramatically so. She was a pretty, healthy, serviceable woman" (p. 10).

Lessing extends the ironic use of "choice"—from her description of Kate's cultivation of herself as the ideally attractive, serviceable suburban housewife—to describing her decision to care for all the others in the household. Before being offered the translation job, Kate had decided not to accompany her husband to the United States because of the expense and her fear that her presence might cramp his style. It never occurred to her to spend a holiday by herself; rather she "chose" to keep the house going for the benefit of the others. "She would be a base for members of the family coming home from university, or dropping in for a day or a week on their way somewhere else; she would housekeep for them, their friends, their friends' friends. She would be available, at everyone's disposal. She was looking forward to it, not only to the many people, but the managing, the being conscious of her efficiency" (p. 12–13).

Kate is not simply dependent upon others' judgment of her appearance and gratitude for her care-taking; she is also detached from it. Lessing conveys Kate's detachment early by sharply juxtaposing her appearance with her thoughts. "A woman stood on her back step, arms folded, waiting. Thinking? She would not have said so. She was tyring to catch hold of something, or to lay it bare so that she could look and define" (p. 3). The reader gradually learns that what Kate is trying to catch hold of is her real self, the basis of authentic choice and feelings. She begins this journey to her real self by detaching herself and becoming an onlooker. Kate observes the conventionality of others' behavior and the way it masks true feelings. "You have to deduce a person's real feelings about a thing by a smile she does not know is on her face, by the way bitterness tightens muscles at a mouth's corner" (p. 33). As an onlooker, Kate discovers the same posturing in herself. "The truth was, she was becoming more and more uncomfortably conscious not only that the things she said, and a good many of the things she thought, had been taken down off a rack and put on, but that what she really felt was something again" (p. 4).

Kate's dissociation of her thought from her behavior grants her some freedom as she conforms to the roles expected of her. After fixing lunch for Michael and the director of the conference, who continue their two-way conversation, Kate retreats. "Having handed them coffee and chocolate wafers, she set an attentive smile on her face, like a sentinel, behind which she could culti-vate her own thoughts" (p. 14). As she realizes that others in the family consider her domestic responsibilities unimportant, her thoughts turn to herself, to her feeling that she has deceived her-self, and to criticizing her idealized image. "Looking back over nearly a quarter of a century, she saw that that had been the charac-teristic of her life—passivity, adaptability to others" (p. 22). With the children nearly grown, she felt obsolete, "an old nurse who had given her years to the family and must now be put up with. The virtues had turned to vices, to the nagging and bullying of other people. An unafraid young creature had been turned, through the long grinding process of always being at other people's beck and call, always having to give out attention to detail, min-uscule wants, demands, needs, events, crises, into an obsessed maniac. Obsessed by what was totally unimportant" (p. 105).

Kate responded to her self-criticism by withdrawing emo-

tionally while continuing to run the large and demanding household. But this very emotional estrangement from the behavior that
others (and she herself) continue to expect from her forms the
basis for a new critical consciousness. She becomes conscious of
both her own behavior and of how others respond to her,
especially after she enters the new social arena of the conference
on world hunger. She realizes that she is expected to provide
maternal care for the delegates—the same job that women are
expected to perform in families—and that she is "unable to switch
herself out of the role of provider of invisible manna, consolation,
warmth, 'sympathy'" (p. 52).

Moreover, Kate observes herself being observed and experi-
ments with manipulating others' responses. "Soon she discovered
that if she wanted to be alone, she should sit badly in a huddled or
discouraged posture, and allow her legs to angle themselves
unbecomingly. If she did this, men did not see her . . . it was really
extraordinary! There she sat, Kate Brown, just as she had always
been, herself, her mind, her awareness, watching the world from
behind a façade only very slightly different from the one she had
maintained since she was sixteen. It was a matter only of a bad
posture" (p. 49).

Kate's growing awareness of the way she has been a "pretty,
healthy, serviceable" object for others opens her eyes to the fact
that all women are objects to others, and thus to themselves. She
reflects on female attendants and stewardesses, whom she sees as
providing not simply care and information but "easily available
and guiltless sex. . . . They have been chosen for their friendly
perky daylight sexiness, and there they are, in ones and twos and
threes, walking up and down, smiling, smiling, smiling, smiling,
and, as you watch them . . . they slowly become inflated with a
warm expanding air. They are intoxicated—but really, literally—
with their own attractiveness, and by their public situation,
dressed and placed where they will draw so many eyes towards
them, and by their own helpfulness. They smile and smile and

smile" (pp. 60–61). Kate's criticism issues not from a superior position but from self-reflective detachment. She sees herself in her role at the conference in the same position as the stewardesses: "smiling, smiling, in the beam of other people's appreciation, turning the beam of her own readiness outward to warm everybody else" (p. 63).

The realization that she has invested so much energy into a falsely idealized self becomes clearer as Kate begins to fail to meet her own perfectionist demands. During a brief romantic tryst with a younger man, Kate catches a flu-like illness from him and suffers alone for weeks from nausea and dehydration. She becomes haggard, unhealthily thin; her gray hair is a noticeable, thick band at the roots of the stylish red dye. In her disheveled and weakened condition, Kate wanders through London looking like an old and slightly demented woman. She stops at a construction site and realizes that the workers don't notice her. "The fact that they didn't suddenly made her angry. She walked away out of sight, and . . . took off her jacket . . . showing her fitting dark dress. She tied her hair dramatically with a scarf. Then she strolled back in front of the workmen, hips conscious of themselves. A storm of whistles, calls, invitations. Out of sight the other way, she made her small transformation and walked back again: the men glanced at her, did not see her. She was trembling with rage: it was rage, it seemed to her, that she had been suppressing for a lifetime. And it was a front for worse, a misery that she did not want to answer, for it was saying again and again: This is what you have been doing for years and years and years" (p. 242).

As an onlooker, Kate becomes aware of her dependence on the judgment of others and of her lifelong obsession with meeting externally defined standards. "The clothes, hair style, manners, posture, voice of Mrs. Brown (or of Jolie Madame, as the trade put it) had been a reproduction the slightest deviation from which had caused her as much discomfort as the scientist's rat feels when the appropriate levers are pushed" (p. 270). In observing herself trying to meet her internalized ideals, she begins to understand that the issue is not how well an individual is able to meet these shoulds but the destruction of the real self that all women experience by trying to do so.

Kate's story begins with her emotional detachment from the feminine behaviors to which she was resigned and ends with her rejection of compliance, symbolized by refusing to dye and style her hair. "Her experience of the last months, her discoveries, her self-definition; what she hoped were now strengths, were concentrated here—that she would walk into her home with her hair undressed, with her hair tied straight back for utility; rough and streaky, and the widening grey band showing like a statement of intent" (p. 269). Flaunting gray hair may seem a superficial symbol for self-acceptance; yet it reflects the trivializing effects of grounding women's identity in their appearance. Kate's "statement of intent" is more than an acceptance of her aging; it is also a rejection of stereotypical femininity.

The Summer before the Dark illustrates how detachment can move beyond resignation to awaken consciousness. Through withdrawing from the very affiliations she also needs, the dependent one can gain the emotional distance from others and from her idealized self that allows for self-awareness. As an observer of herself being observed, she can see the ways her idealized self is external to her. By taking herself as an object, she can realize that she is objectified. Detachment from dependency may awaken consciousness, but it is not the same thing as the realization of the real self. That, according to Horney, requires another journey.

9 | From Feminine Type to Female Hero

As the ideal woman, the feminine type is the stepdaughter of masculine civilization, living the consequences of the cultural practices of sexualization and devaluation. Her estrangement from her real self is accommodation to a culture from which she is alienated. Her suffering is both criticism of that culture and the price she has paid for a flight into dependent safety that "protects" her from opposing the conditions that oppress her.

Therapy is deconstruction of the dependent solution. It is the transformation of the compliantly suffering feminine type into a female hero who is disloyal not to herself but to masculine civilization. The promise of Horney's therapy is criticism and socialization of conflict. The feminine type relinquishes an adaptive other-directedness to create a new inner direction that violates stereotypical femininity. From this position of marginality the female hero opposes and changes the conditions that devalue her.

The socially transforming promise that I find in Horney's approach to therapy pivots on her definition of the real self as the locus of choice and on the importance she attaches to self-responsibility as her primary therapeutic goal. The release of the real self through the therapeutic process is the emergence of the consciousness that one is free to make the choices that affect one's future rather than adapting pliantly to the demands of external circumstance or control. The real self is the existential consciousness of oneself as an intentional, acting subject, rather than an object who merges with established "shoulds" (cf. Beauvoir, 1952, pp. xxiv–xxxiv). It includes the understanding that one's choices are one's own responsibility, both in the making and in the consequences they create. Horney described this self-responsibility in terms of two components:

> First, I (and nobody else) am responsible for my life, for my growth as a human being, for the development of whatever talents I have. It is of no use to imagine that others keep me down. If they actually do, it is up to me to fight them.
>
> Secondly, I (and nobody else) am responsible for what I think, feel, say, do, decide. It is weak to blame others and it makes me weaker. It is useless to blame others, because I (and nobody else) have to bear the consequences of my being and my doing. (Horney, 1942b, p. 86)

In this rather heroic statement, Horney sets the assumptions that throw the feminine type back upon herself in a way that she had avoided. The first part of her statement underscores the existential anguish that accompanies the realization that no other individual, ideology, fad, or organization can be relied upon to define one's intentions and, thus, one's future. The future is an open possibility into which one is thrust with no guarantees. Conversely, the second part emphasizes the awareness that one's actions, thoughts, and so on from the past are the consequence of one's own choices and not of what others "made" one do. Between a past that is interpreted as the accumulation of her choices and a future that is unpredictable as the outcome of choices yet to be made, the feminine type is admonished to accept responsibility for all she has been and will be.

This may seem like a heartless expectation for one who was victimized through sexualization and devaluation. But Horney was sensitive to the difference between the creation of a problem and its solution. "If a tree, because of storms, too little sun, or too poor soil, becomes warped and crooked, you would not call this its essential nature" (Horney, 1952a, p. 68). Nor would you blame it. Like the tree that suffered from unfriendly or indifferent nature, the injured adult has adapted to the deprivation of her past. And, like the tree, the individual is unable to correct past deficiencies: the storms and the soil, as it were, are a matter of recorded history. Yet, unlike the tree, the human being has the capacity to change. Indeed, it is her responsibility. For Horney the imperative for this change is both personal and social.

The personal imperative derives from the suffering that externalized living and inner conflict produce; it is the longing of the real self to overcome dependency on external validation and the tyranny of inner abuse. To be released from externalized living banishes dependency on others, which means opposing their controlling or victimizing behavior. To be released from inner conflict is to deconstruct one's vulnerability to abuse by others. That vulnerability is the paralysis of self-pity, of feeling like a victim. This is not to deny the conditions in which women actually are victimized, but only to change the dependent response to these experiences—a fearful submission which exacerbates inner rage and self-pity, feelings which are projected outward. The sense of being an innocent victim contains a truth, but it also distorts and denies other aspects of reality, including one's own choices and the possibilities for creating change. This is why Horney found that feeling abused is an "intricate mixture of facts and fancy" (Horney, 1951, p. 9). Her therapeutic goal was to deconstruct the dependent character structure that sustains the fantasy, in order to develop the strength to oppose actual abuse. Taking responsibility for one's own actions means opposing victimization. "If others actually do keep me down, it is up to me to fight them."

Horney's therapeutic goal assumes that the feminine type was not responsible for the treatment she received from others, but that her future depends upon her overcoming her defensive reaction. This purpose produces the socialization of conflict and criticism that I associate with the female hero. Whereas the feminine type fled confrontation by accepting abuse and inwardly raged against it, the female hero learns to fight back as a responsibility to herself.

While the feminine type adapted herself uncritically to compulsory femininity and criticized herself, the female hero frees herself from inner criticism to engage in the world from a critical perspective.

This duty to release oneself from the solutions of the past has, for Horney, a social purpose in addition to a personal one. In it lies the resolution of the conflict between the responsibility to self and responsibility to others, a resolution that transcends the distortions of female altruism.

In a symposium on "Psychoanalysis and Moral Values," Horney argued that resolving inner conflicts is a moral obligation. Because intrapsychic problems manifest themselves in interpersonal relations, working through these problems improves one's ability to treat others in an ethically responsible way. Analyzing one's inner conflicts means breaking through the denial of feelings and sloughing off the dictates of the oppressive idealized self. It means cultivating a truthfulness toward oneself that is the basis for honesty toward others. It also means realizing the autonomy of the real self that is the basis for mutuality with—not dependence on—others. Hence, attaining self-knowledge and healthy fulfillment is the primary moral act because it is the means to all other moral acts. It is the act of giving birth to the morally responsible individual (Horney, 1950b).

The morally responsible individual acts in the world from a critical sensibility and is able to take an independent stand (Horney, 1939a). In contrast, the externalized living of the dependent type promotes an uncritical allegience to prevailing ideology: "as their behavior and their feelings are wholly directed by expectations from the outside, they lose whatever power of initiative they may once have had ... and they become easy converts to any ideology that promises guidance. ... It is people with these traits who succumb most easily to Fascist propoganda. ... The individual in a Fascist state is not supposed to stand up for his own wishes, rights, judgments. ... [He] is bolstered up by being submerged in the greater unity of race and nation" (p. 132). If externalized living promotes obedience to political domination, the independent judgment of the real self endorses an engagement in the world based not in egocentric neediness but in a capacity to experience oneself as an active part of a wider human society (Horney, 1950a, p. 365). This is a social responsibility that claims the larger world as one's domain and risks conflict within it (Horney, 1939a).

I suggest that Horney's goal of the individual liberated from inner conflict implies a transformation of the dependent responsibility associated with female altruism. Instead of retreating into a protected sphere, caring for others through a fearful need for them, or recoiling from their authority, the female hero believes that she herself is worthy of care and that the world is her domain. She practices an empowered caring that risks conflict to change the world so that women and the socially necessary need to care for one another are no longer devalued.

This socially transforming promise in Horney's therapy assumes that the devaluation of women and the devaluation of mutual care are linked, as Jean Baker Miller (1976) argues. Overcoming one requires a transformation of the other. But just as the vision remains a possibility, so does the female hero herself. She, like the feminine type, is an ideal type; actual independence and critical social engagement are more complex, less "pure" in flesh and blood. One important reason is that the female hero is discordant with a world that continues to expect feminine submission and presume female inferiority. The hero's self-direction collides with masculine civilization. Indeed, it is this collision that socializes the conflict.

Instead of criticizing herself, the female hero opposes the conditions in which she is devalued and sexualized. Her heroism is not in the fact of her marginality but in her actively living her opposition to externally defined structures and expectations. But the struggle is not easily maintained or straightforward; the conflict can undermine resolve, and active engagement can generate opposition. Cultural expectations and the social forms of masculine civilization can, as Virginia Woolf explained to an anonymous male authority, exert a powerful influence that creates self-doubt. "Inevitably we look upon society, so kind to you, so harsh to us, as an ill-fitting form that distorts the truth; deforms the mind; fetters the will" (Woolf, 1966/1938, p. 105). For Woolf and for Horney, the solution was not in trying to clothe themselves in the forms which fit so poorly. Nor was it in pretending that their perspective was free of the world they criticized. It was, rather, in living their alienation—engaging in the world that they also opposed, daring to create new values for a society whose "unreal loyalties" (Woolf, 1966/1938, p. 80) and "fictitious values" (Horney, 1950b, p. 364) they also rejected.

Living the alienation asserts women's choice against the structures that oppose it. It is a disloyalty to the civilization that demands their sweet compliance and holds out the false promise of triumphant vindication. I argue that Horney's concept of the therapeutic release of the real self implies the individual basis for an ongoing social transformation, but not all who have studied Horney's work interpret it in this way. Critics such as Marcuse (1955) and Jacoby (1975) view her, along with the other cultural neo-Freudians—Adler, Fromm, Sullivan, Thompson—as espousing an adaptive or conformist psychology. Both Marcuse and Jacoby lodge their criticisms in the assumption that Freud's criticism of culture lies in his concept of instinct, and that by rejecting the theoretical primacy of instinct in favor of cultural determinants Horney and the others removed the basis for opposing a repressive culture. From their perspectives the liberation of the real self is nothing more than the adaptation of the individual to socially acceptable roles and behaviors devoid of the opposition that instinctual drive provides (Jacoby, 1975, pp. 29–30; Marcuse, 1955, pp. 217–51).

Essential to this criticism, as to Freud's instinct theory, is a romantic tendency to value the hidden and untamed desires of the uncivilized self as the locus of freedom from social control (Rieff, 1959, p. 200; Gagnon and Simon, 1973, pp. 10–16). The core of this hidden drive is sexual; its opponent is social regulation. This romantic view of a liberating and antisocial libido presumes conditions in which sexual drive can be cherished as exhilarating and daring, the "great personal secret" (Foucault, 1978, p. 35) that maintains the individual's inner integrity and opposition to social control. Libido is for the romantic Freudians the secret, rebellious, authentic self. But this romanticism actually represents the historical reality in which middle-class male sexuality is defined as the "jewel which is so indiscreet," the grand and glorious secret that is the locus of truth (p. 79). The romanticization of sex ignores the reality in which the liberation of men's libido becomes for women and girls the condition of "real danger" (see chapter 4). From the perspective of the sexualized woman, the romantic libido as the great repository of uncivilized urges is not the uncontaminated touchstone of social criticism. It is, rather, a historically created social problem.

By locating critical sensibility in a choosing self, Horney asserted rational judgment against romanticized irrationalism. From Marcuse's and Jacoby's perspective, Horney's solution contaminates social criticism with conscious judgment and cultural values and thus palliates opposition to domination. What these critics ignore is the point that Foucault emphasized: the romanticized libido *is* contaminated; sexuality is historically constituted. In opting for rational choice rather than sexual desire, Horney merely chose to locate criticism in one culturally informed capacity rather than in another. The one she chose— rational judgment—reflects her critique of masculine civilization's trivialization of women's independent judgment and action (Horney, 1932a, p. 146). It also reflects a suspicion of the romantic view of sexuality as liberating.

Horney's solution was to desexualize power, a decision that she apparently also made on a personal level. When she was nineteen, she recorded in her diary:

> To be free of sensuality means great power in a woman. Only in this way will she be independent of a man. Otherwise she will always long for him and in the exaggerated yearning of her senses she will be able to drown out all feeling of her own value. (Horney, 1980, p. 104)

Horney's personal choice to separate power from sexuality was an attempt to liberate herself from subordination in heterosexual relationships. Her later theoretical identification of the real self with the power of conscious choice was a female alternative to the male romanticization that confounded sexuality, power, and truth. By desexualizing power, Horney claimed independent judgment as the capacity of the real self in both men and women. This is the basis from which her theoretical work on neurosis can be read as a gender-neutral psychology. But it is also the androgynous and rationalist premise from which she critiqued masculine civilization's devaluation of women.

Horney's rationalist solution draws on the nineteenth-century opposition between sexuality and intelligence. The idea that sex and intellect were incompatible and that women's intellectual life is determined by their reproductive functions obviously devalued their capacity to reason (Smith-Rosenberg, 1973; Gay, 1984, pp. 213–25). Freud's attitudes toward women also showed the influence of this idea (Rieff, 1959, p. 193). Horney accepted the opposition but not the devaluation. She claimed the power of reason for women but maintained the sex-intellect duality.

Thus Horney's response to the romanticization of libido is as interesting for what it doesn't do as for what it does. By separating power from sexuality, Horney claimed power but avoided sexuality. She left unanswered questions concerning female sexuality, independent female desire, and above all the other

possibility implied in the separation of sexuality and power—
sexual expression free of domination and subordination. That
these issues are just beginning to be explored, and not always with
agreement, attests to the lingering difficulty women have in claiming and speaking of their bodies and erotic pleasure and to the
ways in which the practices of sexuality and power remain entwined (see Vance, 1984; Ferguson et al., 1984; Snitow, Stansell,
and Thompson, 1983).

The absence of sexual interpretation in Horney's work implies
her criticism of the psychoanalytic obsession with sexual meaning. She charged that Freud's instinct theory makes sexual drive
the secret meaning behind all relationships and all actions
(Horney, 1939b, pp. 47–78). The desexualization of her interpretation of behavior is not merely an avoidance of sexuality but an
attempt to understand behavior in terms other than sexual reductionism: "all is not sexuality that looks like it" (Horney, 1937,
p. 151). Freud's theory leads to the conclusion that "any kind of
affection becomes an aim-inhibited expression of libidinal
desires" (p. 53). All friendly relations, positive activities, and even
mistakes are seen as sexually motivated. Similarly, women's
desire for independence and self-assertion are nothing more than
instances of instinctually based penis envy (p. 104). Horney
argued that Freud's reduction of all behavior to sexual instinct
devalues its complicated motives, and that his derivation of
behavior from underlying, uncontrollable, unconscious desires
absolved individuals from responsibility for their behavior.

By making self-responsibility her fundamental therapeutic
goal, Horney reclaimed judgment as a human capacity that is not
reducible to sexuality (libido), guilt (superego), or accommodation
to external reality (ego). Freedom and responsibility of choice that
draw upon a whole real self, not a segmented and managed self,
bring to bear perception, cognition, feeling, and judgment
(Horney, 1939b). In the whole self, judgment is implicit in seeing
and feelings inform understanding (cf. A. Walker, 1979, p. 49). The

self-knowledge that emerges is not an end in itself but a condition that informs action (Horney, 1950a, p. 365; 1947b, p. 87).

The concept of the real self as consciousness in action sets Horney's therapeutic goals apart from those that critics have associated with contemporary therapeutic values. She did not, contrary to Marcuse's (1955) and Jacoby's (1975) views, promote a therapy of conformity. She criticized masculine civilization's treatment of women and promoted a heroic engagement that transforms historically created oppression. The promise of her therapy is not the endless narcissistic self-absorption in consuming techniques of self-gratification that Lasch (1979) associates with contemporary therapies. Nor does it promote the emergence of what Rieff calls "psychological man," the chronically ill wimp who wishes only to "assimilate [himself] to the world as it is" (Rieff, 1959, p. 392). Unlike Lears (1981), Horney did not romanticize neurotic conflict as a ennobling human tragedy that forms the inner basis of cultural criticism, criticism that is silenced by therapy. She did not advocate pursuing culturally prescribed, constantly shifting idealized self-images, nor did she endorse the flattening of feeling in resignation to the world. For her, the therapeutic goal was not the paralysis of action but its realization.

The release of the inner-directed real self is not easily achieved, either through therapy or through active engagement in life (Horney, 1945, p. 240). Dependency is more than an annoying habit. Horney would regard the demand that women give up this trait, espoused in recent popularizations (Dowling, 1981; Gilbert and Webster, 1982), to be not only naive but potentially harmful (Horney, 1945, p. 243). Independence for her means inner independence, and it is made possible only by the often painful process of overcoming the tension between the real and proud selves. To exhort women to give up the "bad habit" of dependence for the good habit of independence is to address the symptoms rather than the problem; and, even more dangerous, it is to create a new idealized self—the Independent Woman—who contemptuously

denies the deeply rooted dependency that remains. Such superficial approaches to psychic change will only deepen self-contempt.

Nor is Horney's therapeutic approach primarily cognitive.
Recent works on cognitive therapy have articulated the central
neurotic conflict in terms that correspond to Horney's real and
perfectionist-idealized selves (see Burns, 1980). However, the
underlying assumption of cognitive psychology is that thought
determines feelings, thus that by thinking differently (that is, by
reducing conceptualized perfectionist demands) the patient can
learn to accept herself. Horney's therapeutic approach, by contrast, holds to a more traditional emphasis on working through
feelings (Rubins, 1980). The patient's knowledge of herself "must
not remain an intellectual knowledge, though it may start that
way, but must become an *emotional experience*. . . . Only when
experiencing the full impact in its irrationality of a hitherto
unconscious or semi-conscious feeling or drive do we gradually
come to know the intensity and the compulsiveness of unconscious forces operating within ourselves" (Horney, 1950a,
pp. 342–43). Hence, self-knowledge for Horney is not simply cognitive awareness but emotional understanding of one's particular
experiences. Without feeling the particularity of one's conflicts,
self-awareness never gets beyond the level of intellectualization.
The knowledge "does not become real . . . ; it does not
become . . . personal property; it does not take roots" (p. 343).

Self-knowledge, for Horney, is knowledge not only of conflicts
and strivings that are relatively easy to identify but also (and more
important) of those that are deep, unconscious, and disallowed. In
attempting to grasp the depths of her feelings and conflicts, the
individual faces a militant defense against self-revelation: the idealized self. It is the proud self that silences these feelings, because
they violate the "shoulds" that pride demands. The proud self is
an integrative solution to feelings of self-contempt. It gives the
individual a sense of unity, a feeling of worth, as well as a protec-

tion against self-hatred. Hence, any insight into the feelings that have been repressed is experienced as a threat to the idealized self, and the individual wards off any realization of not having lived up to the dictates of pride. Such lapses are experienced as unpardonable sins (Horney, 1950a, p. 335) and humiliating accusations. The individual is on the defensive against a sober examination of the self in order to ward off the anxiety and terror self-knowledge threatens to produce.

Thus, analysis reveals that the inner struggle involves layers of conflict. First are the conflicts *within* the neurotic structure: between neurotic solutions such as affection versus ambition, and the conflict brought on by self-hatred as one's actual behavior interferes with and is condemned by the idealized self in its search for glory. In addition, there is the conflict between the real self and the pride system: pride and self-hatred join forces against the real self and its desire for truth. Horney considered the deconstruction of this central inner conflict to be the primary objective of the therapeutic process (Horney, 1950a, p. 112).

The double assault of pride and self-contempt is experienced as the feeling that nothing short of perfection can save one from utter worthlessness. When perfectionist dictates are momentarily achieved, pride temporarily overcomes shame. On the other hand, when the minutest flaw appears, the feelings of worthlessness resurge. One who is caught between these extremes cannot find a middle ground of self-acceptance. Rather, she is constantly seesawing between pride and shame, self-congratulation and self-contempt. In her attempts to realize her real self, she must wage a dual battle against both feelings of worthlessness and the illusory gratification of temporarily meeting externally defined standards of achievement (Horney, 1937, p. 225; 1945, pp. 151–52).

The promise of the real self is the release from this terror of opposing extremes. However, the road of psychoanalytic therapy (Horney, 1950a, p. 333) is circuitous and uncharted. Horney avoided the dogmatic prescription of a universal technique or method of analysis. While she lectured on many aspects of therapeutic technique,[1] she did not presume that, given the great variety among human beings, the road to recovery could be rigidly dictated.

One reason for this flexibility was Horney's openness concerning the outcome of analysis. While the emergence of the real self was her goal, she had no preconceptions about who that real self should be. This was not hazy thinking on her part but an appreciation for the uniqueness of every human being. She saw therapy as a process in which the therapist helped her patient to discover and give birth to her real self. For the therapist to define that real self would not only be presumptuous but would also be the imposition of another idealized self-image.

The release of the real self from the seesawing of the pride system is, I suggest, a triumph of the ordinary. Horney did not define the emergence of the real self in this way, but her analysis suggests it. She saw its realization as freedom from the extremes of deep self-hatred and perfectionistic pride. In simply being herself, with all her capabilities and flaws, a person comes to realize that she does not have to be extraordinary in order to be worthwhile. She can be ordinary, and in that ordinariness lies a "sense of fulfillment which is different from anything . . . [she] has known before" (Horney, 1950a, p. 363).

By *ordinary* I do not mean to suggest an identification with abstractions such as "public opinion"; nor do I imply that acceptance of oneself as ordinary is mindless identification with prevailing ideological symbols of mass-produced popular items. Experiencing ordinariness is instead acceptance of oneself as a

1. Horney's students and associates have collected and published notes from her lectures on psycohanalytic technique. See Morton B. Cantor, "The Quality of the Analyst's Attention"; Emy A. Metzger, "Understanding the Patient as the Basis of All Technique"; and Ralph Slate, "Evaluation of Change"; in *Advances in Psychoanalysis: Contributions to Karen Horney's Holistic Approach* (Kelman, ed., 1964, pp. 220–50). Other lectures on technique have been published in Kelman,ed., *New Perspectives on Psychoanalysis* (1965). See also Morton Cantor, "Karen Horney on Psychoanalytic Technique: Mobilizing Constructive Forces" (1967); and Sara Sheiner, "Karen Horney on Psychoanalytic Technique: Free Association" (1967).

human being who does not correspond to mass-produced abstractions such as "the contemporary mother," "the perfect ten," or "the working woman." It is acceptance of oneself as unique rather than criticism of oneself for not exactly fitting the stereotype. It is the realization that in trying to meet perfectionist and stereotypical ideals of pride one has been "willing the impossible" (Horney, 1952b, p. 7). Released from the overcompensating striving for glory, the patient begins gradually to experience herself as she uniquely is. She begins to feel her inner life—the disallowed and the unrealized—and in this process gains a sense of her own possibility.

The power of the ordinary is an idea of transcendence that is especially appropriate to the feminine type. The feminine type's proud self was originally an attempt to "will the impossible," to fabricate a personality that was loved only insofar as she was not truly herself. Repressing her hostility, becoming alluringly compliant, caring for others, displaying her own body as an object of consumption—in short, compulsively becoming whatever others want her to be—are indeed impossible, not only because the audience is constantly shifting and the demands for perfection—from within and without—are thus infinite, but also because her heart simply is not in it. Her real self rebels, sometimes secretly, sometimes unconsciously, sometimes overtly. The power of the ordinary means that, in rejecting the impossible, she also rejects the self-hatred that generates it. Neither perfect nor contemptible, she discovers the extraordinary power of her ordinary, unique self and what is truly possible.

This process of discovery entails another noted by Alice Miller, a discovery startling in its simplicity. To use R. D. Laing's rendering of Heidegger, "the dreadful has already happened" (Laing, 1967, p. 54; A. Miller, 1981, p. 63). This means for the feminine type that the complex web of defenses, the striving for safety in dependency, is a protection after the fact. The dreaded loss of the self, the alienation from one's true being, has already occurred.

The feminine type had already been sexualized as a child: alluring compliance could not alter that fact. She was also devalued as a person: admiring helpfulness could not reverse that condition. She was deprived of nurturing, yet expected to meet adult needs: no matter how altruistic she became, she would not be given the nurturing she needed. Her proud self is the lie that attempts to deny that what she dreads has indeed happened. With that realization, she recognizes that her elaborate strivings for safety are useless pretensions and that her anger, humiliation, and vulnerability are very human responses to experiences that she cannot undo.

Devaluation and sexualization explain the dependent solution and especially the confounding of the need for love and the fear of authority to which dependency and feminine altruism are a response. Felt self-knowledge thus involves not only understanding that the self was not loved for who she really was but also *feeling* the anger and sadness that this is the truth, the secret, the feminine type had tried to hide, especially from herself. Discovering this secret is not simply a process of demystifying the past. It is experiencing the feelings that have been disallowed. In permitting herself to feel anger, fear, and sadness, the feminine type validates the unmet needs of the daughter and becomes mother to her self. In learning not to fear her feelings and needs, she accepts them and herself as valid. Giving this to herself is an act of affirmation and of love. With this felt self-acceptance, the confounding of fear of others and the need for their love and approval loses its base. No longer fearing others, she no longer feels that she must appease them. She therefore no longer needs her proud self.

For it is the idealized self that is the characterological solution linking the childhood experience of devaluation and sexualization to the dictates of culturally prescribed femininity. The feminine type clings desperately to this internalization of the cultural definition of what she should be as compensation for what she fears she is. In breaking through this inner fear, in embracing what she has dreaded, the female hero shatters the internal form of her victimization. External shoulds are driven from their internal stronghold, and conscious choice rather than fearful compliance informs her actions. She experiences, finally, the extraordinary power of her ordinary real self.

References

Abel, E., Hirsch, M., and Langland, E., eds. 1983. *The Voyage In: Fictions of Female Development*. Hanover, N.H.: University Press of New England.

Abraham, K. 1927. The experiencing of sexual trauma as a form of sexual activity. In P. Bryan and A. Strachey, eds., *Selected Papers on Psychoanalysis*, pp. 47–63. New York: Brunner/Mazel. (Originally published 1907.)

————. 1927. Manifestations of the female castration complex. In P. Bryan and A. Strachey, eds., *Selected Papers on Psychoanalysis*, pp. 338–69. New York: Brunner/Mazel. (Originally published 1920.)

Addams, J. 1961. *Twenty Years at Hull House*. New York: New American Library. (Originally published 1910.)

Adler, A. 1917. *The Neurotic Constitution*. New York: Moffat, Yard.

————. 1956. *The Individual Psychology of Alfred Adler: A Systematic Presentation in Selections from His Writings*. H. L. Ansbacher and R. R. Ansbacher, eds. New York: Basic Books.

Allen, A. T. 1985. Mothers of the new generation: Adele Schreiber, Helene Stocker, and the evolution of a German idea of motherhood, 1900–1914, *Signs* 10, no. 3, pp. 418–38.

Allen G. 1967. *William James: A Biography*. New York: Viking.

Andersen, A. 1985. *Practical Comprehensive Treatment of Anorexia Nervosa and Bulimia*. Baltimore: Johns Hopkins University Press.

Auerbach, J., et al. 1985. Commentary on Gilligan's In a Different Voice. *Feminist Studies* 11, no. 1, pp. 149–61.

Auerbach, N. 1982. *Woman and the Demon: The Life of a Victorian Myth*. Cambridge: Harvard University Press.

Baker, P. 1984. The domestication of politics: Women and American political society, 1780–1920. *American Historical Review* 89, no. 3, pp. 620–47.

Balint, M. 1965. *Primary Love and Psycho-Analytic Technique*. New York: Liveright.

Balswick, J. and Peck, C. 1971. The inexpressive male: A tragedy of American society. *The Family Coordinator 20*, pp. 363–68.

Banner, L. 1983. *American Beauty*. New York: Alfred A. Knopf.

Barker-Benfield, G. J. 1976. *The Horrors of the Half-Known Life: Male Attitudes toward Women and Sexuality in Nineteenth Century America*. New York: Harper & Row.

————. 1979. Mother emancipator: The meaning of Jane Addams' sickness and cure. *Journal of Family History* 4, no. 4, pp. 395–420.

Beauvoir, S. de. 1952. *The Second Sex*. New York: Random House.

Becker, S. 1981. *The Origins of the Equal Rights Amendment: American Feminism between the Wars*. Westport, Conn.: Greenwood Press.

Belotti, E. 1975. *Little Girls*. London: Writers and Readers Publishing Cooperative.

Benedict, R. 1959. *Patterns of Culture*. Boston: Houghton Mifflin. (Originally published 1934.)

Benjamin, J. 1983. Master and slave: The fantasy of erotic domination. In A. Snitow, C. Stansell, and S. Thompson, eds., *Powers of Desire: The Politics of Sexuality*, pp. 280–99. New York: Monthly Review Press.

Berger, J. 1972. *Ways of Seeing*. New York: Penguin Books.

Bernheimer, C., and Kahane, C., eds. 1985. *In Dora's Case: Freud-Hysteria-Feminism*. New York: Columbia University Press.

Blackwell, A. 1968. Losing her privilege. In A. Kraditor, ed., *Up from the Pedestal: Selected Writings in the History of American Feminism*, pp. 204–05. Chicago: Quadrangle Books. (Originally published 1890.)

Blair, K. 1980. *The Clubwoman as Feminist: True Womanhood Redefined, 1868–1914*. New York: Holmes & Meier.

Bledstein, B. 1976. *The Culture of Professionalism*. New York: W. W. Norton.

Bloch, R. 1978a. American feminine ideal in transition: The rise of the moral mother, 1785–1815. *Feminist Studies* 4, no. 2, pp. 100–26.

————. 1978b. Untangling the roots of modern sex roles: A survey of four centuries of change. *Signs* 4, no. 2, pp. 237–52.

Bock, G. 1983. Racism and sexism in Nazi Germany: Motherhood, compulsory sterilization, and the state. *Signs* 8, no. 3, pp. 400–21.

Bogan, L. 1978. From the journals of a poet. *The New Yorker* 53 (January), p. 62.

Bowlby, J. 1969. *Attachment*. Vol. 1 of *Attachment and Loss*. New York: Basic Books.

————. 1973. *Separation: Anxiety and Anger*. Vol. 2 of *Attachment and*

Loss. New York: Basic Books.

———. 1980. *Loss: Sadness and Depression*. Vol. 3 of *Attachment and Loss*. New York: Basic Books.

Braverman, H. 1974. *Labor and Monopoly Capital*. New York: Monthly Review Press.

Breines, W., and Gordon, L. 1983. The new scholarship on family violence. *Signs* 8, no. 3, pp. 490–531.

Bridenthal, R. 1984. "Professional" housewives: Stepsisters of the women's movement. In R. Bridenthal, A. Grossmann, and M. Kaplan, eds., *When Biology Became Destiny: Women in Weimar and Nazi Germany*, pp. 153–73. New York: Monthly Review Press.

Bridenthal, R., Grossmann, A., and Kaplan, M., eds. 1984. *When Biology Became Destiny: Women in Weimar and Nazi Germany*. New York: Monthly Review Press.

Bridenthal, R., and Koonz, C. 1984. Beyond *Kinder, Küche, Kirche*: Weimar women in politics and work. In R. Bridenthal, A. Grossmann, and M. Kaplan, eds., *When Biology Became Destiny: Women in Weimar and Nazi Germany*, pp. 33–65. New York: Monthly Review Press.

Burns, D. 1980. *Feeling Good: The New Mood Therapy*. New York: William Morrow.

Cameron, D. 1954. Karen Horney: A pioneer in the science of human relations. *American Journal of Psychoanalysis* 14, pp. 19–29.

Cantor, M. 1967. Karen Horney on psychoanalytic technique: Mobilizing constructive forces. *American Journal of Psychoanalysis* 27, pp. 188–99.

Caplan, P. 1981. *Barriers between Women*. Jamaica, N.Y.: Spectrum Publications.

———. 1985. *The Myth of Women's Masochism*. New York: E. P. Dutton.

Carpenter, E. 1911. *Love's Coming of Age*. New York: Modern Library.

Chambers-Schiller, L. 1984. *Liberty, a Better Husband*. New Haven: Yale University Press.

Chernin, K. 1981. *The Obsession: Reflections of the Tyranny of Slenderness*. New York: Harper and Row.

Chesler, P. 1972. *Women and Madness*. Garden City, N.Y.: Doubleday.

Chodorow, N. 1978. *The Reproduction of Mothering*. Berkeley: University of California Press.

Christ, C. 1977. Victorian masculinity and the angel in the house. In M. Vicinus, ed., *A Widening Sphere*, pp. 146–62. Bloomington:

Indiana University Press.

Clance, P., and Imes, S. 1978. The impostor phenomenon in high-achieving women: Dynamics and therapeutic intervention. *Psychotherapy: Theory, Research and Practice* 15, no. 3, pp. 241–47.

Cole, D. 1978. A personality sketch of Cain, the son of Adam. *Journal of Psychology and Theology* 6, no. 1, pp. 37–39.

Coles, R. 1974. Karen Horney's flight from orthodoxy. In J. Strouse, ed., *Women and Analysis*, pp. 187–91. New York: Grossman.

Cominos, P. 1963. Late Victorian sexual respectability and the social system. *International Review of Social History* 3, pp. 18–48, 216–50.

———. 1972. Innocent femina sensualis in unconscious conflict. In M. Vicinus, ed., *Suffer and Be Still: Women in the Victorian Age*, pp. 155–72. Bloomington: Indiana University Press.

Commander, L. 1907. *The American Idea.* New York: A. S. Barnes.

Contratto, S. 1984. Mother: Social sculptor and trustee of the faith. In M. Lewin, ed., *In the Shadow of the Past: Psychology Portrays the Sexes*, pp. 226–55. New York: Columbia University Press.

Cooley, C. H. 1964. *Human Nature and the Social Order.* New York: Schocken Books. (Originally published 1902.)

Coolidge, M. 1912. *Why Women Are So.* New York: Henry Holt.

Coser, L. 1977. Georg Simmel's neglected contributions to the sociology of women. *Signs* 2, no. 4, pp. 869–76.

———. 1984. *Refugee Scholars in America.* New Haven: Yale University Press.

Cott, N. 1977. *The Bonds of Womanhood: Woman's Sphere in New England, 1780–1835.* New Haven: Yale University Press.

———. 1978. Passionlessness: An interpretation of Victorian sexual ideology, 1790–1850. *Signs* 4, no. 2, pp. 219–36.

Davidoff, L. 1979. Class and gender in Victorian England: The diaries of Arthur J. Munby and Hannah Cullwick. *Feminist Studies* 5, no. 1, pp. 87–141.

Davies, M. 1982. *Woman's Place Is at the Typewriter: Office Work and Office Workers, 1870–1930.* Philadelphia: Temple University Press.

Degler, C. 1974. What ought to be and what was: Women's sexuality in the nineteenth century. *American Historical Review* 79, no. 5, pp. 1467–90.

———. 1980. *At Odds: Women and the Family in America from the Revolution to the Present.* New York: Oxford University Press.

Deland, M. 1910. The change in the feminine ideal. *The Atlantic Monthly* 105, no. 3, pp. 289–302.

Deutsch, H. 1930. The significance of masochism in the mental life of women, *International Journal of Psycho-Analysis* 11, pp. 48–60.

———. 1942. Some forms of emotional disturbance and their relationship to schizophrenia. *Psychoanalytic Quarterly* 11, pp. 301–21.

Diagnostic and Statistical Manual of Mental Disorders, 3d ed. (DSM-III). 1980. Washington, D.C.: American Psychiatric Association.

Dinnerstein, D. 1976. *The Mermaid and the Minotaur*. New York: Harper & Row.

Donovan, F. 1920. *The Woman Who Waits*. Boston: Gorham Press.

Dowling, C. 1981. *The Cinderella Complex: Women's Hidden Fear of Independence*. New York: Summit Books.

Dubbert, J. 1980. Progressivism and the masculinity crisis. In E. Pleck and J. Pleck, eds., *The American Man*, pp. 305–20. Englewood Cliffs, N.J.: Prentice Hall.

DuBois, E. 1975. The radicalism of the woman suffrage movement: Notes toward the reconstruction of nineteenth-century feminism. *Feminist Studies* 3, nos. 1–2, pp. 63–71.

DuBois, E., et al. 1980. Politics and culture in women's history: A symposium. *Feminist Studies* 6, no. 1, pp. 26–64.

DuBois, E., and Gordon, L. 1983. Seeking ecstasy on the battlefield: Danger and pleasure in nineteenth century feminist sexual thought. *Feminist Studies* 9, no. 1, pp. 7–25.

Dworkin, A. 1979. *Pornography: Men Possessing Women*. New York: G. P. Putnam's Sons.

Dyhouse, C. 1981. *Girls Growing up in Late Victorian and Edwardian England*. London: Routledge & Kegan Paul.

Eckardt, M. 1980., Foreword to *The Adolescent Diaries of Karen Horney*, pp. vii–ix. New York: Basic Books.

Ehrenreich, B. 1983. *The Hearts of Men*. Garden City, N.Y.: Anchor Press/Doubleday.

Ehrenreich, B., and English, D. 1979. *For Her Own Good: 150 Years of the Experts' Advice of Women*. Garden City, N.Y.: Anchor Press/Doubleday.

Eicenbaum, L. and Orbach, S. 1982. *Understanding Women*. New York: Basic Books.

Ellis, H. 1923. *Studies in the Psychology of Sex*. Vol. 6 of *Sex in*

Relation to Society. Philadelphia: F. A. Davis. (Originally published 1910.)

Ellul, J. 1964. *The Technological Society*. New York: Vintage Books.

English, O. S., and Finch, S. M. 1954. *Introduction to Psychiatry*. New York: W. W. Norton.

Erikson, E. 1950. *Childhood and Society*. New York: W. W. Norton.

———. 1968. *Identity, Youth, and Crisis*. New York: W. W. Norton.

Evans, R. 1976. *The Feminist Movement in Germany*. London: Sage.

Faderman, L. 1981. *Surpassing the Love of Men*. New York: William Morrow.

Fairbairn, W. R. D. 1952. *An Object Relations Theory of the Personality*. New York: Basic Books.

Fass, P. 1977. *The Damned and the Beautiful: American Youth in the 1920s*. New York: Oxford University Press.

Ferenczi, S. 1984. Confusion of tongues between adults and the child (J. Masson and M. Loring, trans.). In J. Masson, *The Assault on Truth*, pp. 283–95. New York: Farrar, Straus & Giroux.

Ferguson, A., et al. 1984. The feminist sexuality debates. *Signs* 10, no. 1, pp. 106–35.

Filene, P. 1974. *Him/Her/Self: Sex Roles in Modern America*. New York: New American Library.

Fine, R. 1979. *A History of Psychoanalysis*. New York: Columbia University Press.

Flax, J. 1978. The conflict between nurturance and autonomy in mother-daughter relationships and within feminism. *Feminist Studies* 4, no. 2, pp. 171–89.

Fliegel, Z. O. 1973. Feminine psychosexual development in Freudian theory: A historical reconstruction. *Psychoanalytic Quarterly* 42, no. 3, pp. 385–408.

Foley, A. 1982. A Bolton childhood. In J. Burnett, ed., *Destiny Obscure: Autobiographies of Childhood, Education and Family from the 1820s to the 1920s*, pp. 100–07. New York: Penguin Books.

Fox, G. L. 1977. Nice girl: Social control of women through a value construct. *Signs* 2, no. 4, pp. 805–17.

Foucault, M. 1978. Vol. 1 of *An Introduction. The History of Sexuality*. New York: Vintage Books.

Frank, J. D., et al. 1952. Two behavior patterns in therapeutic groups and their apparent motivation. *Human Relations* 5, pp. 289–317.

Freedman, E. 1974–75. The new woman: Changing views of women in the 1920s. *Journal of American History* 61, pp. 373–93.

————. 1979. Separatism as strategy: Female institution building and American feminism, 1870–1930, *Feminist Studies* 5, no. 3, pp. 512–29.

Freeman, N. 1950. Concepts of Adler and Horney. *American Journal of Psychoanalysis* 10, pp. 18–26.

Freud, S. 1896. The aetiology of hysteria. In J. Strachey, ed., *The Standard Edition of the Complete Psychological Works of Sigmund Freud* (hereafter *SE*), vol. 3, pp. 189–221. London: Hogarth Press, 1964.

————. 1905a. *Fragment of an Analysis of a Case of Hysteria. SE*, vol. 7, pp. 3–122.

————. 1905b. *Jokes and Their Relationship to the Unconscious. SE*, vol. 8, pp. 3–258.

————. 1912. On the universal tendency to debasement in the sphere of love. *SE*, vol. 11, pp. 179–90.

————. 1913. *Totem and Taboo. SE*, vol. 13, pp. 1–162.

————. 1915a. Instincts and their vicissitudes. *SE*, vol. 14, pp. 117–45.

————. 1915b. Repression. *SE*, vol. 14, pp. 146–58.

————. 1915c. The unconscious. *SE*, vol. 14, pp. 166–204.

————. 1917. *Introductory Lectures on Psycho-Analysis. SE*, vol. 16, pp. 243–496.

————. 1920. *Beyond the Pleasure Principle. SE*, vol. 18, pp. 3–64.

————. 1923. The libido theory. *SE*, vol. 18, pp. 255–59.

————. 1924. The dissolution of the Oedipus complex. *SE*, vol. 19, pp. 173–79.

————. 1925a. *An Autiobiographical Study. SE*, vol. 20, pp. 3–74.

————. 1925b. Some psychical consequences of the anatomical distinction between the sexes. *SE*, vol. 19, pp. 248–58.

————. 1926. *The Question of Lay Analysis. SE*, vol. 20, pp. 183–258.

————. 1930. *Civilization and Its Discontents. SE*, vol. 21, pp. 64–145.

————. 1931. Female sexuality. *SE*, vol. 21, pp. 225–43.

————. 1933a. Femininity. *SE*, vol. 22, pp. 112–35.

————. 1933b., *New Introductory Lectures on Psycho-Analysis. SE*, vol. 22, pp. 5–182.

————. 1985. *The Complete Letters of Sigmund Freud to Wilhelm Fliess, 1887–1904*. J. Masson, ed. Cambridge: Harvard University Press.

Frieze, I. H. 1982. Investigating the causes and consequences of marital rape. *Signs* 8, no. 3, pp. 532–53.

Fromm, E. 1941. *Escape from Freedom*. New York: Holt, Rinehart & Winston.

———. 1944. Individual and social origins of neurosis. *American Sociological Review* 9, no. 4, pp. 380–84.

Gagnon, J. and Simon, W. 1973. *Sexual Conduct*. Chicago: Aldine.

Gallop, J. 1982. *The Daughter's Seduction: Feminism and Psychoanalysis*. Ithaca, N.Y.: Cornell University Press.

Garfield, S. 1978. Research on client variables in psychotherapy. In A. Garfield and A. Bergin, eds., *Handbook of Psychotherapy and Behavior Changes*, 2d ed., pp. 191–232. New York: John Wiley & Sons.

Garner, S., Kahane, C., and Sprengnether, M. 1985. *The (M)other Tongue: Essays in Feminist Psychoanalytic Interpretation*. Ithaca, N.Y.: Cornell University Press.

Garnett, A. 1985. *Deceived with Kindness*. San Diego: Harcourt Brace Jovanovich.

Garrison, D. 1981. Karen Horney and feminism. *Signs* 6, no. 4, pp. 672–91.

Gay, P. 1984. *Education of the Senses*. New York: Oxford University Press.

Gelpi, B. C. 1981. Introduction to part 1 of *Victorian Women: A Documentary Account of Women's Lives in Nineteenth Century England, France, and the United States*, pp. 8–21. E. Hellerstein, L. Hume, and K. Offen, eds. Stanford: Stanford University Press.

Gilbert, L., and Webster, P. 1982. *Bound by Love: The Sweet Trap of Daughterhood*. Boston: Beacon Press.

Gilbert, S. M., and Gubar, S. 1979. *The Madwoman in the Attic: The Woman Writer and the Nineteenth Century Literary Imagination*. New Haven: Yale University Press.

Gilligan, C. 1982. *In a Different Voice*. Cambridge: Harvard University Press.

Gilman, C. P. 1929. Sex and race progress. In V. F. Calverton and S. D. Schmalhausen, eds. *Sex in Civilization*, pp. 109–26. New York: MacCauley.

Gilman, S. 1981. Freud and the prostitute: Male stereotypes of female sexuality in fin-de-siecle Vienna. *Journal of the American Academy of Psychoanalysis* 9, no. 3, pp. 337–60.

Glenn, E. N., and Feldberg, R. L. 1984. Clerical work: The female occupation. In J. Freeman, ed., *Women: A Feminist Perspective*, 3d ed., pp. 316–36. Palo Alto, Calif.: Mayfield.

Goffman, E. 1959. *The Presentation of Self in Everyday Life*. Garden City, N.Y.: Doubleday.

Gordon, C. 1980. *Power/Knowledge*. New York: Pantheon Books.

Gordon, L. 1976. *Woman's Body, Woman's Right: A Social History of Birth Control in America*. New York: Penguin Books.

Gordon, M. 1971. From an unfortunate necessity to a cult of mutual orgasm: Sex in American marital education literature, 1830–1940. In J. Henslin, ed., *Studies in the Sociology of Sex*, pp. 53–77. New York: Appleton-Century-Crofts.

Gorham, D. 1978. The "maiden tributes of modern Babylon" reexamined: Child prostitutes and the idea of childhood in late Victorian England, *Victorian Studies* 21, no. 3, pp. 353–79.

——. 1982. *The Victorian Girl and the Feminine Ideal*. Bloomington: University of Indiana Press.

Greenberg, J. and Mitchell, S. 1983. *Object Relations in Psychoanalytic Theory*. Cambridge: Harvard University Press.

Griffin, S. 1981. *Pornography and Silence*. New York: Harper &Row.

Grinker, R. R., Werble, B., and Drye, R. C. 1968. *The Borderline Syndrome: A Behavioral Study of Ego Functions*. New York: Basic Books.

Griswold, R. 1982. *Family and Divorce in California, 1850–1890*. Albany: State University of New York Press.

Grossmann, A. 1983a. Crisis, reaction, and resistance: Women in Germany in the 1920's and 1930's. In A. Swerdlow and H. Lessinger, eds., *Class, Race, and Sex: The Dynamics of Control*, pp. 60–74. Boston: G. K. Hall.

——. 1983b. The new woman and the rationalization of sexuality in Weimar Germany. In A. Snitow, C. Stansell, and S. Thompson, eds., *Powers of Desire: The Politics of Sexuality*, pp. 153–71. New York: Monthly Review Press.

——. 1984. Abortion and economic crisis: The 1931 campaign against paragraph 218. In R. Bridenthal, A. Grossmann, and M. Kaplan, eds., *When Biology Became Destiny: Women in Weimar and Nazi Germany*, pp. 66–86. New York: Monthly Review Press.

Haaken, J. 1983. Sex differences and narcissistic disorders. *American Journal of Psycholanalysis* 43, no. 4, pp. 315–24.

Hackett, A. 1972. The German women's movement and suffrage, 1890–1914: A study of national feminism. In R. Bezucha, ed., *Mod-*

ern *European Social History*, pp. 354–86. Lexington, Mass.: D. C. Heaton.

————. 1976. Feminism and liberalism in Wilhelmine Germany, 1890–1918. In B. Carroll, ed., *Liberating Women's History*, pp. 127–36. Urbana: University of Illinois Press.

Hall, G. S. 1907. *Youth, Its Education, Regimen, and Hygiene*. New York: Appleton.

Haller, J. S., and Haller, R. M. 1974. *The Physician and Sexuality in Victorian America*. Urbana: University of Illinois Press.

Hantover, J. 1978. The Boy Scouts and the validation of masculinity. *Journal of Social Issues* 34, no. 1, pp. 184–95.

Hartocollis, P., ed. 1977. *Borderline Personality Disorders*. New York: International Universities Press.

Hausen, K. 1984. Mother's day in the Weimar republic. In R. Bridenthal, A. Grossmann, and M. Kaplan, eds., *When Biology Became Destiny: Women in Weimar and Nazi Germany*, pp. 131–52. New York: Monthly Review Press.

Hayim, G. 1978. Modern reality strategies: An analysis of Weber, Freud, and Ellul. *Human Studies* 1, no. 4, pp. 315–29.

Helfer, R., McKinney, J., and Kempe, R. 1976. Arresting or freezng the developmental process. In R. Helfer and H. Kempe, eds., *Child Abuse and Neglect: The Family and the Community*, pp. 55–73. Cambridge, Mass.: Ballinger Publishing Co.

Herman, J., with Hirschman, L. 1981. *Father-Daughter Incest*. Cambridge: Harvard University Press.

Hersh, B. 1978. *The Slavery of Sex: Feminist Abolitionists in America*. Urbana: University of Illinois Press.

Hoffman, L. 1977. Changes in family roles, socialization, and sex differences. *American Psychologist* 32, pp. 644–57.

Honeycutt, K. 1979. Socialism and feminism in imperial Germany. *Signs* 5, no. 1, pp. 30–41.

Horney, K. 1924. On the genesis of the castration complex in women. In H. Kelman, ed., *Feminine Psychology* (hereafter *FP*), pp. 37–53. New York: W. W. Norton, 1967.

————. 1926. The flight from womanhood: The masculinity complex in women as viewed by men and by women. *FP*, pp. 54–70.

————. 1926–27. Inhibited femininity: Psychoanalytical contribution to the problem of frigidity. *FP*, pp. 71–83.

————. 1927a. Der Männlichkeitskomplex der Frau. *Archive fur*

Frauenkunde 13, pp. 141–54.

———. 1927b. Psychische Eignung und Nichteignung zur Ehe. In M. Marcuse, ed., *Die Ehe*, pp. 192–203. Berlin: Marcus & Weber.

———. 1927c. Uber die psychischen Bestimmungen der Gattenwahl, In M. Marcuse, ed., *Die Ehe*, pp. 470–80. Berlin: Marcus & Weber.

———. 1927d. Über die psychischen Wurzeln einiger typischer Ehekonflikte. In M. Marcuse, ed., *Die Ehe*, pp. 481–91. Berlin: Marcus & Weber.

———. 1928. The problem of the monogamous ideal. *FP*, pp. 84–88.

———. 1931a. The distrust between the sexes. *FP*, pp. 197–18.

———. 1931b. Premenstrual tension. *FP*, pp. 99–106.

———. 1932a. The dread of woman. *FP*, pp. 133–46.

———. 1932b. Problems of marriage. *FP*, pp. 119–32.

———. 1933a. The denial of the vagina. *FP*, pp. 147–61.

———. 1933b. Maternal conflicts. *FP*, pp. 175–81.

———. 1934. The overvaluation of love. *FP*, pp. 182–213.

———. 1937. *The Neurotic Personality of Our Time*. New York: W. W. Norton.

———. 1939a. Can you take a stand? *Journal of Adult Education* 11, pp. 129–32.

———. 1939b. *New Ways in Psychoanalysis*. New York: W. W. Norton.

———. 1942. *Self Analysis*. New York: W. W. Norton.

———. 1945. *Our Inner Conflicts: A Constructive Theory of Neurosis*. New York: W. W. Norton.

———. 1946a. *Are You Considering Psychoanalysis?* New York: W. W. Norton.

———. 1946b. The future of psychoanalysis. *American Journal of Psychoanalysis* 6, pp. 66–67.

———. 1947a. Inhibitions in work. *American Journal of Psychoanalysis* 7, pp. 18–25.

———. 1947b. Maturity and the individual. *American Journal of Psychoanalysis* 7, pp. 85–87.

———. 1948. The value of vindictiveness. *American Journal of Psychoanalysis* 8, pp. 3–12.

———. 1949. Finding the real self: Foreword to a letter. *American Journal of Psychoanalysis* 9, pp. 3–4.

———. 1950a. *Neurosis and Human Growth*. New York: W. W. Norton.

———. 1950b. Psychoanalysis and moral values: A symposium. *American Journal of Psychoanalysis* 10, pp. 64–65.

———. 1951. On feeling abused. *American Journal of Psychoanalysis* 11, pp. 5–12.

———. 1952a. Human nature can change: A symposium. *American Journal of Psychoanalysis* 12, pp. 67–68.

———. 1952b. The paucity of inner experience. *American Journal of Psychoanalysis* 12, pp. 3–9.

———. 1960. Culture and aggression. *American Journal of Psychoanalysis* 20, pp. 130–38. (Originally published 1931.)

———. 1967. *Feminine Psychology.* H. Kelman, ed. New York: W. W. Norton.

———. 1968. The technique of psychoanalytic therapy. *American Journal of Psychoanalysis* 28, pp. 3–12. (Originally published 1917.)

———. 1980. *The Adolescent Diaries of Karen Horney.* New York: Basic Books.

Jacobson, E. 1964. *The Self and the Object World.* New York: International Universities Press.

Jacoby, R. 1975. *Social Amnesia: A Critique of Conformist Psychology from Adler to Laing.* Boston: Beacon Press.

Jagger, A. 1983. *Feminist Politics and Human Nature.* Totowa, N.J.: Rowman & Allanheld.

James. W. 1981. *The Principles of Psychology,* vols. 1–2. Cambridge: Harvard University Press. (Originally published 1890.)

James, W. T. 1947. Karen Horney and Erich Fromm in relation to Alfred Adler. *Individual Psychology Bulletin* 6, pp. 105–16.

Kanter, R. M. 1977. *Men and Women of the Corporation.* New York: Basic Books.

Kaplan, A., et al. 1983. Women and anger in psychotherapy. In J. Robbins and R. Siegel, eds., *Women Changing Therapy,* pp. 29–40. New York: Haworth Press.

Kaplan, M. 1983. A woman's view of DSM-III. *American Psychologist* 38, no. 7, pp. 786–92.

Kaplan, M. 1984. Sisterhood under siege: Feminism and antisemitism in Germany, 1904–1938. In R. Bridenthal, A. Grossmann, and M. Kaplan, eds., *When Biology Became Destiny: Women in Weimar and Nazi Germany,* pp. 174–96. New York: Monthly Review Press.

Kelman, H., ed. 1964. *Advances in Psychoanalysis: Contributions to Karen Horney's Holistic Approach.* New York: W. W. Norton.

———. 1965. *New Perspectives on Psychoanalysis.* New York: W. W.

Norton.

————. 1971. *Helping People: Karen Horney's Psychoanalytic Approach*. New York: Science House.

Kennedy, D. 1970. *Birth Control in America: The Career of Margaret Sanger*. New Haven: Yale University Press.

Kernberg, O. 1975. *Borderline Conditions and Pathological Narcissism*. New York: Jason Aronson.

————. 1976. *Object Relations Theory and Clinical Psychoanalysis*. New York: Jason Aronson.

————. 1984. *Severe Personality Disorders*. New Haven: Yale University Press.

Kessler-Harris, A. 1982. *Out to Work: A History of Wage-Earning Women in the United States*. New York: Oxford University Press.

Kett, J. 1977. *Rites of Passage: Adolescence in America, 1790 to the Present*. New York: Basic Books.

Key, E. 1911. *Love and Marriage*. New York: Putnam.

Kierkegaard, S. 1941. *The Sickness unto Death*. W. Lowrie, trans. Princeton: Princeton University Press.

Kimsey, L. and Arnold, L. 1977. Precipitating factors in the female borderline syndrome: a dichotomy. *Diseases of the Nervous System* 38, no. 6, pp. 413–19.

Klein, M. 1964. *Contributions to Psychoanalyses: 1921–1945*. New York: McGraw-Hill.

Koehler, L. 1980. *A Search for Power: The "Weaker Sex" in Seventeenth Century New England*. Urbana: University of Illinois Press.

Kohut, H. 1971. *The Analysis of the Self*. New York: International Universities Press.

————. 1977. *The Restoration of the Self*. New York: International Universities Press.

Koonz, C. 1976. Conflicting allegiances: Political ideology and women legislators in Weimar Germany. *Signs* 1, no. 3, pt. 1, pp. 663–83.

————. 1984. The competition for women's *lebensraum*, 1928–1934. In R. Bridenthal, A. Grossmann, and M. Kaplan, eds., *When Biology Became Destiny: Women in Weimar and Nazi Germany*, pp. 199–236. New York: Monthly Review Press.

Kovel, J. 1976. *A Complete Guide to Therapy*. New York: Pantheon Books.

Laing, R. D. 1960. *The Divided Self*. Harmondsworth, Eng.: Penguin Books.

―――. 1967. *The Politics of Experience*. New York: Ballantine Books.

Lasch, C. 1979. *The Culture of Narcissism*. New York: W. W. Norton.

Leach, W. 1980. *True and Perfect Union: The Feminist Reform of Sex and Society*. New York: Basic Books.

Lears, J. 1981. *No Place of Grace*. New York: Pantheon Books.

Lemons, J. S. 1973. *The Woman Citizen: Social Feminism in the 1920s*. Urbana: University of Illinois Press.

Lerner, G. 1969. The lady and the mill girl: Changes in the status of women in the age of Jackson, 1800–1840. *American Studies* 10, no. 1, pp. 5–14.

Lessing, D. 1973. *The Summer before the Dark*. New York: Alfred A. Knopf.

Levin, I. 1972. *The Stepford Wives*. New York: Random House.

Lewis, H. B. 1971. *Shame and Guilt in Neurosis*. New York: International Universities Press.

―――. 1976. *Psychic War in Men and Women*. New York: New York University Press.

Lindner, R. 1952. *Prescription for Rebellion*. New York: Rinehart.

Lindsey, B., and Evans, W. 1972. *The companionate marriage*. New York: Arno Press. (Originally published 1927.)

Lorber, J., et al. 1981. On the reproduction of mothering: A methodological debate. *Signs* 6, no. 3, pp. 482–514.

Lott, B. E. 1981. *Becoming a Woman: The Socialization of Gender*. Springfield, Ill.: Charles C. Thomas.

Lukacs, G. 1971. *History and Class Consciousness*. Cambridge: MIT Press.

Lynd, H. M. 1958. *Shame and the Search for Identity*. New York: Harcourt, Brace.

Lynd, R., and Lynd, H. M. 1956. *Middletown*. New York: Harcourt, Brace & World. (Originally published 1929.)

McHugh, P. 1980. *Prostitution and Victorian Social Reform*. New York: St. Martin's Press.

MacKinnon, C. 1982. Feminism, Marxism, and the state: An agenda for theory. *Signs* 7, no. 3, pp. 515–44.

McMahon, M. 1972. An American courtship: Psychologists and advertising theory in the progressive era. *American Studies* 13, pp. 5–18.

Mahler, M. 1968. *Infantile Psychosis*. Vol. 1 of *On Human Symbiosis and the Vicissitudes of Individuation*. New York: International Universities Press.

———. 1971. A study of the separation-individuation process and its possible application to borderline phenomena in the psychoanalytic situation. *The Psychoanalytic Study of the Child* 26, pp. 403–24.

Mahler, M. 1979. *The Selected Papers of Margaret S. Mahler,* vol. 2. New York: Jason Aronson.

Mann, N. 1980. Needles and pens: "Woman's work" and woman's place in the Victorian novel. Ms., University of Colorado.

Mannheim, K. 1936. *Ideology and Utopia.* New York: Harcourt, Brace & World.

Marcus, S. 1964. *The Other Victorians.* New York: Basic Books.

———. 1984. Freud and Dora: Story, History, Case History. In S. Marcus, *Freud and the Culture of Psychoanalysis,* pp. 42–86. Boston: George Allen & Unwin.

Marcuse, H. 1955. *Eros and Civilization.* New York: Vintage Books.

Maslow, A. H. 1968. *Toward a Psychology of Being.* Princeton, N.J.: Van Nostrand.

Masson, J. M. 1984. *The Assault on Truth: Freud's Suppression of the Seduction Theory.* New York: Farrar, Straus, Giroux.

Masterson, J. F. 1976. *Psychotherapy of the Borderline Adult.* New York: Brunner/Mazel.

———. 1981. *The Narcissistic and Borderline Disorders.* New York: Brunner/Mazel.

Matthaei, J. A. 1982. *An Economic History of Women in America.* New York: Schocken Books.

May, E. 1980. *Great Expectations: Marriage and Divorce in Post-Victorian America.* Chicago: University of Chicago Press.

Mead, G. H. 1962. *Mind, Self, and Society.* Chicago: University of Chicago Press. (Originally published 1934.)

Meiselman, K. C. 1978. *Incest: A Psychological Study of Causes and Effects with Treatment Recommendations.* San Francisco: Jossey-Bass.

Miller, A. 1981. *The Drama of the Gifted Child.* New York: Basic Books. (Originally published as *Prisoners of Childhood.*)

———. 1983. *For Your Own Good: Hidden Cruelty in Child-Rearing and the Roots of Violence.* New York: Farrar, Straus, Giroux.

———. 1984. *Thou Shalt Not Be Aware: Society's Betrayal of the Child.* New York: Farrar, Straus, Giroux.

Miller, J. B. 1976. *Toward a New Psychology of Women.* Boston: Beacon

Press.

Mintz, S. 1983. *A Prison of Expectations: The Family in Victorian Culture.* New York: New York University Press.

Mitchell, J. 1974. *Psychoanalysis and Feminism.* New York: Random House.

Mitscherlich, A. 1969. *Society without the Father.* E. Mosbacher, trans. New York: Harcourt, Brace & World.

Moers, E. 1977. *Literary Women.* Garden City, N.Y.: Anchor Press/ Doubleday.

Morgan, M. 1975. *The Total Woman.* Old Tappan, N.Y.: Revell.

Morris, H. 1976. *On Guilt and Innocence: Essays in Legal Philosophy and Moral Psychology.* Berkeley: University of California Press.

Moulton, R. 1975. Early papers on women: Horney to Thompson. *American Journal of Psychoanalysis* 35, pp. 207–23.

Neumann, E. 1963. *The Great Mother: An Analysis of the Archetype.* Bollingen Series 47. Princeton: Princeton University Press.

Nietzsche, F. 1967. *On the Genealogy of Morals.* W. Kaufmann and R. J. Hollingdale, trans. New York: Random House.

O'Connell, A. 1980. Karen Horney: Theorist in psychoanalysis and feminine psychology. *Psychology of Women Quarterly* 5, no. 1, pp. 81–92.

Paris, B. J. 1978. Horney's theory and the study of literature. *American Journal of Psychoanalysis* 38, no. 4, pp. 343–53.

Peiss, K. 1983. "Charity girls" and city pleasures: Historical notes on working-class sexuality, 1880–1920. In A. Snitow, C. Stansell, and S. Thompson, eds., *Powers of Desire: The Politics of Sexualtiy,* pp. 74–87. New York: Monthly Review Press.

Person, E. 1980. Sexuality as the mainstay of identity: Psychoanalytic perspectives. *Signs* 5, no. 4, pp. 605–30.

Piers, G., and Singer, M. 1971. *Shame and Guilt.* New York: W. W. Norton.

Pivar, D. 1973. *Purity Crusade: Sexual Morality and Social Control, 1868–1900.* Westport, Conn.: Greenwood Press.

Plaza, M. 1981. Our damages and their compensation. Rape: The will not to know of Michel Foucault. *Feminist Issues* 1 (Summer), pp. 25–35.

Pleck, J. 1980. Men's power with women, other men, and society. In E. H. Pleck and J. H. Pleck, eds., *The American Man,* pp. 305–20. Englewood Cliffs, N.J.: Prentice Hall.

Poloma, M. M., and Garland, T. N. 1971. The myth of the egalitarian family: Familial roles and the professionally employed wife. In A. Theodore, ed., *The Professional Woman*, pp. 741–66. Cambridge, Mass.: Schenkman.

Poster, M. 1978. *Critical Theory of the Family*. New York: Seabury Press.

Quinn, S. 1987. *Karen Horney*. New York: Summit Books.

Radway, J. 1984. *Reading the Romance: Women, Patriarchy, and Popular Literature*. Chapel Hill: University of North Carolina Press.

Ramas, M. 1980. Freud's Dora, Dora's hysteria: The negation of a woman's rebellion. *Feminist Studies* 6, no. 3, pp. 472–510.

Rank, O. 1972. *Will Therapy*. New York: Alfred A. Knopf. (Originally published 1936.)

Rapp, R., and Ross, E. 1983. The twenties backlash: Compulsory heterosexuality, the consumer family, and the waning of feminism. In Swerdlow, A. and Lessinger, H., eds., *Class, Race, and Sex: The Dynamics of Control*, pp. 93–107. Boston: G. K. Hall.

Rich, A. 1976. *Of Woman Born*. New York: W. W. Norton.

———. 1979. Disloyal to civilization: Feminism, racism, and gynephobia. *Chrysalis* 7, pp. 9–27.

———. 1980. Compulsory heterosexuality and lesbian existence. *Signs* 5, no. 4, pp. 631–60.

Ricoeur, P. 1970. *Freud and Philosophy: An Essay on Interpretation*. D. Savage, trans. New Haven: Yale University Press.

Rieff, P. 1959. *Freud: The Mind of the Moralist*. Garden City, N.Y.: Anchor Press/Doubleday.

Robbins, J. H., and Siegel, R. J., eds. 1983. *Women Changing Therapy*. New York: Howarth Press.

Rohrbaugh, J. B. 1981. Psychology of women, 1980. In B. Haber, ed., *The Women's Annual*, pp. 200–25. Boston: G. K. Hall.

Rosen, R. 1982. *The Lost Sisterhood: Prostitution in America: 1900–1918*. Baltimore: Johns Hopkins University Press.

Rosenberg, C. 1973. Sexuality, class and role in 19th century America. *American Quarterly* 25, pp. 131–53.

Rosenberg, R. 1982. *Beyond Separate Spheres: Intellectual Roots of Modern Feminism*. New Haven: Yale University Press.

Ross, E., and Rapp., R. 1981. Sex and society: A research note from social history and anthropology. *Comparative Studies in Society and History* 23, pp. 51–72.

Rothman, E. 1984. *Hands and Hearts: A History of Courtship in America.* New York: Basic Books.

Rothman, S. 1978. *Woman's Proper Place: A History of Changing Ideals and Practices, 1870 to the Present.* New York: Basic Books.

Rubin, G. 1975. The traffic in women: Notes on the "political economy" of sex. In R. Reiter, ed., *Toward an Anthropology of Women,* pp. 157–210. New York: Monthly Review Press.

Rubin, L. 1983. *Intimate Strangers.* New York: Harper & Row.

Rubins, J. L. 1978. *Karen Horney: Gentle Rebel of Psychoanalysis.* New York: Dial Press.

————. 1980. On cognition, affects, and Horney theory. *The American Journal of Psychoanalysis* 40, no. 1, pp. 195–211.

Rupp, L. J. 1981. Reflections on twentieth-century American women's history. *Reviews in American History* 9, no. 2, pp. 275–84.

Rush, F. 1977. Freud and the sexual abuse of children. *Chrysalis* 1, pp. 31–45.

————. 1980. *The Best Kept Secret: Sexual Abuse of Children.* Englewood Cliffs, N.J.: Prentice-Hall.

Ryan, M. 1983. *Womanhood in America: From Colonial Times to the Present,* 3d ed. New York: Franklin Watts.

Sahli, N. 1979. Smashing: Women's relationships before the fall. *Chrysalis* 8, pp. 17–27.

Satre, J. P. 1966. *Being and Nothingness.* Hazel F. Barnes, trans. New York: Washington Square Press.

Scanzoni, J. 1972. *Sexual Bargaining: Power Politics in the American Marriage.* Englewood Cliffs, N.J.: Prentice-Hall.

Schechter, S. 1982. *Women and Male Violence: The Visions and Struggles of the Battered Women's Movement.* Boston: South End Press.

Schmalhausen, S. D. 1929. The sexual revolution. In V. F. Claverton and S. D. Schmalhausen, eds., *Sex in Civilization,* pp. 349–436. Garden City, N.J.: Garden City Publishing.

Schneider, D. 1968. *American Kinship: A Cultural Account.* Englewood Cliffs, N.J.: Prentice-Hall.

Sears, H. 1977. *The Sex Radicals: Free Love in High Victorian America.* Lawrence: University Press of Kansas.

Sheiner, S. 1967. Karen Horney on psychoanalytic technique: Free association. *American Journal of Psychoanalysis* 27, pp. 200–08.

Shields, S. 1984. "To pet, coddle, and 'do for'": Caretaking and the concept of maternal instinct. In M. Lewin, ed., *In the Shadow of the*

Past: Psychology Portrays the Sexes, pp. 256–73. New York: Columbia University Press.

Shorter, E. 1975. *The Making of the Modern Family*. New York: Basic Books.

Showalter, E. 1978. Introduction to *These Modern Women*, pp. 3–29. E. Showalter, ed. Westbury, N.Y.: Feminist Press.

Simmel, G. 1911. *Philosophische Kultur*. Leipzig: Werner Klinkhardt.

———. 1984. *Georg Simmel: On Women, Sexuality, and Love*. G. Oakes, trans. New Haven: Yale University Press.

Simmons, C. 1979. Companionate marriage and the lesbian threat. *Frontiers* 4, pp. 54–59.

Sklar, K. K. 1973. *Catharine Beecher*. New Haven: Yale University Press.

Skolnick, A. 1978. *The Intimate Environment*, 2d ed. Boston: Little, Brown.

Smith, D. 1973. Family limitation, sexual control, and domestic feminism in Victorian America. *Feminist Studies* 1, pp. 40–57.

Smith-Rosenberg, C. 1971. Beauty, the beast, and the militant woman: A case study in sex roles and social stress in Jacksonian America. *American Quarterly* 23, pp. 562–84.

———. 1972. The hysterical woman: Sex roles in nineteenth-century America. *Social Research* 13, pp. 652–78.

———. 1973. Puberty to menopause: The cycle of femininity in nineteenth-century America. *Feminist Studies* 1, no. 3/4, pp. 58–72.

———. 1975. The female world of love and ritual: Relations between women in nineteenth-century America. *Signs* 1, no. 1, pp. 1-29.

———. 1985. *Disorderly Conduct: Visions of Gender in Victorian America*. New York: Alfred A. Knopf.

Snitow, A., Stansell, C. and Thompson, S. 1983. Introduction. *Powers of Desire: The Politics of Sexuality*, pp. 9–47. New York: Monthly Review Press.

Sours, J. 1980. *Starving to Death in a Sea of Objects: The Anorexia Nervosa Syndrome*. New York: Jacob Aronson.

Stacey, J. 1983. The new conservative feminism. *Feminist Studies* 9, no. 3, pp. 559–83.

Stanton, E. C. 1972. Address to the New York State Legislature, 1860. In M. Schneir, ed., *Feminism: The Essential Historical Writings*, pp. 117–21. New York: Vintage Books.

Stone, L. 1977. *The Family, Sex and Marriage in England 1500–1800*.

New York: Harper and Row.

Strouse, J. 1980. *Alice James: A Biography*. Boston: Houghton Mifflin.

Sullivan, H. S. 1940. *Conceptions of Modern Psychiatry*. New York: W. W. Norton.

———. 1953. *The Interpersonal Theory of Psychiatry*. New York: W. W. Norton.

Surrey, J. 1983. The relational self in women. No. 82–02 in the Work in Progress Series of the Stone Center of Wellesley College. Wellesley, Mass.

Swan, J. 1974. Master and nannie: Freud's two mothers and the discovery of the Oedipus complex. *American Image* 31, pp. 1–64.

———. 1985. Difference and silence: John Milton and the question of gender. In S. Garner, C. Kahane, and M. Sprengnether, eds., *The (M)other Tongue: Essays in Feminist Psychoanalytic Interpretation*, pp. 142–93. Ithaca, N.Y.: Cornell University Press.

Symonds, A. 1971. Phobias after marriage: Women's declaration of dependence. *American Journal of Psychoanalysis* 31, no. 2, pp. 144–52.

———. 1973. The myth of femininity: A symposium. *American Journal of Psychoanalysis* 33, no. 1, pp. 42–55.

———. 1974. The liberated woman: Healthy and neurotic. *American Journal of Psychoanalysis* 34, no. 3, pp. 177–83.

———. 1978. The psychodynamics of expansiveness in the success-oriented woman. *American Journal of Psychoanalysis* 38, no. 3, pp. 195–205.

———. 1979. Violence against women: The myth of masochism. *American Journal of Psychotherapy* 33, no. 3, pp. 161–73.

Tarbell, I. 1916. *The Ways of Woman*. New York: Macmillan.

Tentler, L. W. 1979. *Wage-Earning Women: Industrial Work and Family Life in the United States, 1900–1930*. New York: Oxford University Press.

Thomas, W. I. 1967. *The Unadjusted Girl*. New York: Harper & Row. (Originally published 1923.)

Tilly, L. A., and Scott, J. W. 1978. *Women, Work, and Family*. New York: Holt, Rinehart, & Winston.

Trimberger, E. K. 1983. Feminism, men, and modern love: Greenwich Village, 1900–1925. In A. Snitow, C. Stansell, and S. Thompson, eds., *Powers of Desire: The Politics of Sexuality*, pp. 131–52. New York: Monthly Review Press.

Trumback, R. 1978. *The Rise of the Egalitarian Family*. New York: Academic Press.

Van Herik, J. 1982. *Freud on Femininity and Faith*. Berkeley: University of California Press.

Vance, C. (ed.) 1984. *Pleasure and Danger: Exploring Female Sexuality*. Boston: Routledge & Kegan Paul.

Veblen, T. 1953. *The Theory of the Leisure Class*. New York: New American Library. (Originally published 1899.)

Walker, A. 1979. One child of one's own. *Ms.* 8, no. 2 (August), p. 49.

Waites, E. 1982. Fixing women: Devaluation, idealization, and the female fetish. *Journal of the American Psychoanalytic Association* 30, no. 2, pp. 435–59.

Walker, L. E. 1979. *The Battered Woman*. New York: Harper & Row.

Walkowitz, J. 1980 . *Prostitution and Victorian Society: Women, Class, and the State*. Cambridge: Cambridge University Press.

Watson, J. B. 1919. *Psychology from the Standpoint of a Behaviorist*. Philadelphia: Lippincott.

———. 1924. *Behaviorism*. New York: W. W. Norton.

Weber, M. 1971. Ideal types and the study of social change. In J. E. T. Eldridge, ed., *Max Weber: The Interpretation of Social Reality*, pp. 226–28. New York: Charles Scribner's Sons.

Weeks, J. 1981. *Sex, Politics, and Society: The Regulation of Sexuality Since 1800*. London: Longman.

Weisskopf, S. C. 1980. Maternal sexuality and asexual motherhood. *Signs* 5, no. 4, pp. 766–82.

Weitzman, 1979. *Sex Role Socialization*. Palo Alto, Calif.: Mayfield.

Welter, B. 1973. The cult of true womanhood: 1820–1860. In J. E. Friedman and W. G. Shade, eds., *Our American Sisters: Women in American Life and Thought*, pp. 96–123. Boston: Allyn & Bacon.

Westkott, M. 1977. Dialectics of fantasy. *Frontiers* 2, no. 3, pp. 1–7.

———. 1978. Mothers and daughters in the world of the father. *Frontiers* 3, no. 2, pp. 16–22.

———. 1979. Feminist criticism of the social sciences. *Harvard Educational Review* 49, no. 4, pp. 422–30.

Wiebe, R. 1967. *The Search for Order: 1877–1920*. New York: Hill & Wang.

Wilson, M. G. 1979. *The American Woman in Transition: The Urban Influence, 1870–1920*. Westport, Conn.: Greenwood Press.

Winnicott, D. W. 1965. *The Maturational Processes and the Facilitat-*

ing Environment. New York: International Universities Press.

Witenberg, E. 1974. American neo-Freudian school: The interpersonal and cultural approaches. In S. Arieti, ed., *American Handbook of Psychiatry,* 2d ed., vol. 1, pp. 843–61. New York: Basic Books.

Wohl, A. S. 1978. Sex and the single room: Incest among the Victorian working classes. In A. S. Wohl, ed., *The Victorian Family,* pp. 197–216. New York: St. Martin's Press.

Wolfenstein, M., and Leites, N. 1950. *Movies: A Psychological Study.* New York: Free Press.

Wolman, B. 1960. *Contemporary Theories and Systems in Psychology.* New York: Harper & Row.

Wood, G. 1986. *The Myth of Neurosis: Overcoming the Illness Excuse.* New York: Harper & Row.

Woolf, V. 1944. The new dress. In *A Haunted House and Other Short Stories,* pp. 47–57. New York: Harcourt, Brace & World.

———. 1955. *To the Lighthouse.* New York: Harcourt, Brace & World.

———. 1966. *Three Guineas.* New York: Harcourt, Brace, Jovanovich. (Originally published 1938.)

———. 1976. *Moments of Being.* New York: Harcourt, Brace, Jovanovich.

Wright, G. 1980. *Moralism and the Model Home: Domestic Architecture and the Cultural Conflict in Chicago, 1873–1913.* Chicago: University of Chicago Press.

———. 1981. *Building the Dream: A Social History of Housing in America.* New York: Pantheon Books.

Wurmser, L. 1981. *The Mask of Shame.* Baltimore: Johns Hopkins University Press.

Index